IMAGES OF WAR
NORMANDY BEYOND THE BEACHES

RARE PHOTOGRAPHS FROM WARTIME ARCHIVES

Jon Diamond

Pen & Sword
MILITARY

First published in Great Britain in 2024 by
PEN & SWORD MILITARY
an imprint of Pen & Sword Books Ltd
Yorkshire – Philadelphia

Copyright © Jon Diamond, 2024

ISBN 978-1-39903-206-3

The right of Jon Diamond to be identified as the author of this work has been asserted by him in accordance with the Copyright, Designs and Patents Act 1988.

A CIP catalogue record for this book is available from the British Library.

All rights reserved. No part of this book may be reproduced or transmitted in any form or by any means, electronic or mechanical including photocopying, recording or by any information storage and retrieval system, without permission from the Publisher in writing.

Typeset by Concept, Huddersfield, West Yorkshire, HD4 5JL.
Printed and bound in England by CPI Group (UK) Ltd, Croydon, CR0 4YY.

Pen & Sword Books Ltd incorporates the imprints of After the Battle, Atlas, Archaeology, Aviation, Discovery, Family History, Fiction, History, Maritime, Military, Military Classics, Politics, Select, Transport, True Crime, Air World, Frontline Publishing, Leo Cooper, Remember When, Seaforth Publishing, The Praetorian Press, Wharncliffe Local History, Wharncliffe Transport, Wharncliffe True Crime and White Owl.

For a complete list of Pen & Sword titles please contact
PEN & SWORD BOOKS LTD
47 Church Street, Barnsley, South Yorkshire, S70 2AS, England
E-mail: enquiries@pen-and-sword.co.uk
Website: www.pen-and-sword.co.uk
or
PEN & SWORD BOOKS
1950 Lawrence Rd, Havertown, PA 19083, USA
E-mail: uspen-and-sword@casematepublishers.com
Website: www.penandswordbooks.com

Contents

Introduction 4

Abbreviations 5

Chapter One
Strategic Situation and Aims of the Normandy Campaign 7

Chapter Two
The Allied Landings at Normandy, 5–6 June 1944 27

Chapter Three
Commanders and Combatants 65

Chapter Four
Initial Inland Movements from the Beaches . . 111

Chapter Five
US First Army's Capture of Cherbourg and Movement Towards St Lô 133

Chapter Six
The Anglo-Canadian Siege of Caen and the Falaise-Argentan 'Pocket' 165

Epilogue 201

Bibliography 207

Introduction

There are an enormous number of highly detailed volumes in print delineating the combat within Normandy that commenced on 6 June 1944 with the Allied invasion, Operation *Overlord*. This Images of War book is not an attempt to reiterate the mountain of information about the Normandy campaign already well documented by numerous historians and military participants. Rather it is a photographic catalogue, principally culled from the National Archives and Records Administration (NARA) and the Library of Congress. It aims to demonstrate with memorialized images the critical sectors comprising the combat, weapons, tactics based on terrain features, and the various personnel involved in securing an Allied lodgment following the initial June landings, leading on to the ultimate breakout in pursuit of the Germans that started in late July and ended in late August with the crossing of the Seine river and the liberation of Paris. Focus will be primarily directed towards combat beyond the beaches at vital locations such as Cherbourg, Caen, and St Lô as well as at other battlefields and sites including Bayeux, Sainte-Mère-Église, Carentan, La Haye-du-Puits, Lessay, and Marigny. As the Allied breakout started after Operation *Cobra* at the end of July, other areas such as Coutances, Avranches, and the Falaise-Argentan 'Pocket' will be depicted.

* * *

Gratitude is due to the archivists at the above mentioned institutions for their expert curating and maintenance of the photographic record, without which this book could not have been compiled.

Abbreviations

AF – Air Force
AG – Army Group
ANZAC – Australian and New Zealand Army Corps
AP – Armour-piercing
ARV – Armoured Recovery Vehicle
AT – Anti-tank
AVRE – Armoured Vehicle Royal Engineers
BEF – British Expeditionary Force
BG – Brigadier General
BGS – Brigadier General Staff
CCA – Combat Command A
CCB – Combat Command B
C-in-C – Commander-in-Chief
CIGS – Chief, Imperial General Staff
CNO – Chief of Naval Operations
CO – Commanding Officer
COS – Chief of Staff
CP – Command Post
DAK – Deutsches Afrika Korps
DD – Duplex Drive
DSC – Distinguished Service Cross
DSO – Distinguished Service Order
ETO – European Theater of Operations
FM – Field Marshal
GIR – Glider Infantry Regiment
GMC – Gun Motor Carriage
GOC – General Officer Commanding
HE – High Explosive
IR – Infantry Regiment
JCOS – Joint Chiefs of Staff
LC – Lieutenant Colonel
LCA – Landing Craft, Assault
LCI – Landing Craft, Infantry
LCM – Landing Craft, Mechanized
LCT – Landing Craft, Tank
LCVP – Landing Craft, Vehicle, Personnel
LG – Lieutenant General
LOC – Line of Control
LST – Landing Ship, Tank
MG – Major General
MO – Medical Officer
MP – Military Policeman
OP – Observation Post
QF – Quick Firing
PIR – Parachute Infantry Regiment
RA – Royal Artillery
RAF – Royal Air Force
RAMC – Royal Army Medical Corps
RASC – Royal Army Service Corps
RE – Royal Engineers
RM – Royal Marines
RN – Royal Navy

RTR – Royal Tank Regiment
SHAEF – Supreme Headquarters Allied Expeditionary Force
SMG – Submachine Gun
SMLE – Short Magazine Lee Enfield
SPA – Self-Propelled Artillery
TAF – Tactical Air Force
TD – Tank Destroyer
USA – United States Army
USAAF – United States Army Air Force
USCG – United States Coast Guard
USMC – United Stated Marine Corps
USN – United States Navy
USS – United States Ship

Chapter One

Strategic Situation and Aims of the Normandy Campaign

The British Expeditionary Force (BEF) was sent into northern France and the Low Countries after the outbreak of the Second World War on 1 September 1939. Possessing inadequate equipment and weapons for a modern continental war, the German blitzkrieg of 10 May 1940 forced them into a disastrous retreat to the French coastal city of Dunkirk in late May–early June. Although presented as the miraculous rescue of 340,000 Allied soldiers from military catastrophe, thereby providing Britain with the nucleus of its army and future veteran army commanders and leaders, Dunkirk was nonetheless a major setback that would continue to haunt British military planners. Coupled with the later disaster at Dieppe (Operation *Jubilee*), during a small-scale Canadian-British amphibious assault on a fortified French coastal town in August 1942, it meant that senior Allied military leaders were concerned about the risk of another ill-planned and executed seaborne invasion of Occupied France. Even the Germans, after the failed Dieppe raid on a defended port, suspected that the real invasion would be an over-the-beach one.

At the operational level the Germans expected such an attack, but could not pinpoint its exact location due in part to an Allied misformation campaign. Field Marshal (FM) Erwin Rommel, in charge of all Western defences from the Bay of Biscay to Denmark, initially leaned towards Calais but considered a Normandy invasion also likely. He focused his attention on the defences of what the Allies had codenamed 'Omaha Beach' (because of its long concave waterfront resembling Salerno, which the Allies assaulted in September 1943 and almost had to abandon). After being put in charge of Fortress Europe by Hitler in early 1944, Rommel saw to it that the defences were improved drastically, with hundreds of pill-boxes, tank traps, thousands of obstacles and millions of mines intentionally placed to be underwater at high tide. Hitler thought the attack would come in Normandy, yet was at the same time duped by the Allies' plan to make the assault on Calais look like the main invasion – by fortifying both locales he lacked sufficient concentration of his forces.

The initial seaborne attack on 6 June 1944 launched five Allied divisions at four nearly contiguous beaches and one outlier on the Cotentin Peninsula, Utah Beach. The goal of the Americans was to cut the Peninsula in two at its southern base to prevent the Germans from supplying and strengthening Cherbourg and its deep-water port. Once the problem of Cherbourg was solved, attention could be directed towards an offensive to the south and when the entire Cotentin Peninsula was secured, a movement towards Brittany could begin.

Caen, the regional capital of Calvados, is situated astride the Orne river, 7 miles inland from the coast, and is linked to the Bay of the Seine by the Orne river and the ship canal. The city has rich undulating farmland surrounding it, making it suitable for armoured operations, unlike the *bocage* (pasture enclosed by hedgerows). The imposing Colombelles steelworks was part of an industrial area east of the Orne river. Radiating from Caen was a web of roads and railways vital to Allied plans to drive from the beaches into the heart of northern France.

The manner in which US forces broke out from the bridgehead and the delays incurred, also fuelled acrimony about the initial results of this most complex and daring amphibious assault on a heavily defended and fortified enemy-occupied coastline. After winning the battle of the hedgerows, the entire Allied force moving southward would have to realign itself with a pivot to the east for the capture of the Seine river crossings and also the advance west into Brittany. This would be almost simultaneous with the movement of initially the US First Army toward the Loire river, followed by LG George S. Patton's Third Army towards this waterway, once it was activated on 1 August 1944. Having raced across France during August and liberated Paris, the Allies were then poised to move into Belgium and Holland. They would capture the Belgian port of Antwerp and seize the Dutch V-1 and V-2 rocket launch sites, respectively, from which pilotless planes carrying explosives had devastated London and its surrounding area since mid-June 1944.

Minister of Munitions, Winston Churchill (*centre*), seated at the 1918 Lille liberation parade with LC Bernard Montgomery, COS of the 47th (London) Division (*left, foreground*). This occurrence presaged a military relationship that began at El Alamein in August 1942 and continued throughout the invasions of Sicily (July 1943), the Italian mainland (September 1943) and ultimately Operation *Overlord*, the Normandy invasion (6 June 1944), its lodgment, and breakout into the interior of France. (*Author's collection*)

(**Above**) A bayonet charge on a Turkish trench on the Gallipoli Peninsula by ANZAC infantrymen is shown during the Dardanelles campaign in the First World War (from 19 February 1915 to 9 January 1916). The fighting was between 489,000 Allied soldiers, which included 345,000 British, 50,000 Australians, 15,000 New Zealanders, and 79,000 French, against 315,000 Turkish combatants with approximately 700 German advisors. First Lord of the Admiralty Winston Churchill (1911–15), was a proponent for the amphibious assault and subsequent carnage on the tenuous lodgment within a small perimeter. The Allied campaign was plagued by ill-defined goals, poor planning, insufficient artillery, inexperienced troops, poor intelligence, overconfidence, and an inability to use the terrain to their advantage. On the other side, the Ottoman commanders made use of the high ground above the Allied landing beaches to prevent a penetration inland. Churchill resigned in November 1915 and left London for the Western Front, taking command of a Royal Scots Fusiliers' infantry battalion in early 1916. Lessons learnt in the Dardanelles campaigns were applied to the Normandy landings and amphibious operations conducted by the USMC throughout the Pacific War. (*NARA*)

(**Opposite, above**) Sinking and burning *Kriegsmarine* destroyers in the Ofotfjord leading into Narvik on 10 April 1940, during combat between elements of the German and Royal Navies while two of the ten German destroyers dock after the battle. On 9 April, the Nazis, who had a non-aggression pact with Denmark, had invaded and forced the latter's surrender within hours. Also on that date, the Germans seized Oslo, Stavanger, Bergen, Trondheim and Narvik, violating Norway's neutrality. An Anglo-French force counterattacked at Narvik, despite its location within the Arctic Circle, based on a strategic recommendation of the British Military Co-ordination Committee under the chairmanship of Winston Churchill, then First Lord of the Admiralty. The objective was to establish a naval base for the Allies in the far north of Norway at Narvik, which could be a staging point to seize the Gällivare iron ore fields in Sweden. The conflict in Norway continued from 9 April through 8 June 1940. Allied shortcomings in the attempted seizure of Narvik included poor communications and control between ships and ground troops, lack of landing craft, inadequate air cover and support, faulty provision for re-supply, inexperienced troops, and wrong-sized equipment for the specialized land conditions. (*Library of Congress*)

(**Opposite, below**) Dead British soldiers lie amid abandoned BEF vehicles of the Anglo-French armies on the beaches at Dunkirk in early June 1940. The German blitzkrieg captured France's Channel ports, including Dunkirk, from 26 May to 4 June. Over 350,000 Allied troops were lifted off Dunkirk's beaches and taken to England during Operation *Dynamo*, in which the RN, the RAF, and a civilian boat armada were employed, ensuring a nucleus for a re-formed British Army. Images like this haunted and deterred Prime Minister Winston Churchill and Britain's military leaders from making a hasty large-scale return to Occupied France, despite exhortations from many American generals in 1942–3. They had joined the Allied cause after Adolf Hitler's declaration of war on the United States in December 1941. (*NARA*)

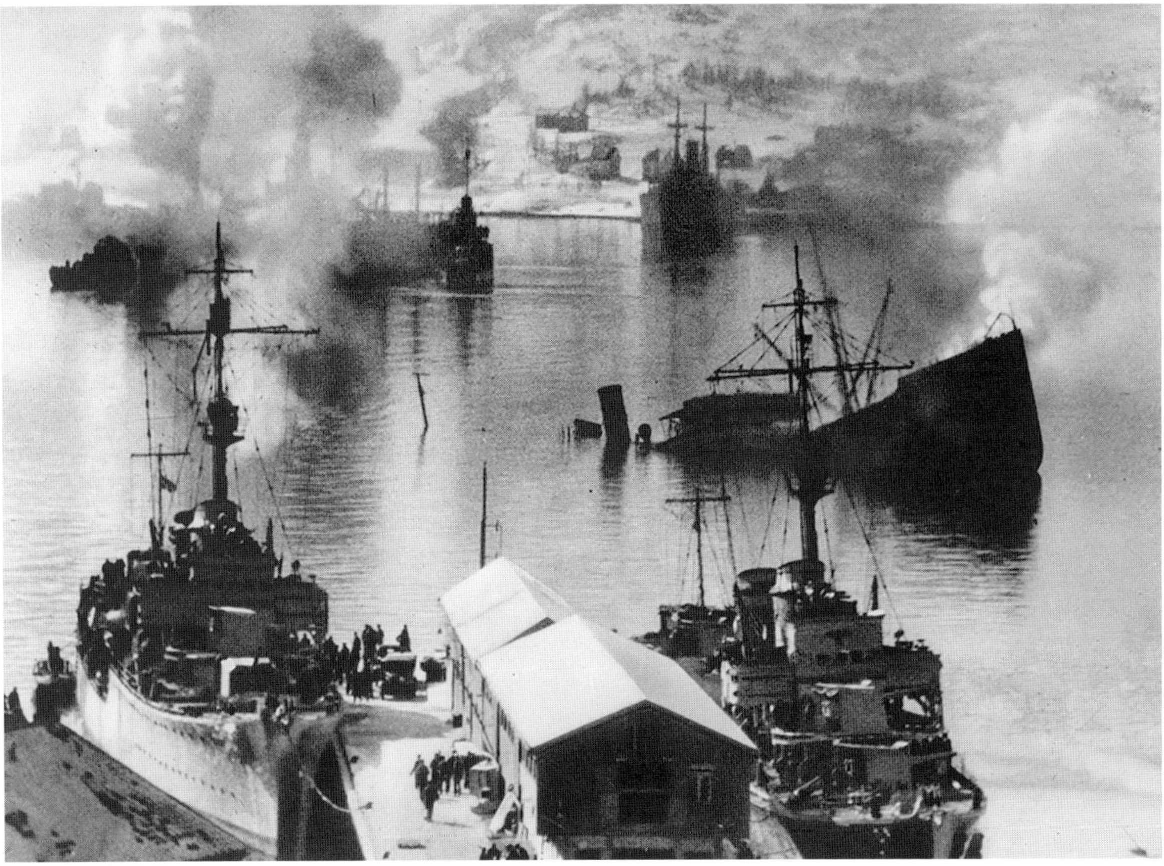

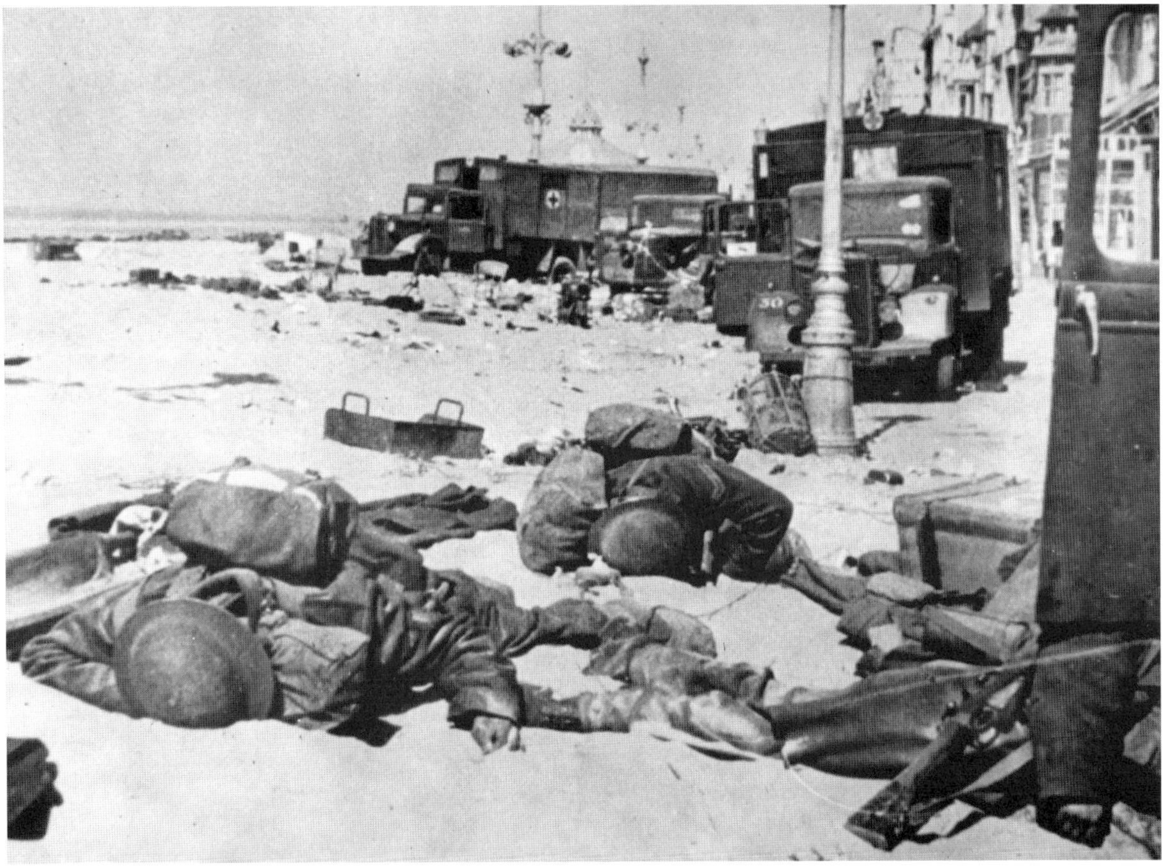

Dead Canadian infantrymen lie among disabled Churchill Infantry tanks on a landing beach at the port of Dieppe, after the failed Operation *Jubilee* of 19 August 1942. In Churchill's *The Hinge of Fate*, the assault on this French coastal town takes only three pages; however, it is one of the most widely examined offensives against German-held territory on the European continent during the period of Commando-style attacks by Combined Operations prior to the Normandy operation. The Prime Minister grandiloquently refers to it as 'a costly but not unfruitful reconnaissance-in-force ... tactically it was a mine of experience ... revealing many shortcomings in our outlook ... we learnt the value of heavy naval guns in an opposed landing.' Such lessons did indeed have a frightful cost, with approximately one fifth of the 5,000 men in the Canadian 2nd Division dying on the beaches of Dieppe, and 2,000 soldiers becoming prisoners-of-war (1,874 Canadian and the rest British Commandos or RN seamen and officers). Additionally, 106 of participating 650 RAF aircraft were destroyed, along with 33 of 179 landing craft lost at sea or on the beaches and one of the eight destroyers sunk, in addition to the deaths of 500 RN personnel. As Lord 'Haw-Haw', the English-born German propagandist commented on the Dieppe raid, it was 'too large to be a symbol, too small to be a success'.

Originally conceived in April 1942 by Admiral Lord Louis Mountbatten's Combined Operations HQ and codenamed Operation *Rutter*, the raid involved General Bernard Montgomery, CG Southeastern Command. Montgomery had been involved in the planning aspect of *Rutter* and was responsible for one of its key decisions, namely a frontal assault across the beaches at the port of Dieppe. He said, 'To assault and capture a port quickly, both troops and tanks would have to go in over the main beaches confronting the town, relying on heavy bombardment and surprise to neutralize the defenses.' Montgomery had no critical feedback regarding this amphibious assault tactic; however, once *Rutter* was postponed on 7 July largely due to weather concerns, the requirement for heavy bombardment for a Dieppe raid was also altered. And shortly after the decision to postpone *Rutter*, Montgomery was ordered to Egypt to take command of British Eighth Army. Pragmatically, the critical error of the Dieppe raid was the attempt to attack and capture a French port-town, which in essence trapped the Allied tanks. At Normandy, the decision was made to assault across open beaches. (*Author's collection*)

A British-crewed LST unloads a truck from its hull so it can traverse matting on the sand to facilitate its movement onto the landing beach at Salerno (Operation *Avalanche*), on Italy's western coast south of Naples, 9 September 1943. The LST is making smoke as the landings took place under both Nazi artillery fire and aerial attacks. LG Mark Clark's Fifth Army was comprised of US VI and British X Corps. FM Albert Kesselring, C-in-C South, had amassed his Tenth Army comprising a panzer corps and the Hermann Göring Division near Naples. The Allied forces met determined resistance and had to fight their way ashore with the aid of naval gunfire. An immediate link-up of the two Allied Corps did not occur. LSTs were hit and LCTs veered away from the Nazi bombardment at the shoreline. By the end of the first day, Fifth Army units made some gains. However, Luftwaffe planes mounted 450 sorties on 9/10 September. Over eighty Allied ships were hit by German bombs off Salerno. By 12 September, Clark's Fifth Army was short of infantry at the beachhead. (NARA)

RAMC personnel within the British beachhead zone are shown burying some of their dead at Salerno's Green Beach. The German counterattack, which began on 13 September 1943, was so intense at the confluence of the Sele and Calore rivers that it had to be stopped by Allied artillery firing over open sights and naval gunfire. Clark's staff reportedly crafted plans for shifting Allied Corps sectors and even a withdrawal from the Salerno beachhead. However, the naval commanders protested that they would be unable to reverse the landing process and advised Clark to continue fighting. (NARA)

(**Above**) A Nazi shell sends up a water plume near a DUKW at Nettuno on 27 April 1944. The Allies initially landed at Anzio and Nettuno (Operation *Shingle*) along Italy's west coast to the north of Salerno, on 22 January 1944, with the intent to outflank the German forces on the Winter Line to enable the advance on Rome. Rather than advancing promptly from the beachhead, US VI Corps commander, MG John Lucas, chose to entrench his troops against an expected Nazi counterattack. The Germans quickly built up a defensive ring around the Allied beachhead as Nazi artillery could shell every Allied position. The breakout from Anzio did not occur until early June 1944. Churchill quipped, 'I had hoped we were hurling a wildcat onto the shore, but all we got was a stranded whale.' (*NARA*)

(**Opposite, above**) At Anzio on 15 May 1944, RA signallers take near-permanent shelter in a slit trench from Nazi shellfire around the beachhead. On 23 May, 1,500 Allied artillery pieces commenced a 40-minute bombardment and a simultaneous aerial assault on German positions was made, to support Allied infantry and armoured movement out of the beachhead. They captured Cisterna on 25 May nearly four months after the landings at Anzio. (*NARA*)

(**Opposite, below**) FM Gerd von Rundstedt, C-in-C West commander, inspects a Wehrmacht AT gun crew on the French coast in 1944. The German gunners are wearing camouflage smocks and are most likely from a more elite, battle-hardened formation than many other units comprised of Wehrmacht 'sick battalions' or former Soviet POWs (referred to as 'Hiwis' – a short form of *Hilfswilliger*, or 'voluntary assistants'). FM von Rundstedt believed that there was no way to stop the Allies near the beaches because of the massive Allied naval firepower, which had saved the US Fifth Army at Salerno in September 1943. He urged that panzer forces be held inland and massed for a large counterattack after the Allies had extended themselves deep into France, rather than squandering elite panzer units with piecemeal commitment and attrition. After the July plot to kill Hitler failed, von Rundstedt was relieved and replaced by FM Günther von Kluge. (*NARA*)

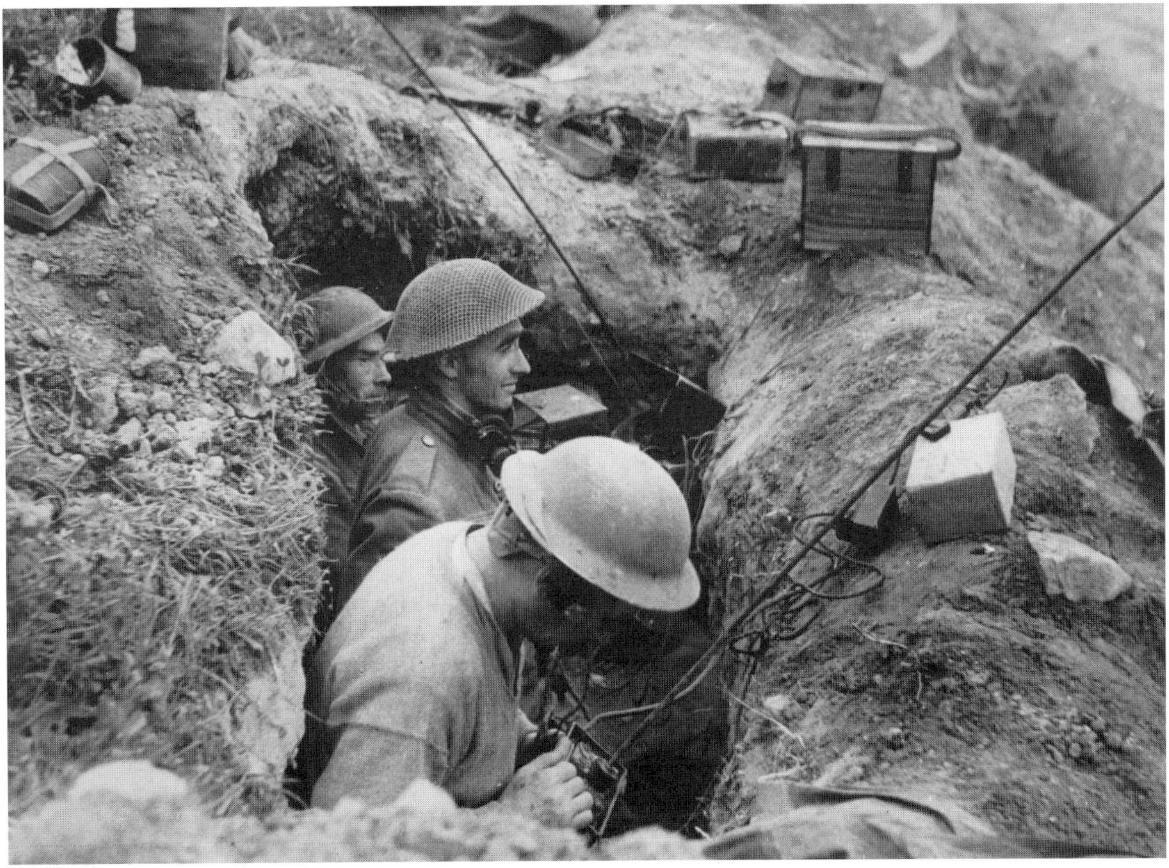

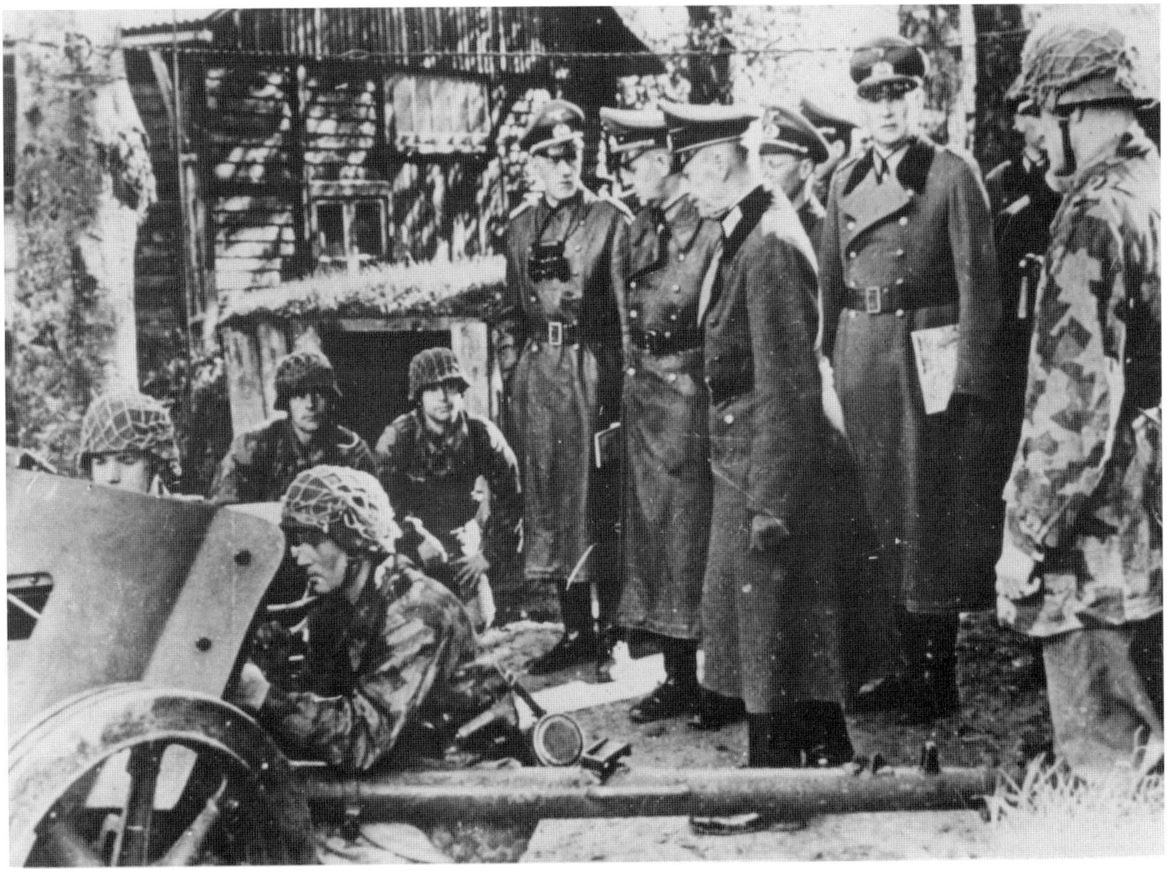

(**Above**) FM Erwin Rommel, commander of AG B, which combated the Allied Normandy invasion of 6 June 1944, is shown with Wehrmacht and *Kriegsmarine* subordinate officers reviewing a map before the invasion. Rommel was instrumental in fortifying Hitler's vaunted Atlantic Wall to stop the Allies at the water's edge. On 4 November 1943, Rommel became General Inspector of the Western Defences and was perplexed by the overall lack of defensive works constructed. After being appointed commander of AG B on 15 January 1944, his mission was to strengthen the Atlantic Wall with millions of mines and obstacles ('Rommel's asparagus') on presumed landing beaches and fields suitable for glider aircraft landings. At the time of the Normandy landings Rommel's fortifications, although formidable, were still incomplete. *(NARA)*

(**Opposite**) British Prime Minister Winston S. Churchill reviews American paratroopers of the US 101st Airborne Division under MG Maxwell Taylor at Newbury Burke in England on 23 March 1944. This elite American formation, along with the US 82nd and 6th British Airborne Divisions, were to seize vital locales and secure the flanks of the invasion beaches to facilitate Allied seaborne assault infantry movement inland. On 7 July, General Montgomery would award Taylor the British DSO for valour during the Normandy airborne assaults. *(NARA)*

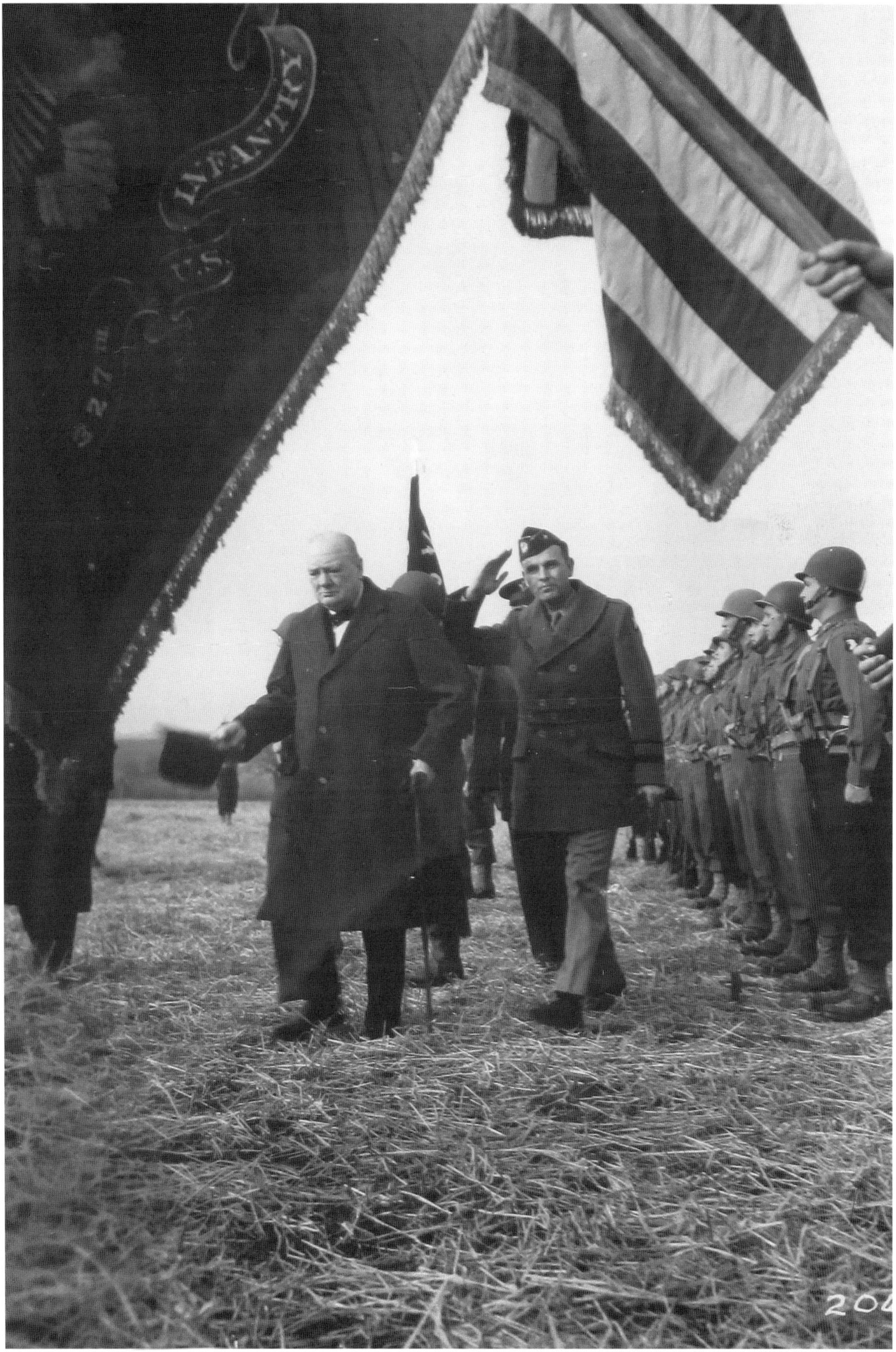
INFANTRY
U.S.

On 1 March 1944, Air Chief Marshal Arthur Tedder (*left*), Deputy Supreme Commander at SHAEF, with General Dwight D. Eisenhower, Supreme Commander at SHAEF, and General Bernard L. Montgomery, to be CG Allied Ground Forces at Normandy (*right*), review armour manoeuvres in England. The Allies (American, British, Canadian and French) committed thirteen armoured divisions and several independent tank brigades to the upcoming campaign. Montgomery planned for a 6 June capture of Caen in the eastern Anglo-Canadian sector so that his armoured formations could break into open tank country south of the Calvados capital. (*NARA*)

Low tide along a Normandy beach reveals wooden obstacles with attached mines planted several hundred feet from the shoreline (*right*). Numerous 'Belgian gates' (*left*) are arrayed in a line closer to the water's edge. The Belgian gate was a movable steel barricade AT obstacle. (*NARA*)

A German *Teller* mine is affixed on top of a wooden pole at Utah Beach at low tide. At high tide these obstacles sat just below the water line so that assault tanks and other vehicles would not notice them and would cause the mines to detonate. (NARA)

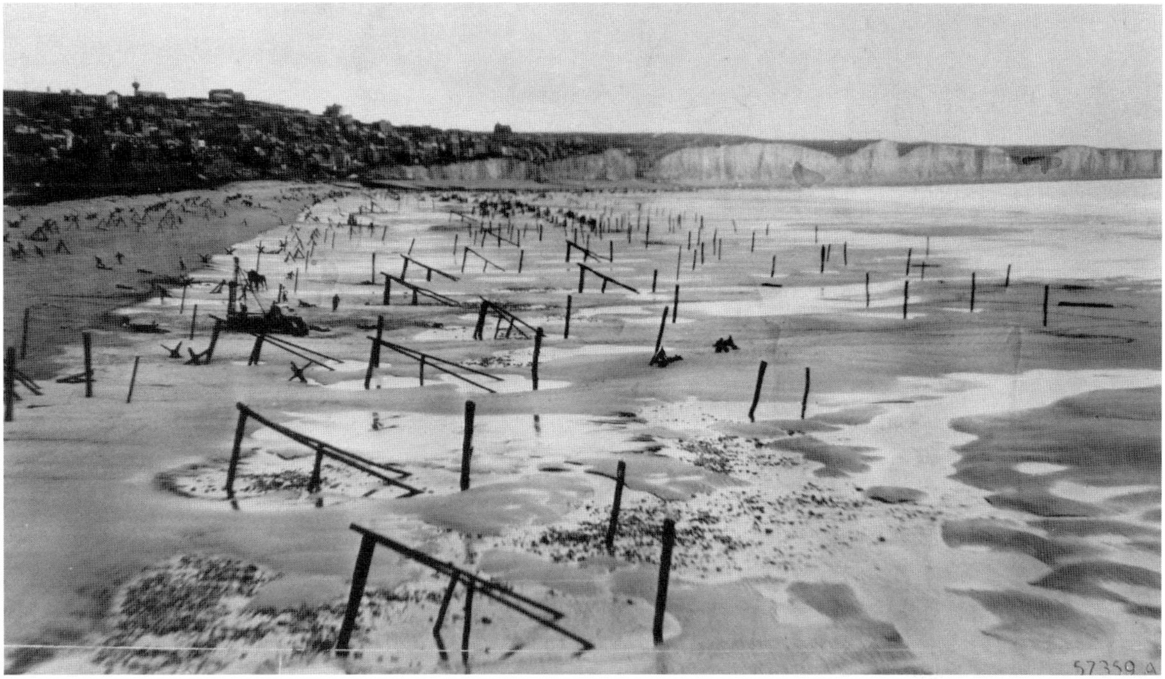

German workers along the French coastline had run from a P-38 reconnaissance fighter that had been 'buzzing' their low-tide positions on 6 May 1944, this photograph showing the wooden poles with attached mines atop them and saw-toothed wooden beam obstacles which were intended to be invisible at high tide to damage or destroy the bottoms of Allied landing craft. Other obstacles were 'hedgehogs' or large steel crossed beams (*far left*) designed to pierce the bottom of landing craft and make them easy targets for German MG positions. (*NARA*)

A German short-barrelled 75mm *Kampfwagenkanone* (Kwk) 37L/24 howitzer housed within the turret of an early Panzer Mk IV serves as a Nazi coastal defence weapon at Omaha Beach. This gun was designed as a close support weapon firing a HE shell, which was also effective against tanks. (*NARA*)

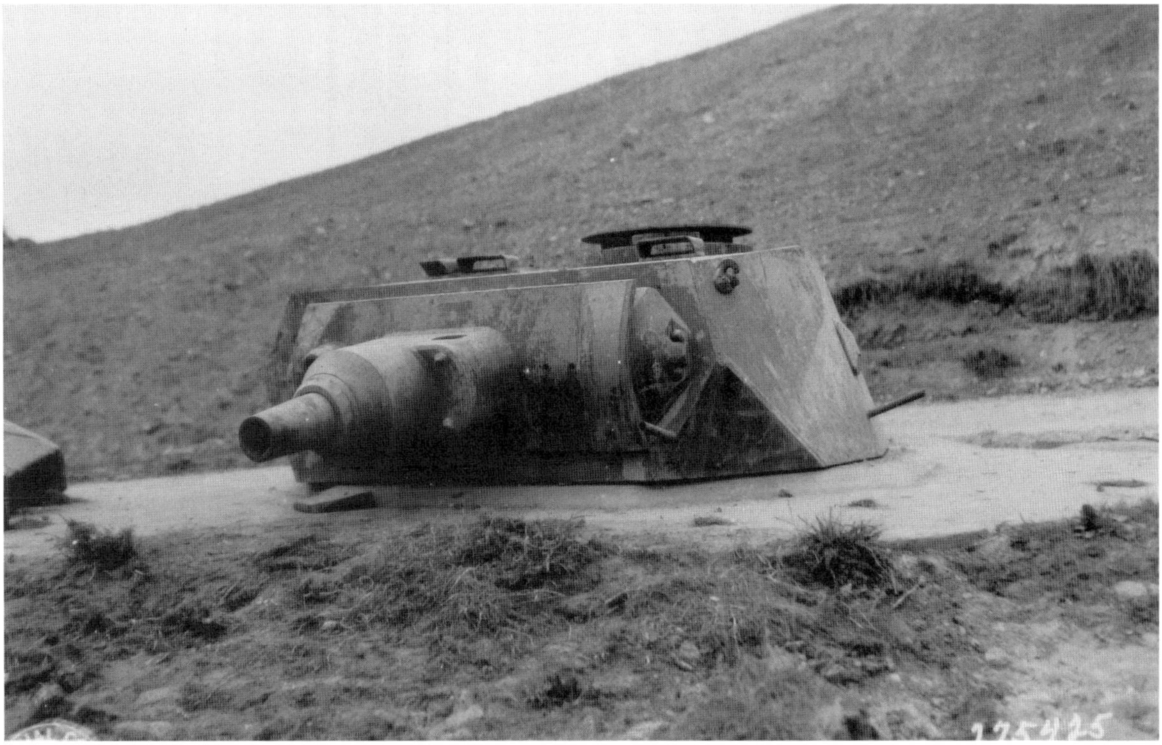

A German 88mm AT gun emplacement in a concrete fortification at Utah Beach is shown. These Nazi defences had to be neutralized by naval gunfire, aerial bombardment, Allied tank gunfire, and infantry with explosive charges. (NARA)

A camouflaged German concrete OP near Pointe du Hoc with a direct view of the Bay of the Seine is mostly destroyed by Allied aerial bombardment prior to the invasion and during the pre-landing naval gunfire barrages. The vertical structure at the centre-top of this reinforced concrete fortification is most likely a ventilator shaft. (NARA)

A German concrete blockhouse at Normandy houses a high-calibre naval gun, which had to be neutralized early on in the invasion by naval bombardment and subsequent aerial sorties so that offshore Allied transports would not be destroyed. (NARA)

A German gun turret, previously part of the French coastal defence of Cherbourg harbour, with numerous shell holes showing the punishment it took from Allied bombardment before this city fell to US VII Corps on 26 June 1944. (NARA)

A London fire brigade works on a blaze started by a pilotless Nazi V-1 missile or 'flying bomb' on 18 June 1944. The German name was *Vergeltungswaffe* 1 or 'Vengeance Weapon 1', an early cruise missile. Because of its limited range, the thousands of V-1 missiles launched against England were fired from facilities along the French and Dutch coasts. The first V-1s against London were launched on 13 June 1944, one week after, and perhaps prompted by, the Allied landings in Normandy. At the peak, more than a hundred were launched daily at southeast England, the total reaching over 9,500 V-1s fired, until the Allies overran the launch sites in October 1944. *(NARA)*

On 1 July 1944, British Prime Minister Winston Churchill talks with an American MP in an English town struck by a V-1 missile the night before. Approximately 2,400 V-1s landed inside Greater London, causing 6,000 fatalities, 18,000 seriously wounded, and 1.5 million Britons evacuated. After the war, Churchill wrote that the V-1 missile 'imposed upon the people of London a burden perhaps even heavier than the air raids of 1940 and 1941. Suspense and strain were more prolonged.... The blind, impersonal nature of the missile made the individual on the ground feel helpless. There was little that he could do, no human enemy that he could see shot down.' The months long deadlock in Normandy added to the concern as the V-1 missile launch sites in the Pas de Calais could not be reached in a timely manner. (NARA)

Chapter Two

The Allied Landings at Normandy, 5–6 June 1944

General Dwight D. Eisenhower, Supreme Commander at SHAEF, talks with paratroopers of Company E, 502nd PIR of the US 101st Airborne Division at Greenham Common airfield in England, on 5 June 1944. This took place directly before the take-off for a nocturnal drop at the western end of the Allied beachhead astride the Douve and Merderet rivers, paralleling the Carentan–Montebourg road in the vicinity of Sainte-Mère-Église and Saint-Côme-du-Mont, inland from Utah Beach. Standing behind Eisenhower is Commander Harry Butcher, USN, his naval aide. Despite apprehension, Eisenhower's message to the paratroopers could not have been more decisive: 'Full victory – nothing else.' The US 101st and 82nd Airborne Divisions were dropped behind Utah Beach to reinforce the invasion flank and secure the causeways across the lowland to enable the US 4th Infantry Division to exit from the beach. In reality, the paratroopers were dispersed over a wide area and took heavy losses seizing causeways across the swamp behind Utah Beach – they had initial difficulty taking Sainte-Mère-Église. (NARA)

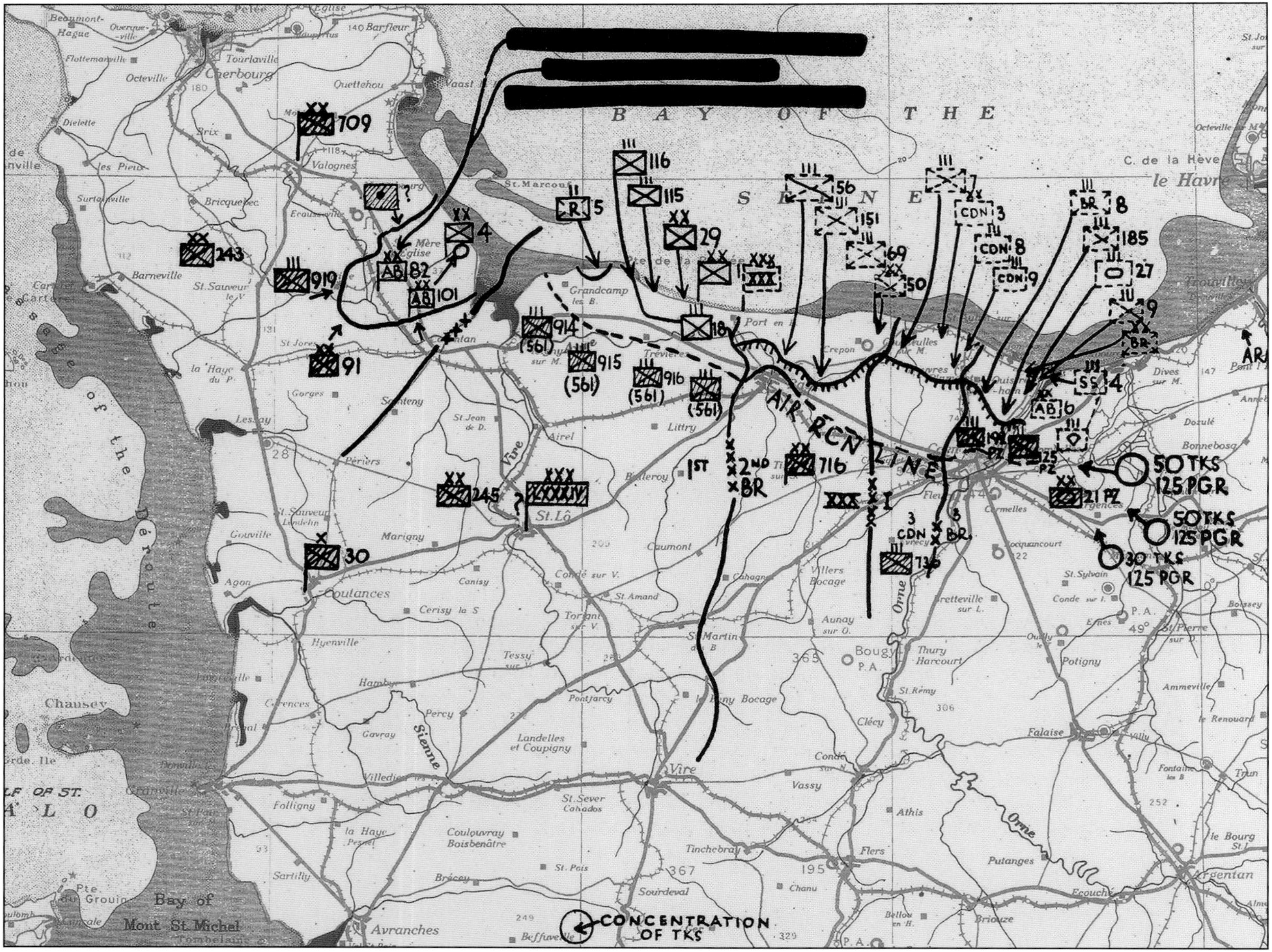
[redacted]
BAY OF THE SEINE
709
243
919
91
AB 82
AB 101
4
R 5
116
115
29
XXX
914 (561)
915 (561)
916 (561)
(561)
18
56
151
69
50
CDN 3
CDN 8
CDN 9
BR 8
185
27
9
BR
SS 4
AB 6
21 PZ
125 PZ
716
245
XXXXIV
30
1ST
2ND BR
I
3 CDN
3 BR.
736
AIR RCN LINE
50 TKS 125 PGR
50 TKS 125 PGR
30 TKS 125 PGR
CONCENTRATION OF TKS
Cherbourg
Barfleur
Valognes
St. Marcouf
Grandcamp les B.
Port en B.
Crepon
Trevieres
Littry
Balleroy
Caumont
St. Lô
Périers
Coutances
Vire
Villers Bocage
Thury Harcourt
Falaise
Argentan
Flers
Avranches
Granville
le Havre
C. de la Hève
Trouville
Dives sur M.
Orne
Sienne
Bay of Mont St. Michel
Passage of the Déroute
Chausey

A US First Army HQ Situation Map from 2400 hrs, 7 June 1944, denoting the Allied assault troops that participated in the initial phases of the amphibious invasion of Normandy and the German units that were present to resist the seaborne attack of 6 June. The right of the Allied attack began on 5–6 June, with the US 101st Airborne (AB) Division parachuting in north of Carentan in the vicinity of Vierville and Sainte Marie-du-Mont and the US 82nd Airborne (AB) Division making a scattered drop in the vicinity of Sainte-Mère-Église and the marshlands of the Douve and Merderet rivers, which flow parallel to the Montebourg–Valognes road in a northwesterly direction towards Cherbourg.

As for the American seaborne assault, elements of the US 4th Infantry Division (MG J. Lawton Collins's VII Corps) landed at Utah Beach meeting limited resistance. This area of the Cotentin Peninsula was defenced by the Wehrmacht's 709th (with its forward 919th Grenadier Regiment), 243rd, 91st Infantry Divisions. The other major American assault on 6 June was at Omaha Beach to the east of the Vire river, by the 116th IR of the US 29th Infantry Division and the 16th IR (regimental insignia not shown) of the US 1st Infantry Division (all of MG Leonard Gerow's V Corps). Other regiments soon followed up including the 115th IR of the 29th Division and 18th IR of the 1st Infantry Division. Elements of the 2nd (battalion insignia not shown) and 5th Ranger Battalions scaled Pointe du Hoc at the western end of Omaha Beach near Grandcamp les Bains.

Reinforced German fortifications and a terrain favouring the Wehrmacht's 352nd Infantry Division's 914th, 915th, 916th Grenadier Regiments and an artillery regiment exacted a heavy toll on the American assault troops. Further east in the British Second Army zone, the 69th, 151st, 56th, and 231st (brigade insignia not shown) Brigades of the British 50th Infantry Division (LG Gerard Bucknall's XXX Corps) landed along Gold Beach to the north of the Norman city of Bayeux. To the east of Gold Beach, the Canadian 7th, 8th, and 9th Brigades of the Canadian 3rd Infantry Division assaulted Juno Beach from Courseulles-sur-Mer to Saint-Aubin-sur-Mer. These assault beaches were defended by the Wehrmacht's 716th Infantry Division. At Sword Beach, the farthest east, the 8th, 9th, 185th Brigades of the British 3rd Division (LG John Crocker's I Corps) landed from Lion-sur-Mer to Ouistreham near the Orne river. British 6th Airborne's 5th and 3rd Parachute Brigades dropped on 5–6 June near the Orne river bridge and canal. No. 4 British Commandos of the 1st Special Service Brigade landed at Sword Beach to take the German gun batteries at Ouistreham, with the support of British tanks from the 27th Armoured Brigade and then, with other units of the 1st Special Service Brigade, relieved elements of British 6th Airborne inland at the Orne bridges. Sword Beach was also defended by elements of the Wehrmacht's 716th Infantry Division; however, what most concerned the British 3rd Division CG, MG Tom G. Rennie, was the German 21st Panzer Division stationed further inland. Movements by the 192nd and 125th *Panzergrenadier* Regiments of the 21st Panzer Division contributed to the inability of the British to capture Caen on 6 June. The German 12th SS-Panzer Division *Hitlerjugend* was also in the vicinity to defend the Caen area, while the Panzer *Lehr* Division was in movement to the battlefield. (NARA)

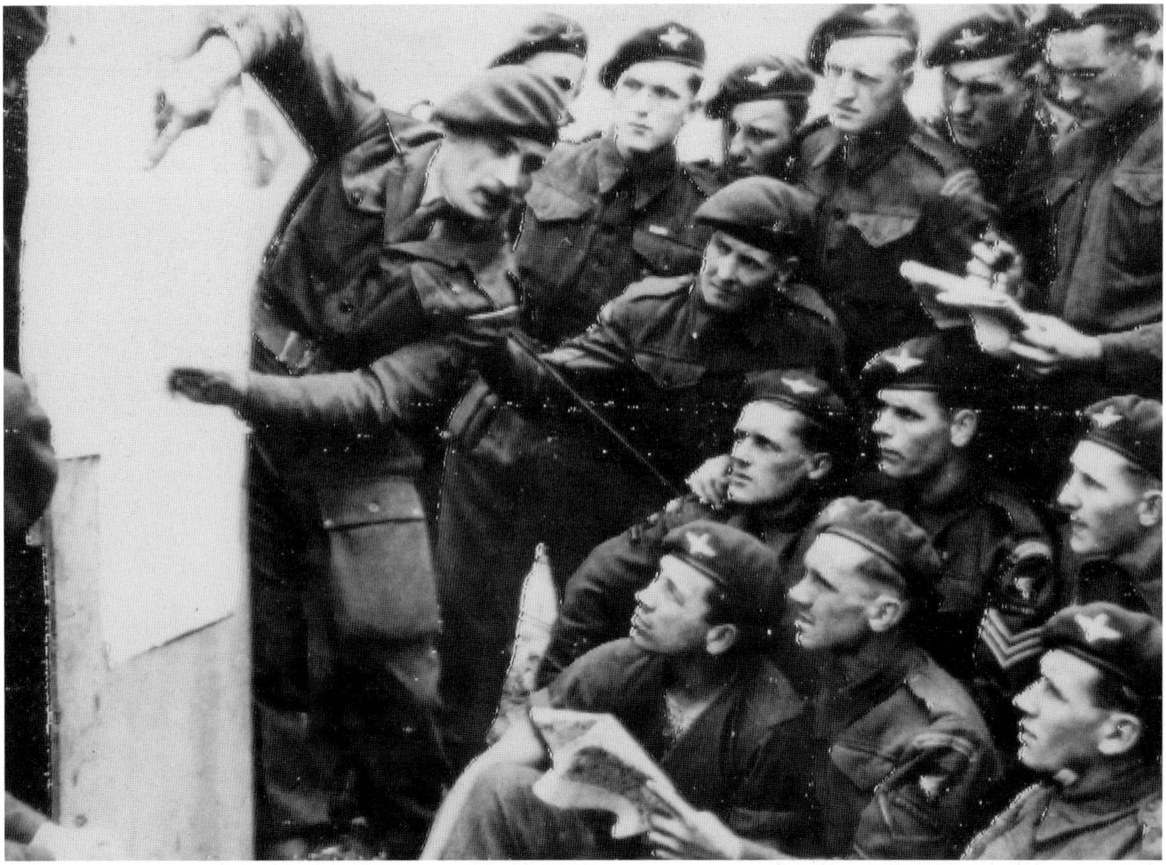

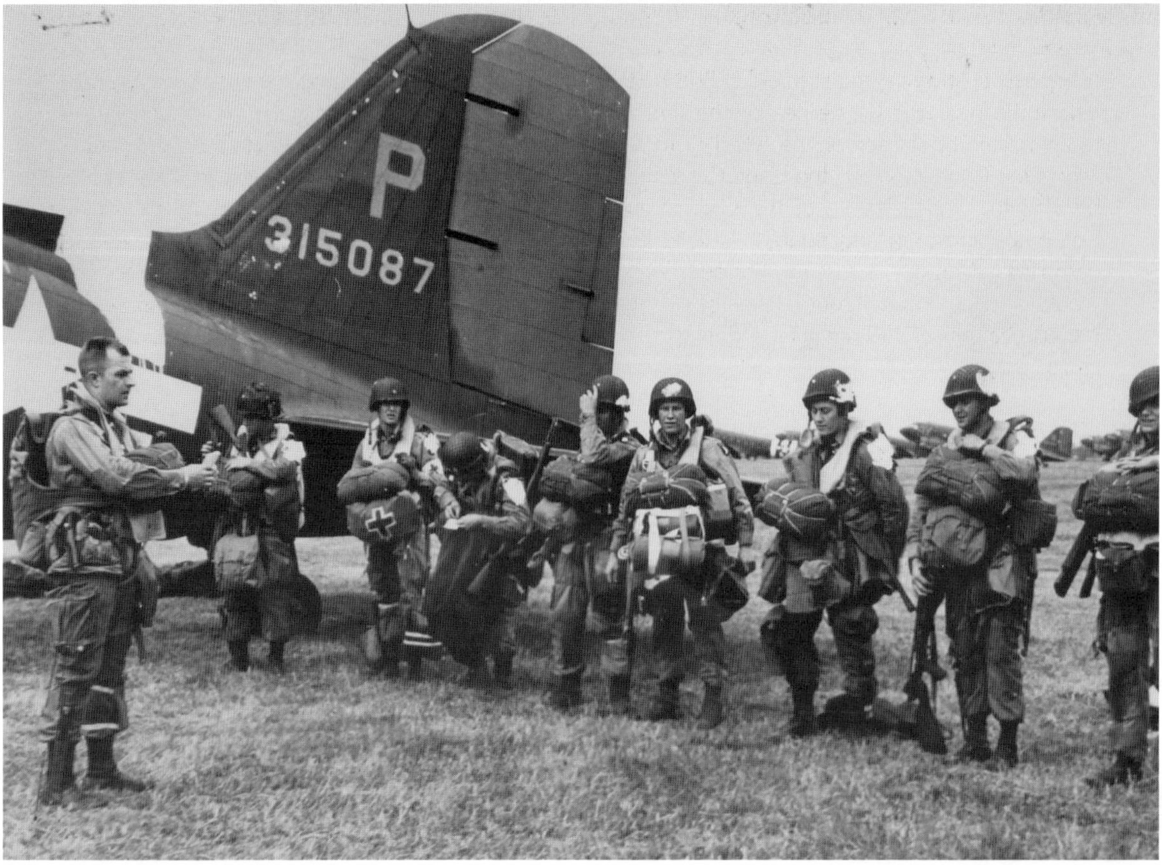
P
315087

(**Opposite, above**) Paratroopers of British 6th Airborne Division receive drop instructions with a map before the invasion flight delineating the landing zones. These drop zones and glider landing areas were to the northeast of Caen on the Allied eastern flank. The 5th Parachute Brigade was to seize the bridges across the Orne river and the Caen Canal north of Ranville and protect landing zones for their gliders bringing the 2nd Battalion of the Oxford and Bucks Light Infantry, and REs to capture the above waterways' crossings and establish a solid bridgehead. The 3rd Parachute Brigade's mission was to demolish the bridges across the flooded Dives river at Troarn, Bures, Robehomme and Varaville. This would block and hold all routes leading in from the southeast. They also needed to destroy the powerful Merville battery of 155mm guns and its garrison before it could enfilade the left flank of the seaborne attack. (NARA)

(**Opposite, below**) US paratroopers of the 101st Airborne Division (denoted by the 'Screaming Eagle' left shoulder patch on the man in the middle, others having had their identifiers censored). They are receiving instructions from their CO before boarding the C-47 transport on 5 June 1944, to be ferried from southern England across the Bay of the Seine to their drop zones inland from Utah Beach. (NARA)

(**Above**) A heavily kitted US paratrooper with his main and reserve parachutes, field gear, ammunition and his 0.45in calibre Thompson SMG sits aboard a C-47 transport, which getting onto was a formidable task given the weight of his gear. In the ETO, the C-47 also had a specialized paratroop variant, the C-53 Skytrooper, with a capacity of twenty-eight troops. (NARA)

(**Above**) A US 9th TAF Martin B-26 Marauder medium bomber releases its load of 26 100lb bombs on German installations just before the amphibious invasion. The B-26 had up to fourteen 0.5in calibre MGs with a crew of seven. Allied air power attained and maintained a situation where the Luftwaffe was rendered incapable of effective interference with Allied landing operations and they disrupted German communications and supply channels for reinforcement against the Allied beachhead. (NARA)

(**Opposite, above**) A Douglas A-20 (DB-7) Havoc of the US 9th TAF passes over elements of the Allied invasion armada on its way to blast German installations along the Normandy coastline on 6 June 1944. This American medium bomber evolved into an excellent attack aircraft in both theatres of war, as well a night fighter and reconnaissance plane. French DB-7s were the first to see combat; however, after the fall of France, this bomber served with the RAF as the Boston. During Operation *Torch*, during the Allied invasion of Vichy French Northwest Africa in November 1942, the A-20 made its American combat debut. The plane had a crew of three and mounted six fixed forward-firing 0.5in calibre Browning MGs in the nose and two 0.5in Browning MGs in a dorsal turret. There was also a flexible 0.5in calibre MG mounted behind the bomb bay. The A-20 Havoc had a maximal 4,000lb bomb load. (NARA)

(**Below**) A Republic P-47 Thunderbolt had an unfortunate conclusion on D-Day, crashing into the sea wall of a Normandy town shortly after the 6 June 1944 invasion. Having been a successful high-altitude fighter in its escort role of US 8th AF bombers during the daylight bombing campaign over Europe, the P-47 transitioned into the foremost American fighter-bomber in its ground-attack role. The Thunderbolt had eight 0.5in calibre MGs and carried a 2,500lb bomb load. In addition, it could carry 5in rockets, which devastated German railroad transport in France, greatly contributing to the isolation of Normandy from Nazi reinforcements. (NARA)

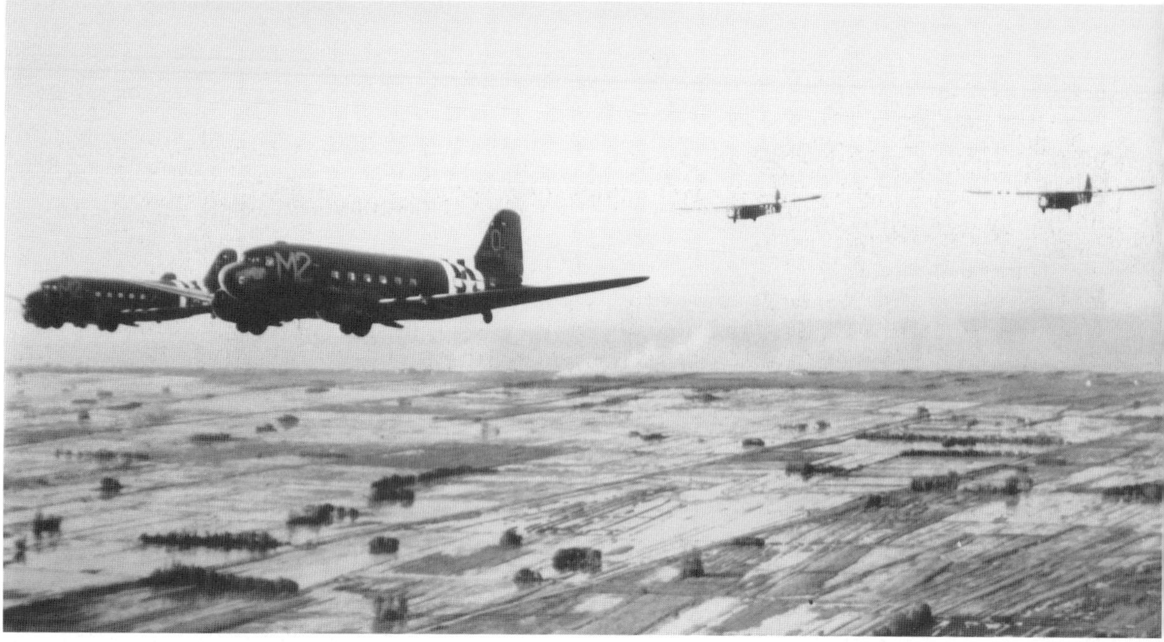

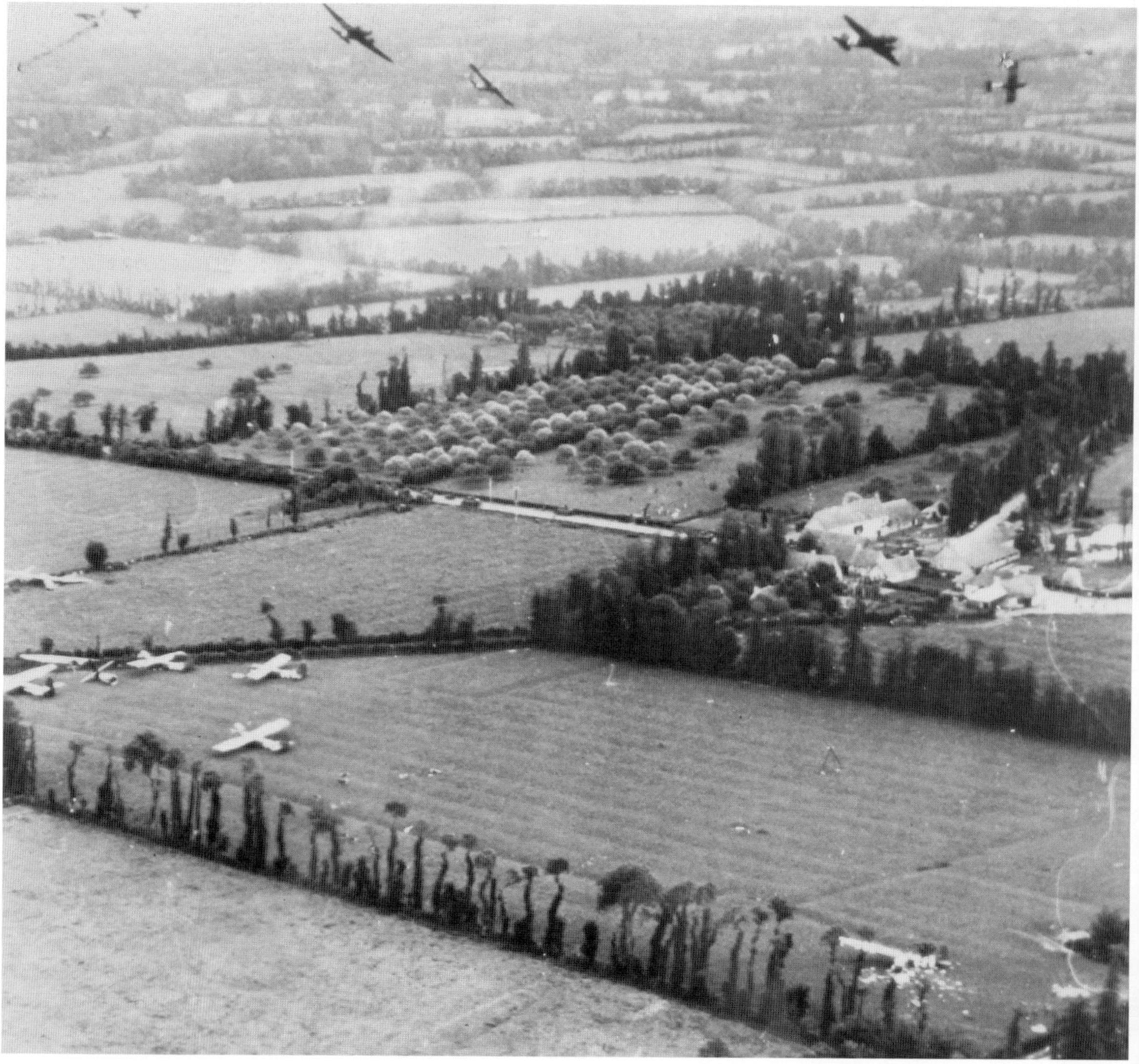

(**Opposite, above**) Two Douglas C-47 Skytrain transport planes (also referred to as R4D to the USN and Dakota to the RAF), each towing a CG-4A Waco glider (known as 'Hadrian' to the British) towards Normandy landing fields on 6 June 1944. The C-47 transport was developed from the civilian Douglas DC-3 airliner, entering service in late December 1941 and extensively utilized in all theatres, with over 10,000 produced. The C-47 Skytrain had a crew of four and a range of 1,600 miles. The glider was manufactured by the Waco Aircraft Company and mass produced by Ford and Cessna, with 14,000 built for all combat theatres entering service in 1942. Being smaller, the Waco could land in more confined spaces, in contrast to the British General Aircraft Hamilcar and the Airspeed Horsa; however, the latter gliders could carry more troopers or a jeep and AT gun. (*NARA*)

(**Opposite, below**) Allied gliders within adjacent Normandy fields are either intact (*left*) or crashed (*lower right*). Above, two C-47 Skytrain transports release their attached gliders to begin their descent to landing zones. Normandy's *bocage* terrain can be seen, with hedgerows demarcating cultivated fields, orchards, and farmhouses with roads and lanes traversing them. (*NARA*)

(**Above**) A Normandy field with several destroyed Horsa gliders and one intact Waco glider (*middle, far left*) near a huge shell crater on 6 June 1944. The *bocage* terrain has tall, tree-lined hedgerows surrounding the fields' perimeter with parallel-running country lanes, which made excellent defensive works for the Germans as predominantly American forces moved inland from their landing beaches. (*NARA*)

(**Above**) Close-up of two wrecked Waco gliders (left) and a Horsa (right) after rough landings in a Normandy field on 6 June 1944. Of the 517 Allied gliders involved in the airborne landings, 222 were Horsas, most of which were destroyed in landing accidents or by German gunfire. Most of the 295 Waco gliders were repairable; however, combat on the beaches and the inland location prevented troop carrier service units from reclaiming them and almost all were left abandoned. (*NARA*)

(**Opposite, above**) An Allied Airspeed Horsa glider has crashed through a hedgerow into a country lane, with its front wheel snapped off. The Horsa was first used in November 1942 in an unsuccessful raid on a Nazi heavy water production facility in Norway. About 250 were deployed by the Allies in Normandy, including elements of the British 6th Airborne Division's Operation *Tonga*, which was a *coup-de-main* landing by six Horsas to capture the Caen Canal and Orne river bridges to prevent German approaches to the British invasion flank. Capable of accommodating thirty glider troops, the Horsa was bigger than the 13-troop capacity CG-4A Waco and was towed by four-engined heavy bombers such as the Short Stirling and the Handley Page Halifax. Twin-engined bombers such as the Armstrong Whitworth Albemarle and Whitley, as well as the C-47 Skytrain/Dakota, were utilized less frequently due to the Horsa's weight. (*NARA*)

(**Opposite, below**) Eight American glider troops lie dead, their faces covered with parachutes, beside their wrecked 437th Troop Carrier Group Horsa glider in a Normandy field near Hiesville on 6 June 1944. Casualties for the airborne divisions were calculated in August 1944 as 1,240 and 1,259 for the US 101st Airborne and 82nd Airborne Divisions, respectively. At dawn, when the seaborne landings were arriving at Utah Beach, the 101st Airborne Division mustered 1,100 men out of 6,600. By evening, its strength had grown to 2,500 paratroopers. The 82nd Airborne Division was at least 4,000 men short of its full complement on 6 June 1944, and three days later it was still at one-third of operational strength. Both divisions lost large quantities of equipment and almost all their glider-borne artillery, much of it sinking in the flooded Merderet and Douve rivers inland from Utah Beach. The glider co-pilot of the destroyed aircraft in the photograph, 1st Lt. George Parker, survived to fly gliders during Operation *Market Garden* in Holland (September 1944) and across the Rhine, in Operation *Varsity* in March 1945. (*NARA*)

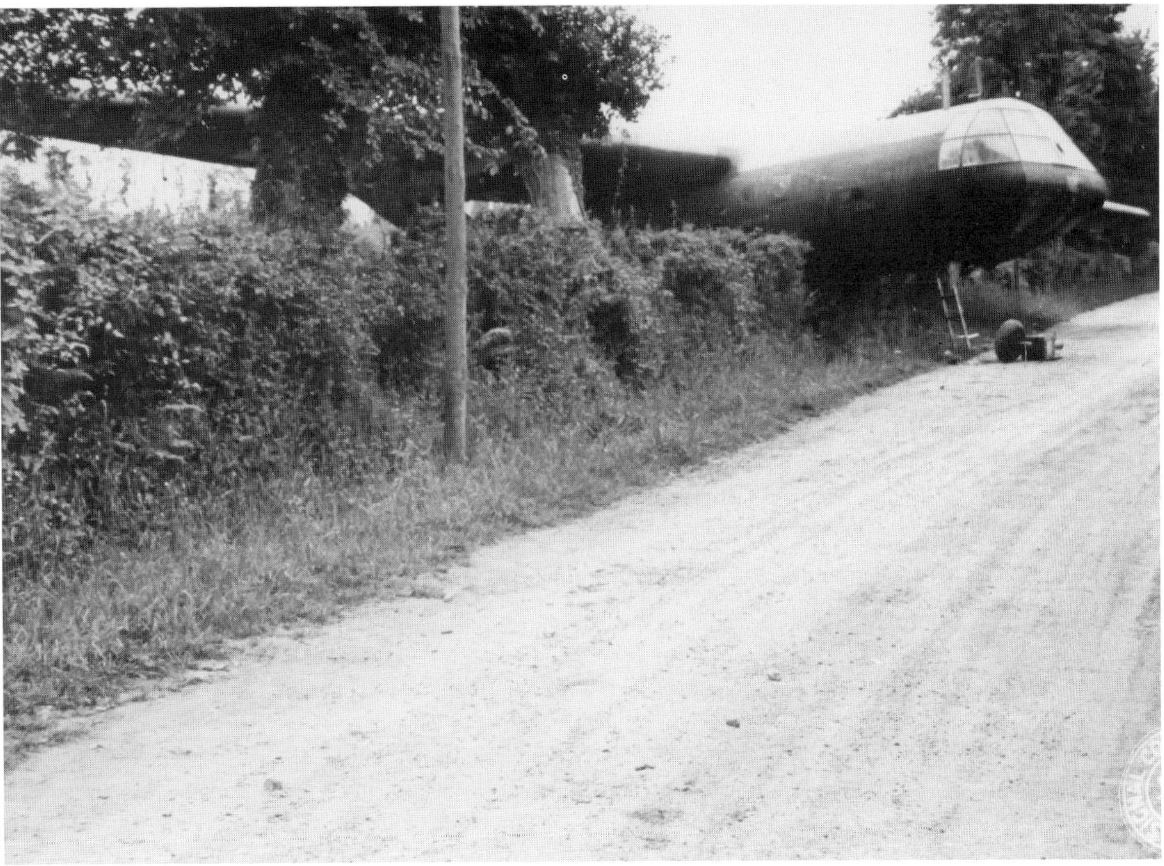

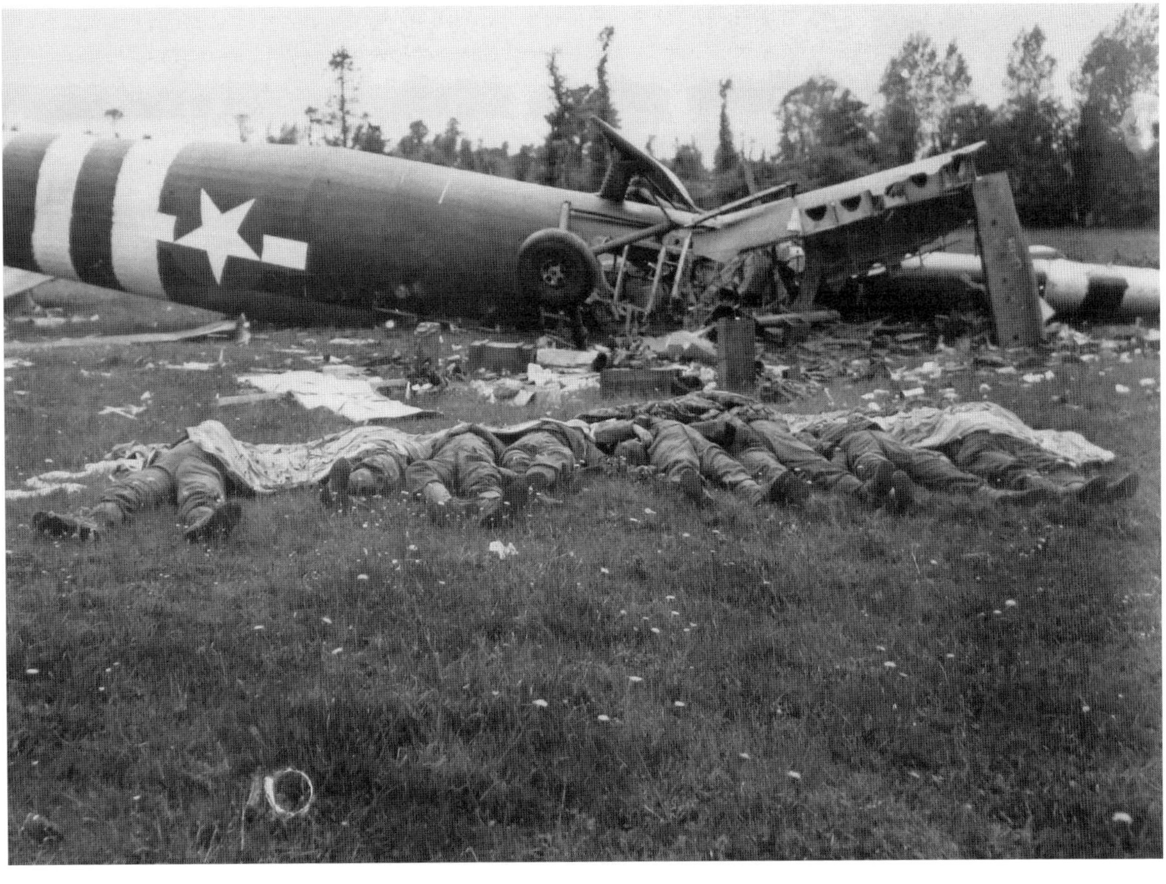

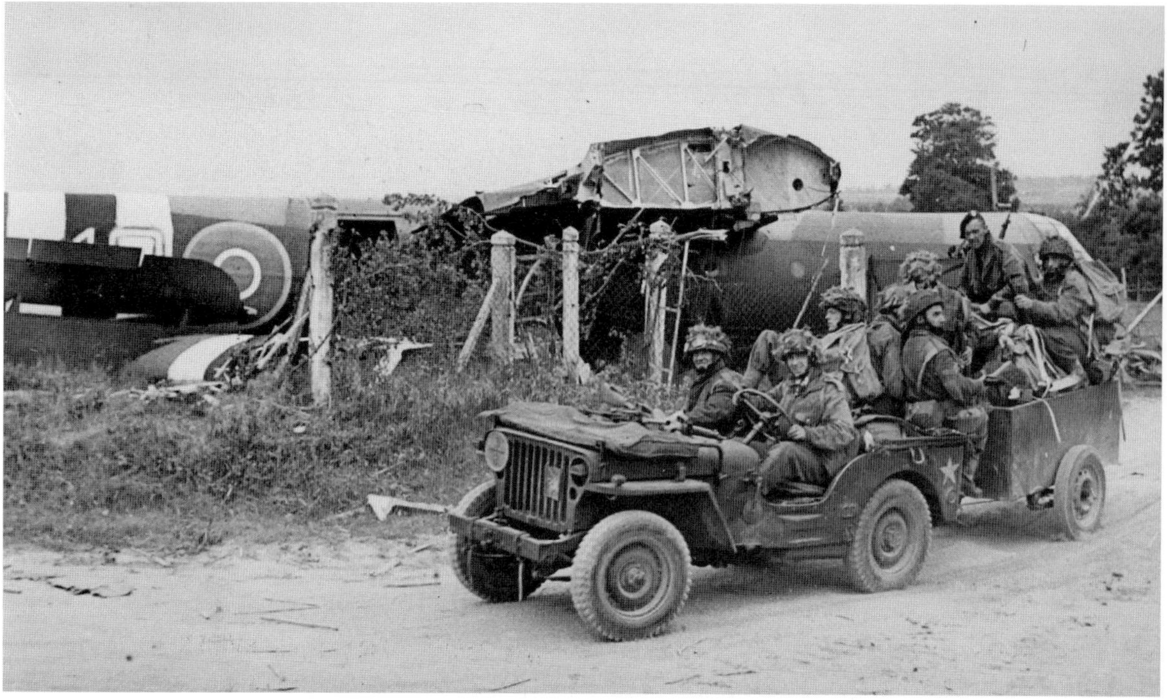

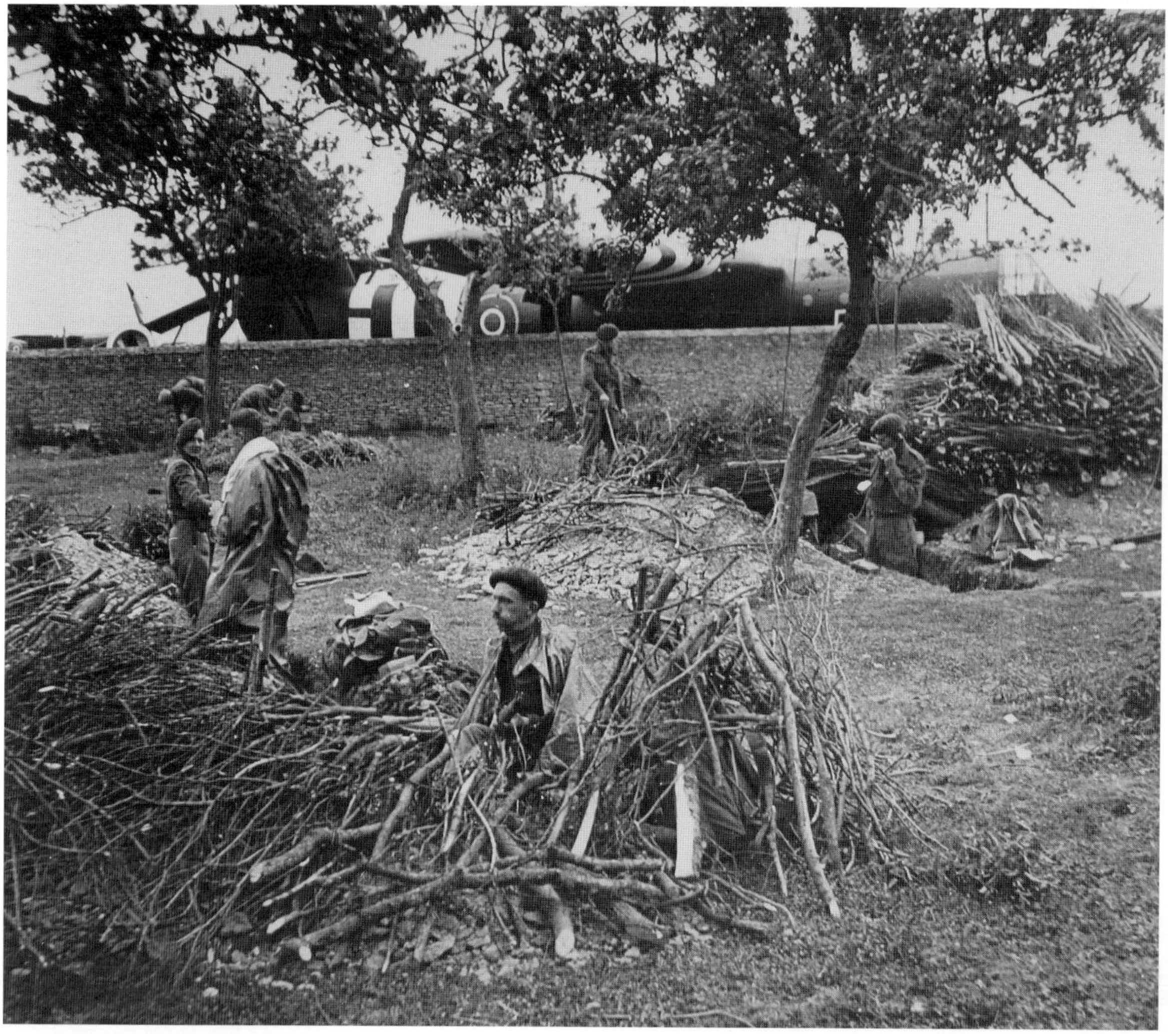

(**Opposite, above**) A British 6th Airborne Division's 716 Company RASC jeep and trailer remove pilots and supplies from damaged Hamilcar gliders, as part of a second wave of the division's later air landing during the morning of 6 June 1944 at Ranville. The British 5th and 3rd Parachute Brigades landed on 5–6 June in the midst of enemy defenders and seized their objectives to prevent German reinforcements from reaching the British flank at Sword. (NARA)

(**Opposite, below**) Men of No. 3 Commando, 1st Special Service Brigade, after linking with British 6th Airborne glider troops, fortify their position with wood-covered foxholes as breastworks. An improvised CP is to the right while an intact Horsa glider and part of another are in an adjacent field near La Haute Ecarde, on western end of DZ 'N' between Ranville and Sallenelles on 6 June 1944. (NARA)

(**Above**) A line of Allied ships sails from English ports to the Bay of Seine to commence the seaborne invasion of Normandy on 5 June 1944. Barrage balloons above the vessels deterred any low-flying Luftwaffe sorties. By sunrise on 5 June, 5,000 vessels were moving from their anchorages to steam in convoy through the overnight hours amid buoyed channels cleared of mines. Allied warships, 50 miles wide of the edges of the armada, made sure no enemy surface craft approached. Before sunset on 5 June, two flotillas of mine-sweepers stood off the Normandy coast. From 0200hrs on 6 June, the HQ ships of the amphibious assault moved into their transport areas to put their landing craft into the water. (NARA)

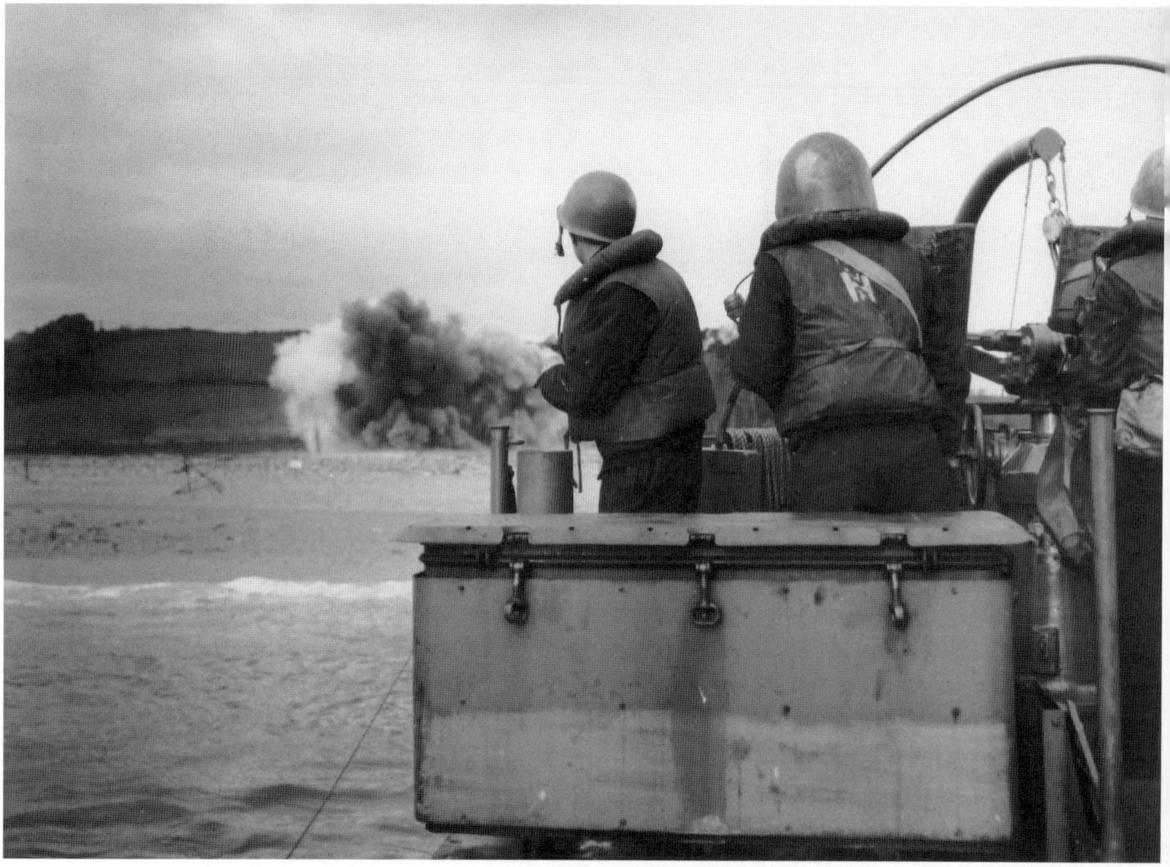

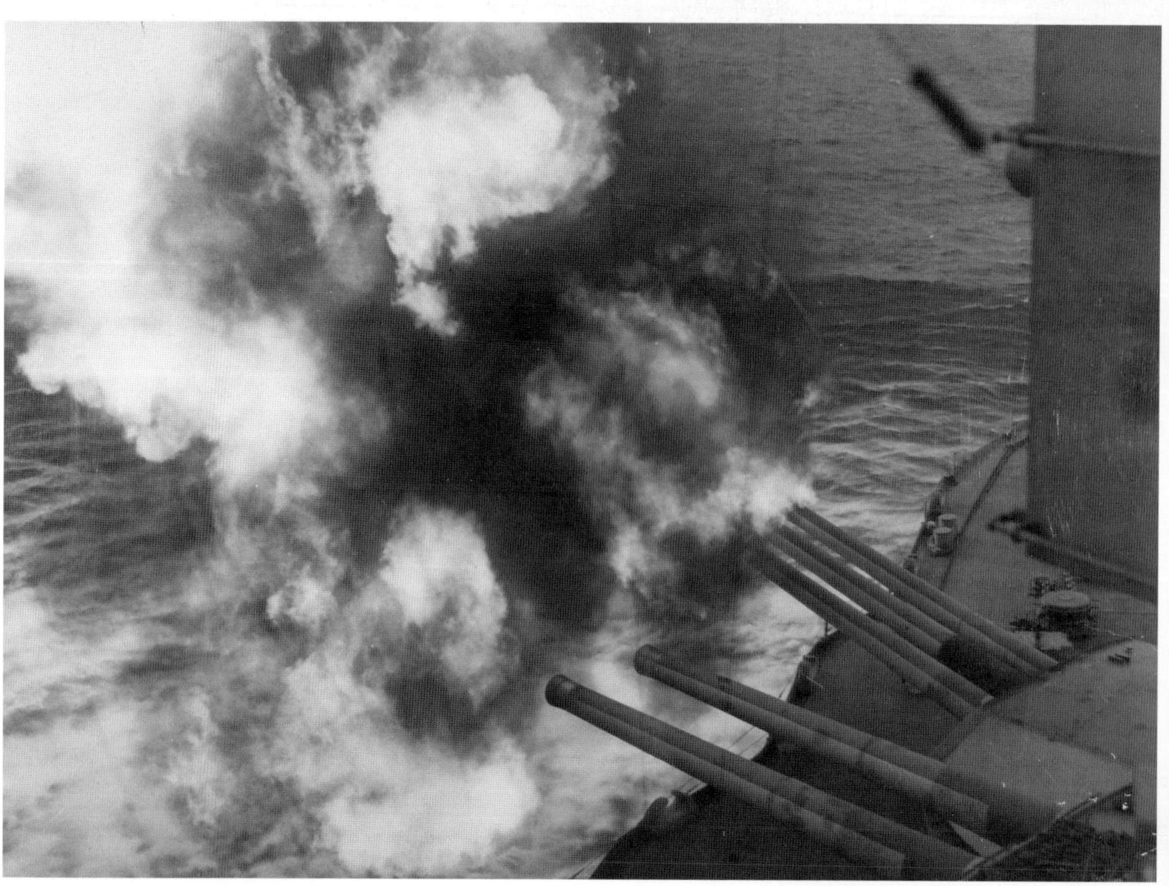

(**Opposite, above**) A USCG attack vessel, probably an LCI, approaches the Normandy shore on 6 June 1944. A German mine is seen exploding ashore off the port bow of the ship. The Coast Guardsman (*right*) mans a 20mm AA gun to provide indirect fire against German targets ashore as infantrymen have to wade through the surf to the beach. (*NARA*)

(**Opposite, below**) The USS *Nevada*, a battleship that survived the Pearl Harbor attack of December 1941 and was redeployed to the Atlantic in mid-1943, fires a 14in salvo at German installations in the Utah Beach area on 6 June 1944. The ship's complement of 5in guns also engaged enemy targets that day. It was deployed as a flagship during Operation *Neptune* and then in the bombardment concentrated on the German batteries of Azeville and Saint-Marcouf. In late June, the USS *Nevada* bombarded the Nazi batteries of Cherbourg, supporting the US VII Corps forces attacking the port city. (*NARA*)

(**Above**) An aerial view on 6 June 1944 shows an American sector at Omaha Beach. Infantrymen are sprawled on the beach sand trying to make it to the height above (*top, background*). Amphibious DD tanks are in column trying to clear the surf to the shore. LSTs and LCIs are further back in the water. Assaulting infantry is bogged down by German gunfire at the water's edge. (*NARA*)

(**Above**) An aerial view from a US 9th TAF Martin B-26 Marauder, of 6 June 1944 Utah Beach landings at 0630hrs. Several LCIs are close to the shoreline disembarking infantry while LSTs are at the left. American vehicles are moving along the narrow beachfront while others move inland (*left*). Numerous shell holes from aerial and naval pre-invasion bombardment are visible. Utah Beach was an isolated operation with the US 4th Infantry Division's 8th IR establishing a bridgehead. The 8th IR's 1st Battalion was at Green Beach and the 2nd Battalion at Red Beach. Twenty landing craft carried 600 men with two companies of amphibious DD tanks of the 70th TB in the initial wave. Fortuitously, the tide had carried this initial wave more than a mile south of their target. Within two hours the leading troops were off the beach with enemy strongpoints being neutralized. By noon, the beach had been cleared at a cost of six men killed and thirty-nine wounded. By day's end the 8th and 22nd IRs had lost twelve men. (*NARA*)

(**Opposite, above**) American soldiers are loaded into an LCVP from a USN transport for the run-in to either Omaha or Utah Beach on 6 June 1944. These landing assault craft were put into the water several miles offshore. Although the sea appears calm, these smaller craft on the run-in to Omaha Beach were exposed to the full force of the northwesterly wind, bringing waves up to 6 feet high. Some assault craft foundered immediately, leaving scores of troops in the water struggling for their lives. (*NARA*)

(**Opposite, below**) A USN-crewed LCVP awaits its turn to approach a USN transport to begin loading infantrymen aboard for the final ride to the beachhead. The sailors wearing helmets keep a lookout to the sky and shore for any sign of a Luftwaffe sortie, 6 June 1944. (*NARA*)

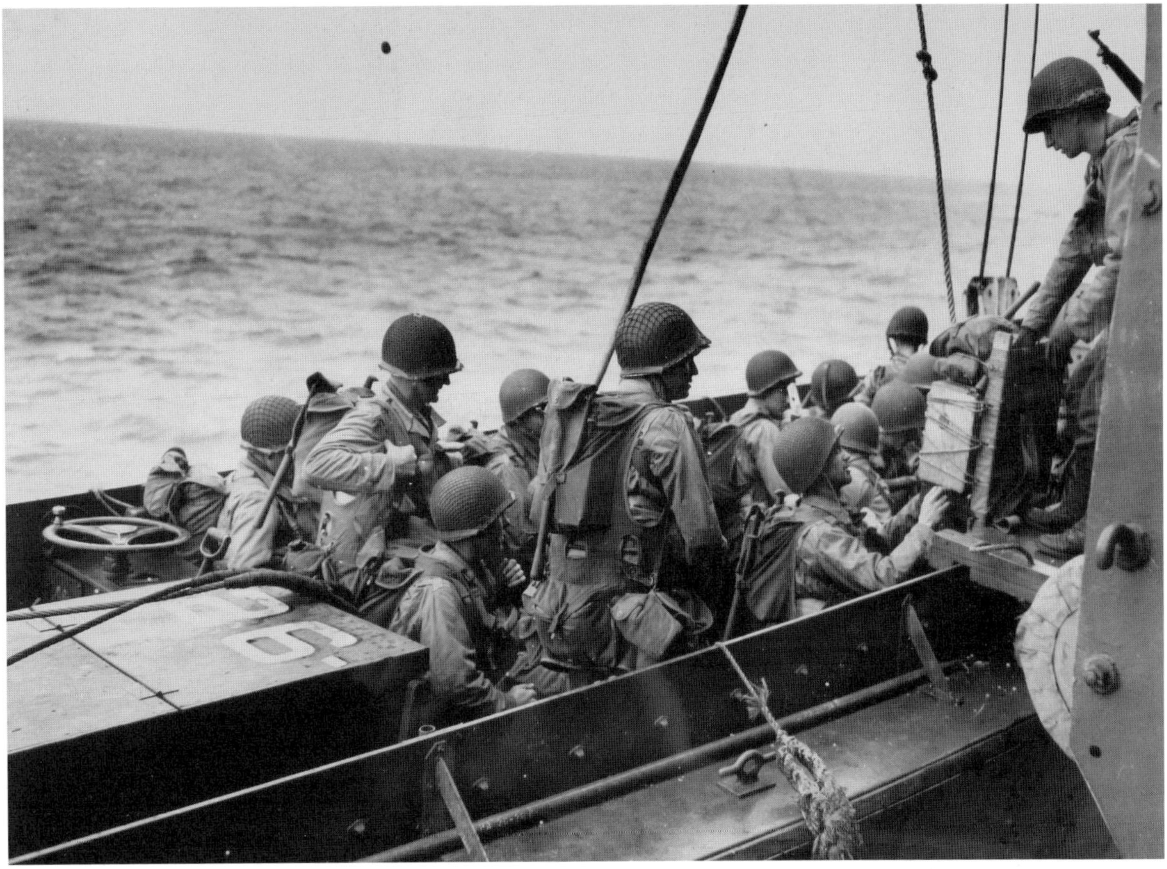

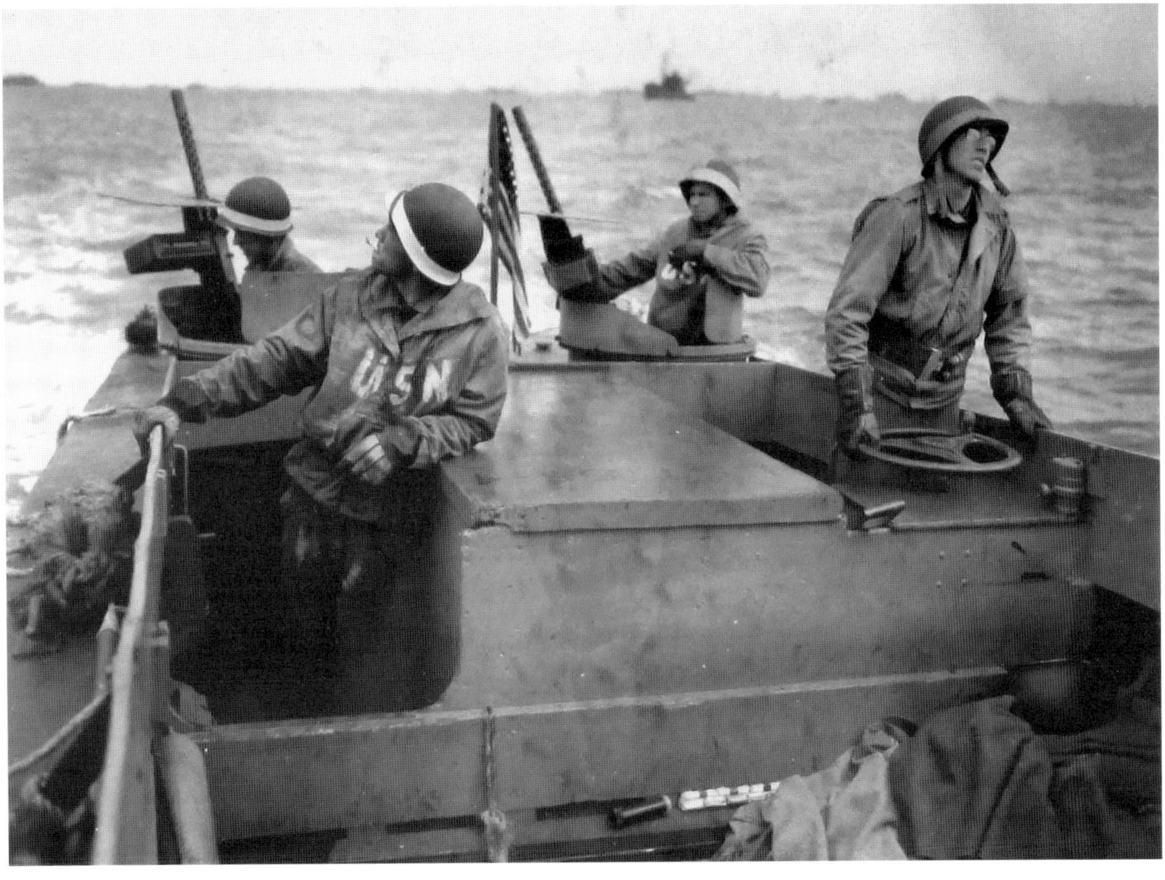
USN

USCG-crewed LCVP off Omaha Beach on 6 June 1944 heads toward the smoke hanging over the hotly contested shoreline, as infantrymen from earlier-arriving LCVPs wade through rough surf to the beach with its obstacles. German gunfire zones and a tall cliff await them. (NARA)

The LCVP ramp has been lowered and the troops of Company E, 16th IR, US 1st Infantry Division, wade toward the Omaha Beach shoreline on 6 June 1944 under withering German fire with beach obstacles, casualties and a disabled US M4 DD amphibious tank. Smoke from naval and aerial bombardment obscures the chalk cliff above the beach beyond the shoreline. (NARA)

Men of the 16th IR, US 1st Infantry Division come ashore at Omaha Beach at 0630hrs on 6 June 1944. The high tide covers some of the German beach obstacles. Only 5 out of 32 amphibious DD M4s of the 741st TB survived the poor surf conditions and German defensive gunfire. The line of the Omaha bluff is visible in the distance. Infantrymen lie prone on the beach or take cover behind the amphibious DD tanks still in the surf or German 'hedgehog' steel obstacles. (NARA)

One of the surviving classic images of the Omaha Beach assault on 6 June 1944 taken by celebrated photographer Robert Capa, shows American infantrymen seeking refuge behind German steel 'hedgehog' obstacles. Empty LCVPs are attempting to move against the surf to return to the transports while other soldiers are trying to swim or are dead and floating in the water. (NARA)

(**Above**) US Ranger infantrymen, from A, B, or C Companies of the 2nd Ranger Battalion, as suggested by the numeral '2' within the diamond-shaped insignia on the back of the helmet of the soldier kneeling (*lower left*) and (*far right*), level their 0.3in calibre LMG behind a sand mound. They landed with the 5th Ranger Battalion to support the 116th IR of the 29th Infantry Division at Omaha Beach on 6 June 1944. Strong sea currents carved such hillocks in the wet ribbed sands. Omaha lies between the outcropping rocks of Pointe de la Percée to the west, and Port-en-Bessin in the east, forming a shallow arc of sand enclosed inland by bluffs. The 5th Ranger Battalion with A, B, and C Companies of the 2nd Ranger Battalion and elements of the 116th IR broke across the seawall and barbed wire entanglements and up the pillbox-rimmed heights of the chalk cliff under intense enemy MG and mortar fire. They advanced 4 miles inland to the key town of Vierville-sur-Mer, thus opening the breach for supporting troops to follow up as the beachhead began to expand. (*NARA*)

(**Opposite, above**) A US soldier sits on a German 47mm AT gun atop a hillock at a landing site at Utah Beach on 12 June 1944. Fortuitously, due to the tides, the 2nd Battalion, 8th IR of the US 4th Infantry Division landed south of their intended target which was not heavily defended at the shoreline. (*NARA*)

(**Opposite, below**) On 21 June 1944 a US soldier inspects the maze of entrenchments situated on the bluff above Omaha Beach that had housed German infantry with heavy automatic weapons, that wreaked havoc on the assaulting infantrymen in the surf and at the shoreline on 6 June. The rocky shoulders of the bluffs flanking the American landing beaches had enabled the Germans to conceal their gun positions to enfilade the shore approaches. Behind the forward enemy defences, the slopes of the bluffs further obscured more German trench systems, MG nests and minefields. (*NARA*)

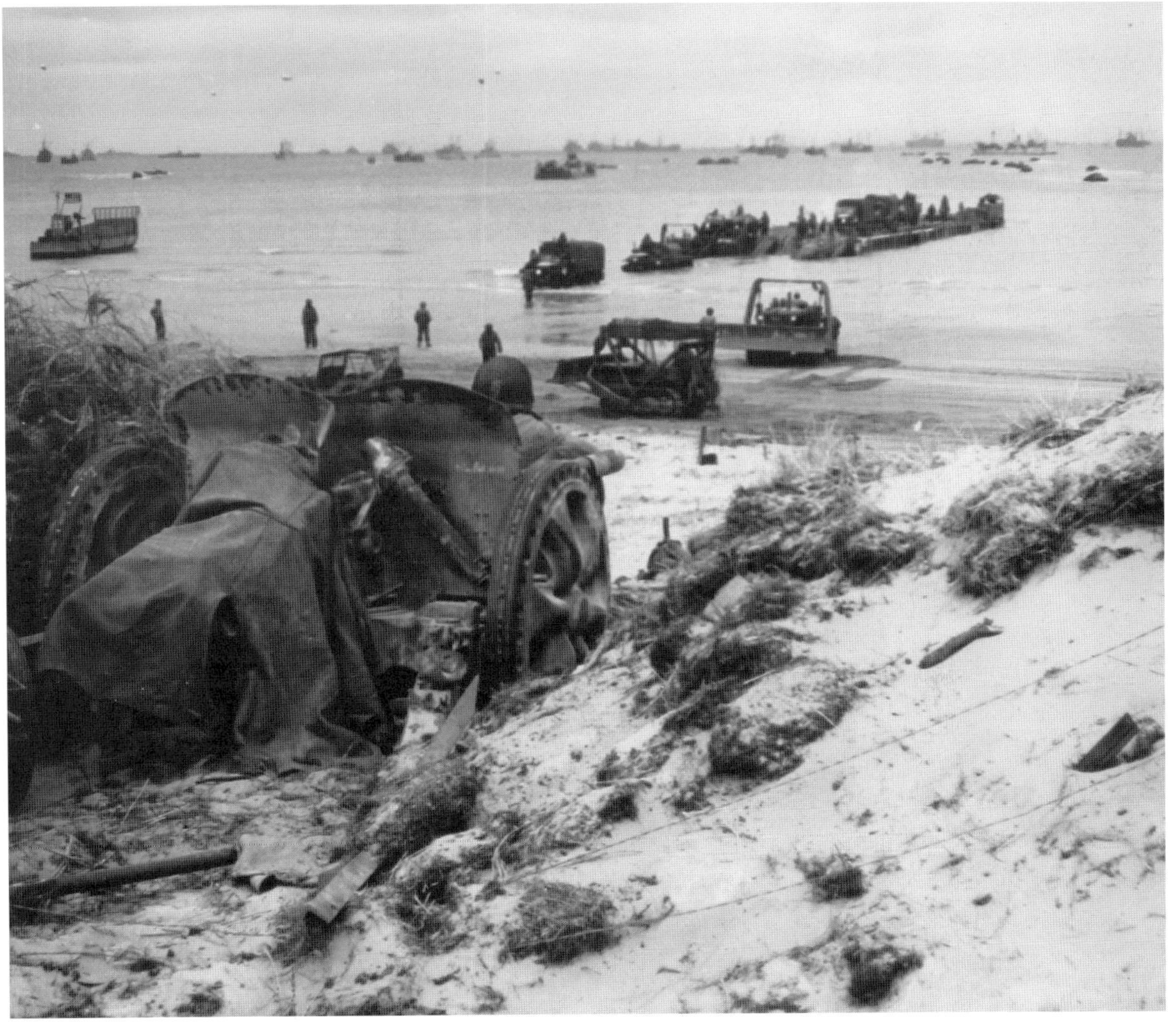

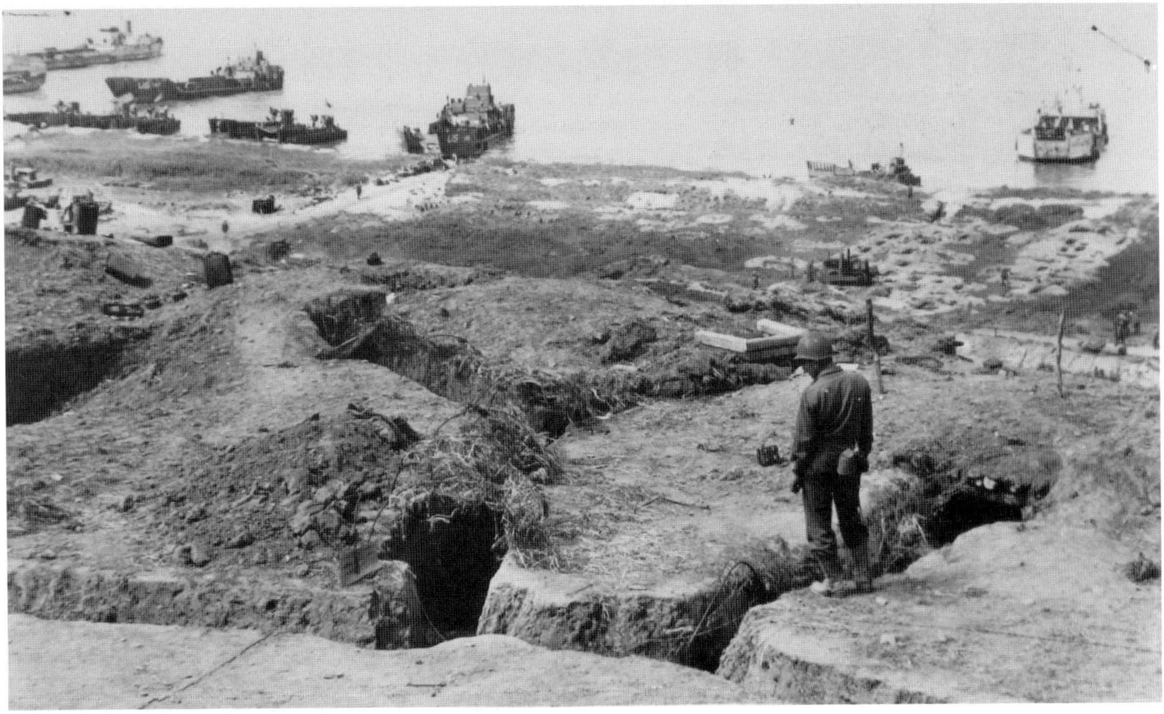

(**Above**) A member of the American shore party examines the interior of a log-fortified slit trench that Rommel's troops and workers carved into the bluff above Omaha Beach. These enabled German defenders to move about overlooking the beach with the protection of the trench's earthen walls. *(NARA)*

(**Opposite, above**) A German dual-purpose 88mm AT/AA gun in one of four concrete beach revetments that were destroyed by either Allied bombing or naval gunfire on 6 June 1944. If they had not been taken out casualties at Omaha Beach in terms both of men and assault craft would have been much higher. *(NARA)*

(**Opposite, below**) The interior of a concrete-walled German 88mm AT gun emplacement is shown; it has a reinforced steel ceiling to minimize Allied gunfire or naval bombardment damage. This emplacement, although it was neutralized, clearly survived the pre-invasion bombardment. *(NARA)*

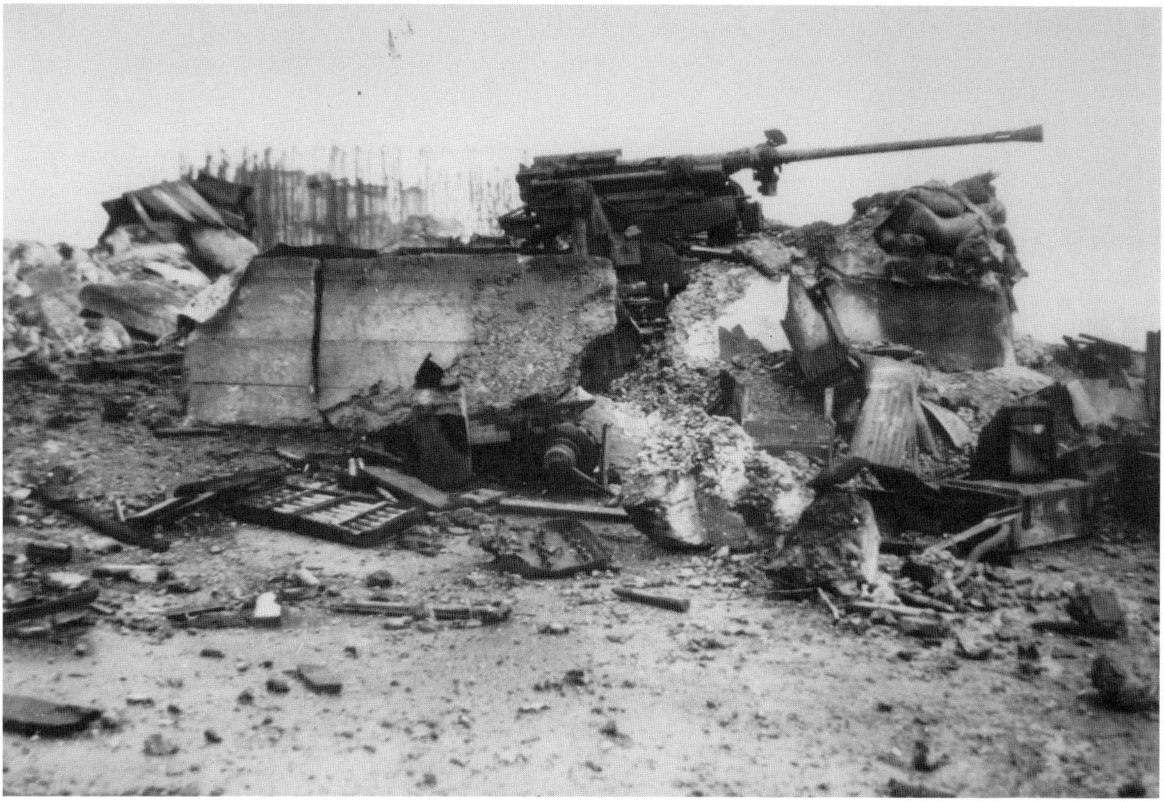

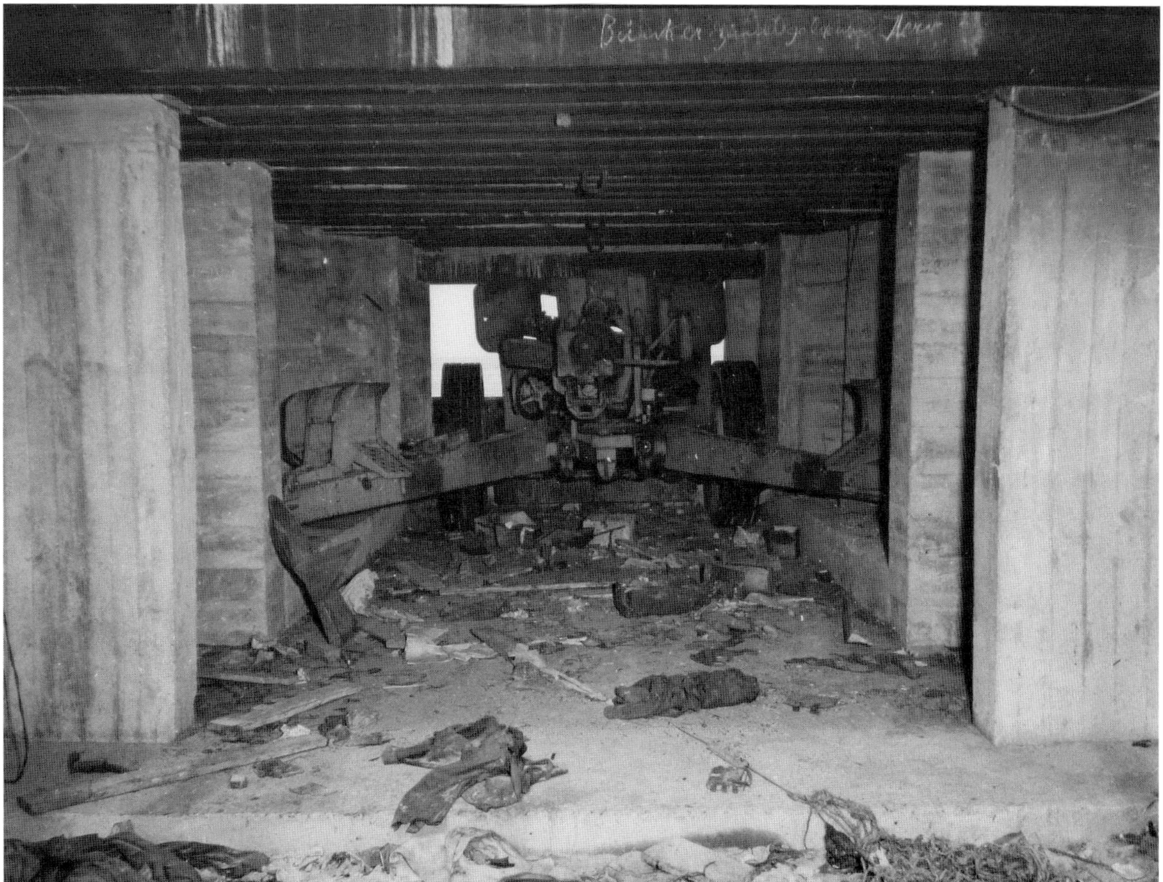

A US LCI loaded with assault troops lists heavily before sinking in the Bay of Seine on 6 June 1944. Many of the troops and ship's crew were saved by smaller USCG rescue craft before it sank. This particular vessel was a victim of German defensive gunfire or struck a mine. (NARA)

A USCG-crewed LCVP is ablaze during its run-in for Omaha Beach on 6 June 1944. Several LCVPs were damaged by mines or German gunfire from the beach. The bluff overlooking the beach and German steel obstacles ('hedgehogs') are clearly visible. The terraced slopes of the bluff gave cover to a deeper defensive ring of trench systems, MG nests, and minefields. *(NARA)*

American shore-party soldiers at Omaha Beach assist one of their fellow assault troops onto the beach from the life raft after their landing craft was sunk by the Germans. The beach here was rocky with very strong surf, meaning any soldier weighed down with gear was unlikely to survive swimming to the shore. The three soldiers without helmets that left the raft are wearing inflatable waist life vests. *(NARA)*

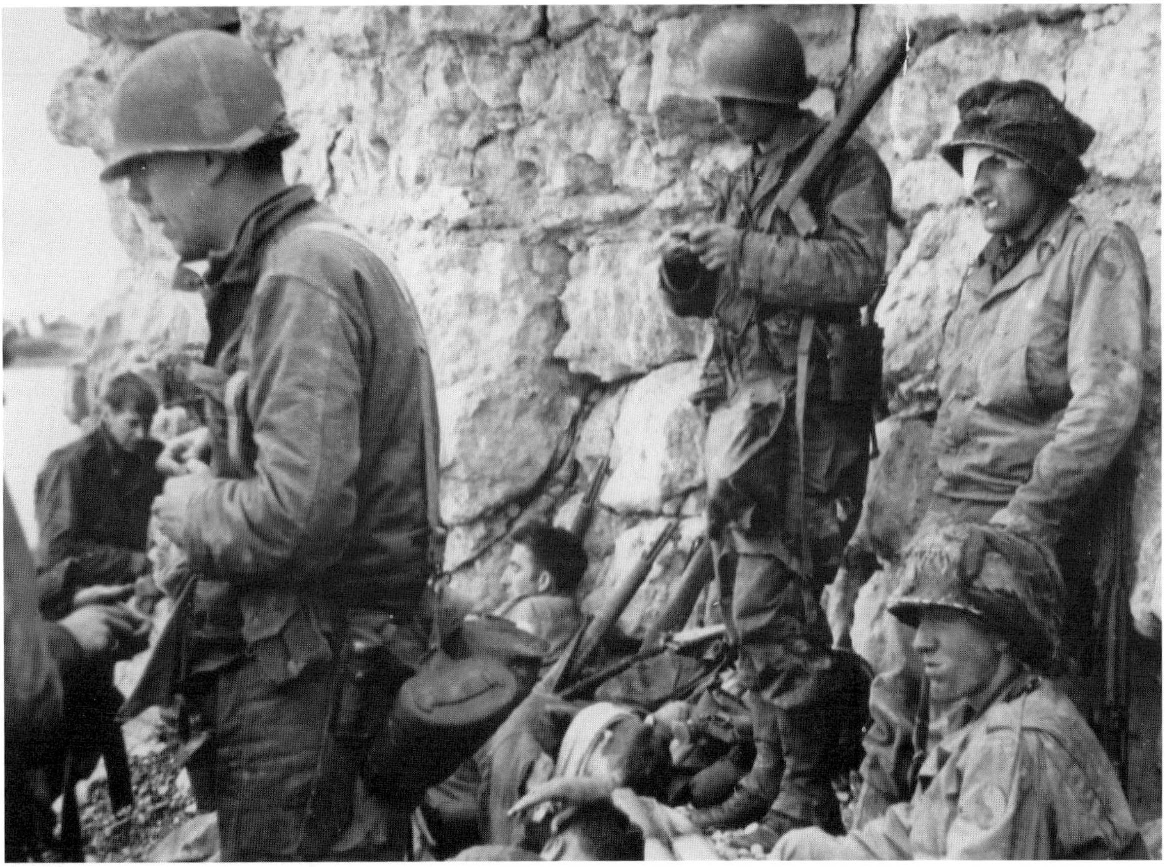

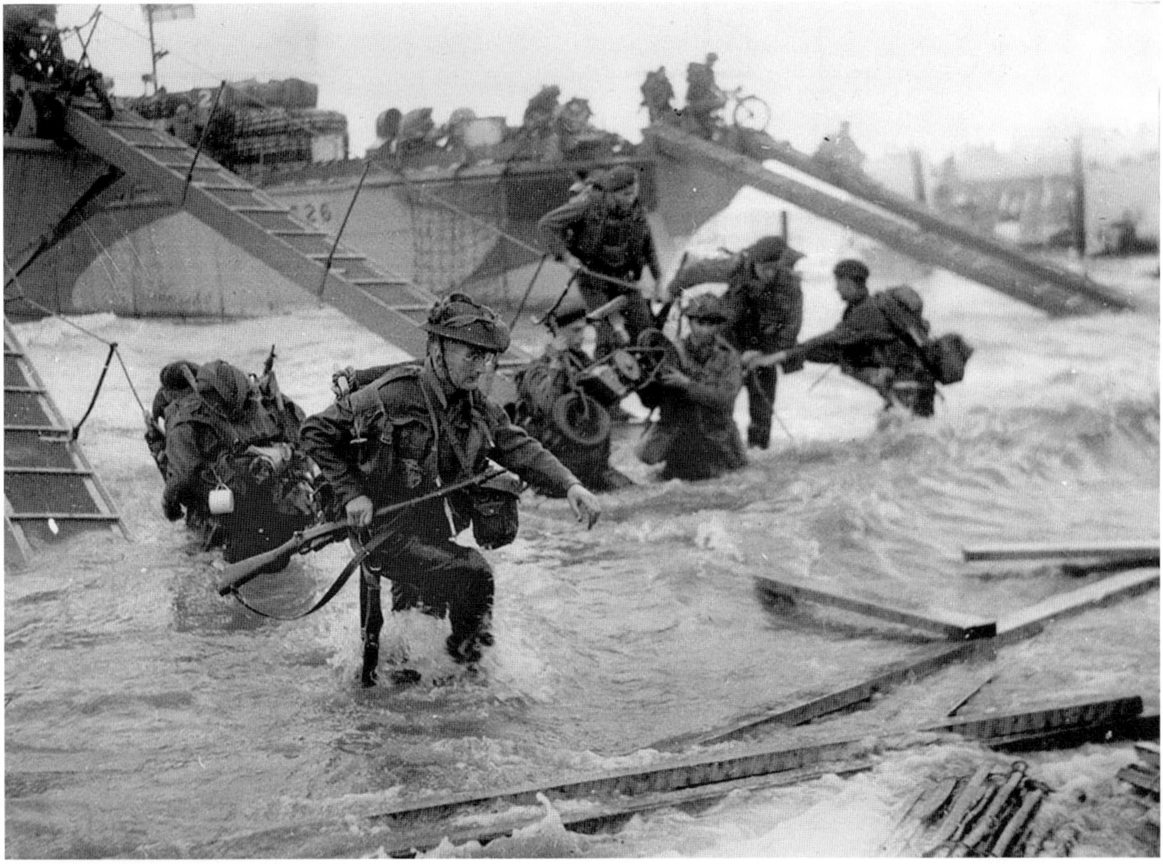

(**Opposite, above**) American assault troops compose themselves after reaching the relative safety of the chalk cliff at Omaha Beach on 6 June 1944. The men reveal a variety of facial expressions, wounds, and exhaustion. Within half an hour of H-Hour, there were at least 1,000 assault infantry and engineers alive on the beach; however, they were not fighting the Germans, merely struggling to survive. As is evident, many were too exhausted to drag their equipment across the beach and too few were able to assault the Nazi strongpoints head-on. The two soldiers at the right have the distinctive left shoulder patch of the US 29th ('Blue and Gray') Infantry Division. *(NARA)*

(**Opposite, below**) On 6 June 1944, members of the HQ No. 48 RM Commandos, 4th Special Service Brigade disembark from the LCI assault craft in strong surf at Nan Red Beach, in support of the Canadian 8th Brigade at Saint-Aubin-sur-Mer, at the far end of Juno Beach bordering with Sword Beach. The Canadians and RM Commandos were part of British I Corps, under the command of LG John Crocker. *(Author's collection)*

(**Above**) Canadian infantrymen at Juno Beach wait to move inland after securing their assault zones and clearing the beach of obstacles, debris and undetonated mines. These were infantry of the Canadian 8th and 9th Brigades. Their advance inland ended at nightfall due to reports of counterattacks by the 21st Panzer Division against the gap between Sword and Juno Beaches. *(NARA)*

(**Above**) The 2nd Battalion, East Yorkshire Regiment land at Queen Red sector of Sword Beach with DD amphibious tanks confronting German defences. H-Hour for Sword Beach was 0730hrs, with that beach's DD tanks put into the water 3 miles out. Thirty-three of forty DD tanks of the 13/18th Hussars made it ashore with some succumbing to enemy AT gunfire, sited on Périers Ridge. (*Author's collection*)

(**Opposite, above**) The 2nd Battalion, Middlesex Regiment, an MG battalion of the 3rd British Division comes ashore with the second wave in support of the 1st Battalion, South Lancashire Regiment, at the Queen Red sector of Sword Beach at 0745hrs on 6 June 1944. Every British division had an extra MG battalion equipped with Vickers medium MGs. Some of the wounded are being led out of the water to the beach by medical orderlies of 8 Field Ambulance, RAMC. Attached REs of 84 Field Company have the white band around their helmets. Commandos of 1st Special Service Brigade disembark from LCIs (*background*). The South Lancashires reached Hermanville, over a mile inland and confronted the vital Périers Ridge with the German AT guns and infantry of the Wehrmacht's 716th Division. British armoured and infantry units reached Biévelle, south of Périers, at 1600hrs, 3 miles short of Caen, before two dozen tanks of the 21st Panzer Division clashed head-on with the King's Shropshire Light Infantry and accompanying tanks of the Staffordshire Yeomanry. (*NARA*)

(**Opposite, below**) British No. 6 Commandos race inland from combat after landing at Sword Beach for Ouistreham on 6 June 1944, to aid the small force of the Oxford and Bucks Light Infantry and a battalion from the 3rd Parachute Brigade at the Orne river bridgehead. By then, the Commando unit had fought its way through enemy strongpoints, destroyed a German battery against the landing beaches, and marched 9 miles. The Commandos arrived only two and a half minutes behind schedule. The British paratroops and glider troops had held for 12 hours against powerful Nazi counterattack supported by enemy artillery and mortars. One company of the Oxford and Bucks, with all its officers killed or wounded, held on without relief for 17 hours. It was 1400hrs when No. 6 Commando crossed the Orne river bridge on its way to reinforce the 9th Battalion, 3rd Parachute Brigade. (*NARA*)

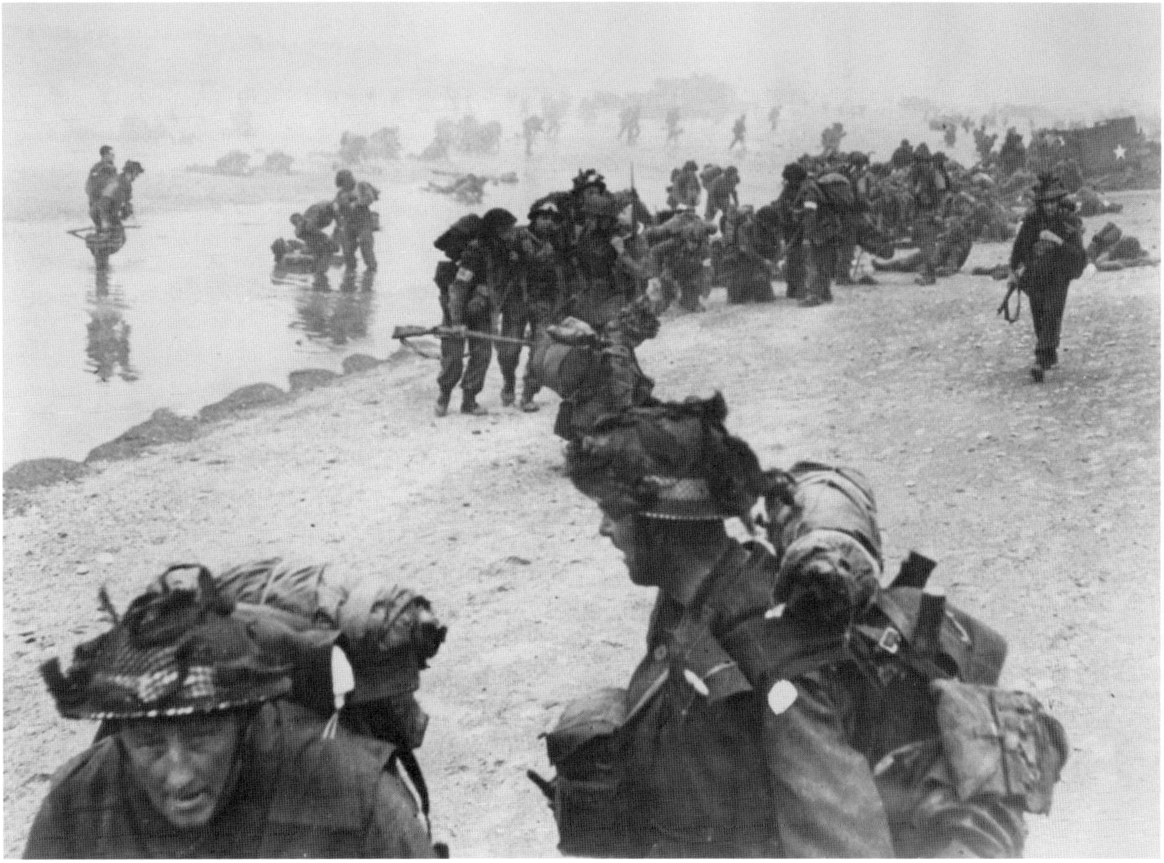

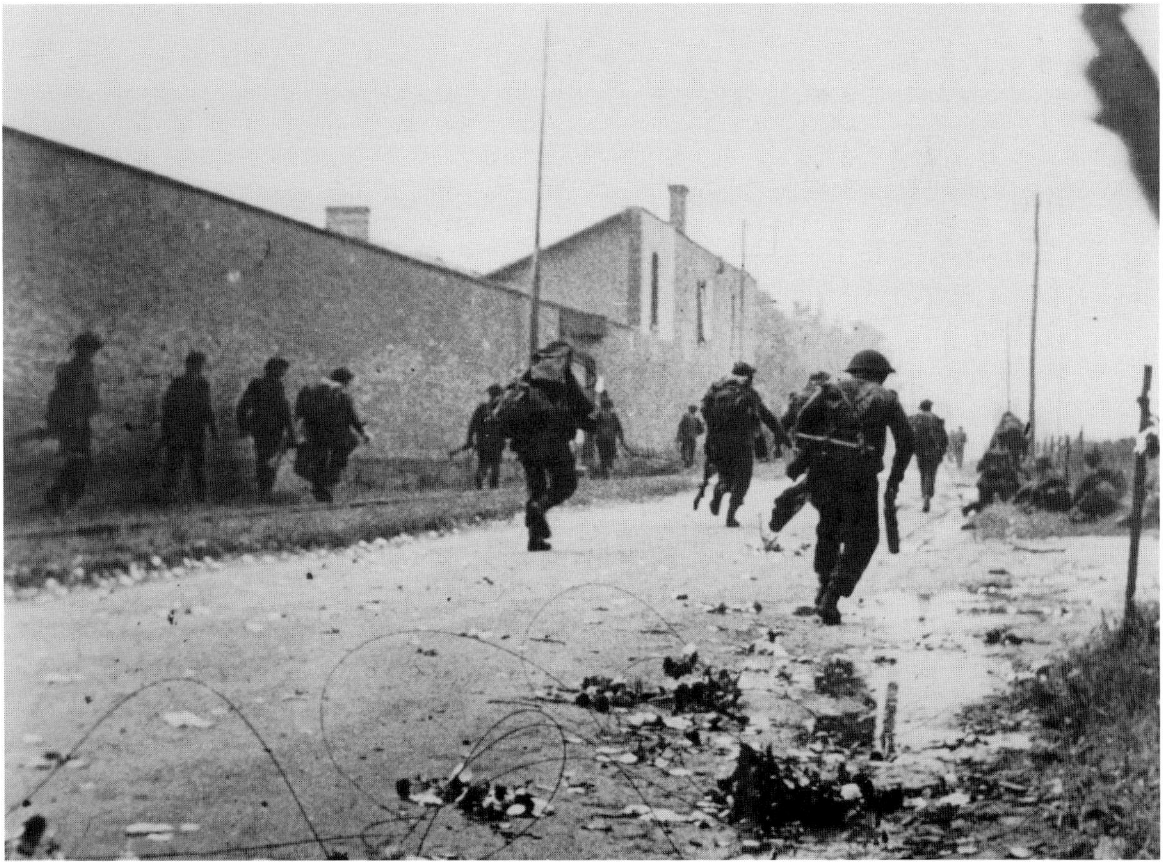

(**Above**) British No. 47 RM Commandos attached to the British 50th Northumbrian Infantry Division splash ashore from their LCA at Gold Beach between Arromanches and Le Hamel on 6 June 1944. The RM Commandos then moved west of Arromanches toward Port-en-Bessin to the east of Omaha Beach. The main weight of the British amphibious assault was centred on Gold Beach, a shallow arc streaked with soft clay behind which, to the west, were the powerful Nazi strongpoints and fortified villages of Arromanches and Le Hamel and to the east, La Rivière.

Within an hour of landing, MG Percy Hobart's 79th AVRE Armoured Division's RE specialized tanks emerged onto the beach and created four safe lanes over the Le Hamel beaches. AVRE Petard tanks moved across the landing beach to neutralize fortified houses and strongpoints to facilitate British infantry moving inland with fewer casualties. Other AVREs filled craters and AT ditches with fascines and bulldozed tracks for other vehicles. At La Rivière, British tanks and assault teams initially faced intense mortar, AT and MG fire directed from well-sited pillboxes and strongpoint houses linked together. However, within an hour both armour and infantry were more than a mile inland. Arromanches was to be the site of a British artificial harbour or 'Mulberry'. The success at Gold Beach on D-Day enabled a relatively early entry into Bayeux, the first French city to be reclaimed by the Allies. (*Author's collection*)

(**Opposite, above**) Infantrymen and SBs of the US 8th IR, 4th Infantry Division are seen with full equipment wading onto Utah Beach, where they were relatively unscathed by German defences due to a landing zone 'error' – the unit arrived southeast of the planned assault area that was closer to the stronger German troop areas near the Dunes of Varreville. This was also fortuitous since Utah Beach was not contiguous with the other Allied beaches and would rely heavily on the US 82nd and 101st Airborne Divisions to secure the causeways and the Carentan-to-Montebourg road, paralleling the Douve and Merderet rivers, heading towards a major objective, Cherbourg. (*NARA*)

(**Below**) Pointe du Hoc is a series of cliffs that reportedly housed several German artillery bunkers and MG posts, 4 miles west of the centre and overlooking Omaha Beach. Companies D, E, and F of the US 2nd Ranger Battalion were pitted against the German 914th Grenadier Regiment of the Wehrmacht's 352nd Infantry Division, and captured the cliffs by scaling them with rope ladders. After some initial delay because of German fire on British LCAs, the Rangers began to fire grappling hooks and ropes up onto the cliffs. They made it up with only fifteen casualties but once on top the Rangers found that their primary target, the artillery battery of six captured French 155mm guns of First World War vintage, had been removed. Two Rangers patrolling found five of the six guns 550 yards from their casemates and destroyed their firing and traversing mechanisms with thermite grenades. The sixth German gun was being fixed elsewhere. Counterattacks by elements of the German 914th Grenadier Regiment were fended off by the Rangers but produced casualties among the Americans, who were now holding on to a small pocket on the Pointe du Hoc until relief came on 8 June 1944. (NARA)

(**Above**) A dead German soldier lies sprawled before his pillbox at Utah Beach at Les Dunes de Madeleine on 6 June 1944. The pillbox was part concrete and wooden battery reinforced with sandbags on its roof, overlooking the Bay of Seine. The aperture visible is a rear entrance for German troops to move in and out. (*NARA*)

(**Opposite, above**) A German soldier digs his way out from sand that had buried him alive following the Allied naval bombardment at Omaha Beach. Three veteran battalions of the German 352nd Division defending Omaha lost 20 per cent of their strength with 1,200 casualties on 6 June 1944 and lacked reserves to continue the fight. (*NARA*)

(**Opposite, below**) An American infantryman lies dead abutting one of the numerous German wooden pole obstacles at low tide on Omaha Beach. Other steel hedgehog obstacles (*left*), which would not have been visible to American landing craft at high tide on 6 June 1944, are seen in the background with the rising bluffs above the sea wall. The beach itself was mined, especially in the areas between the gullies and from low to high water mark, along with an elaborate system of staggered lethal obstacles, so it seemed at first glance impregnable to the US landing craft and assaulting infantry on the beach and in the surf. (*NARA*)

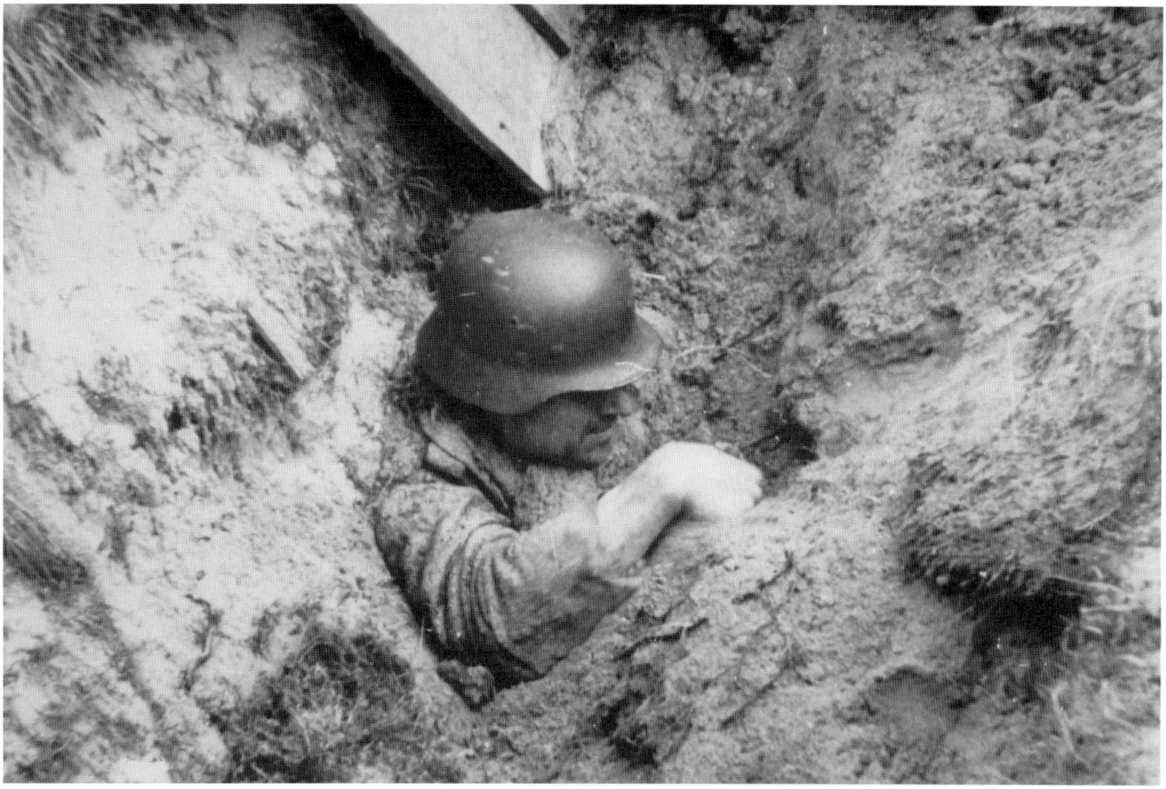

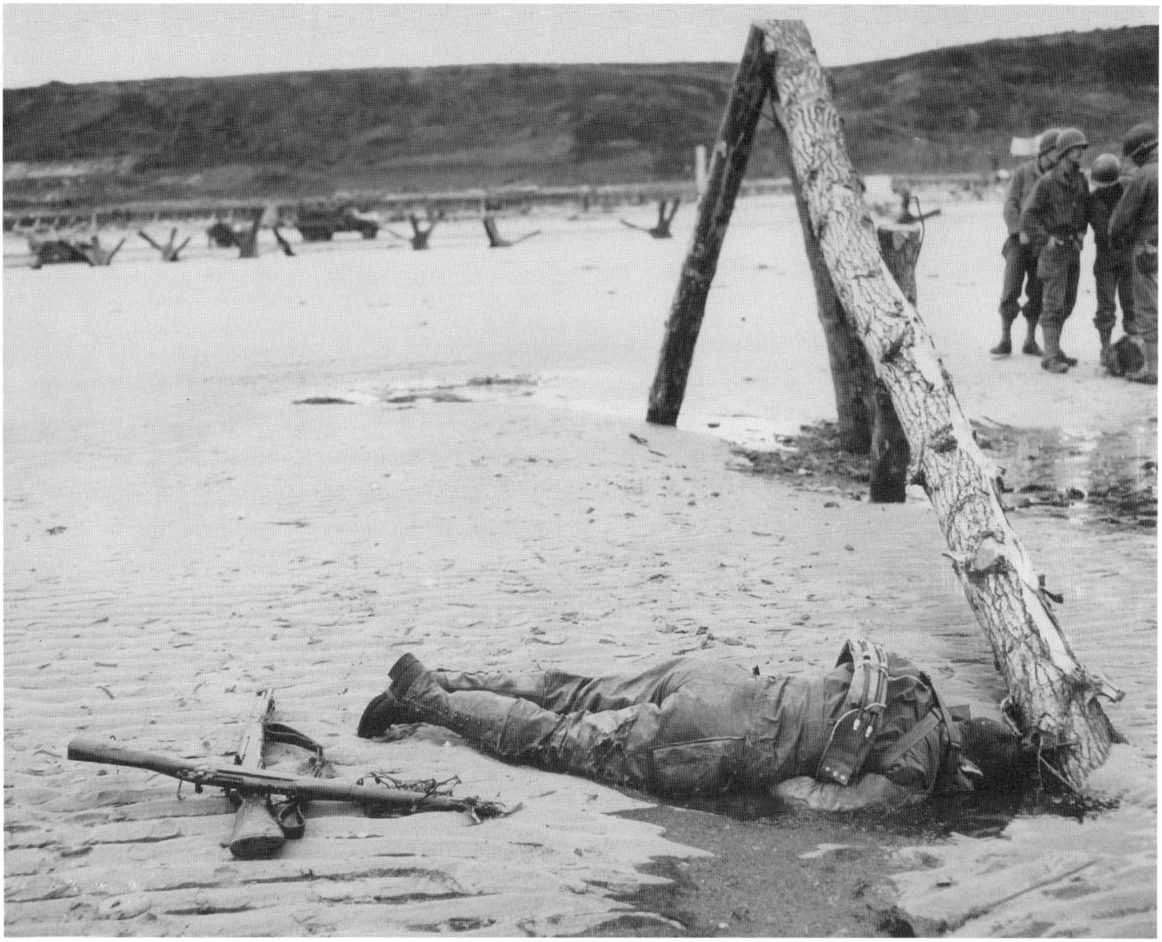

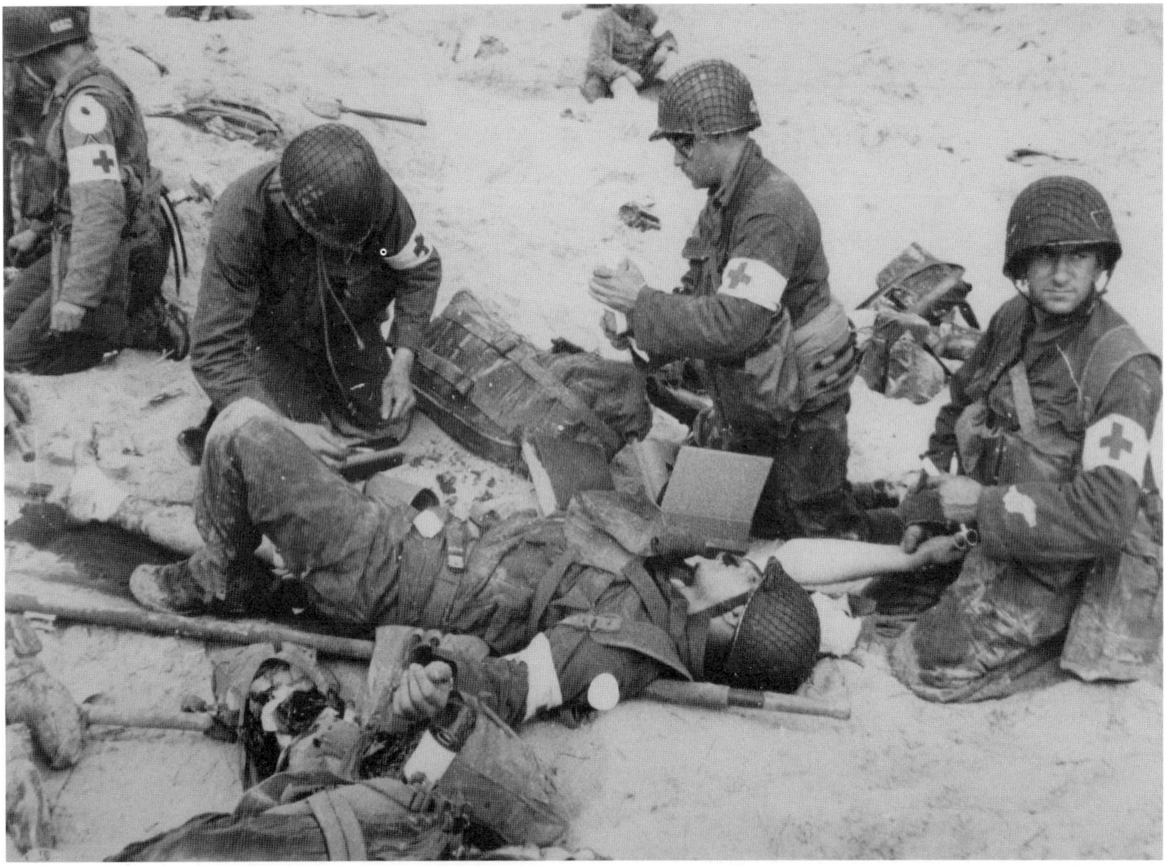

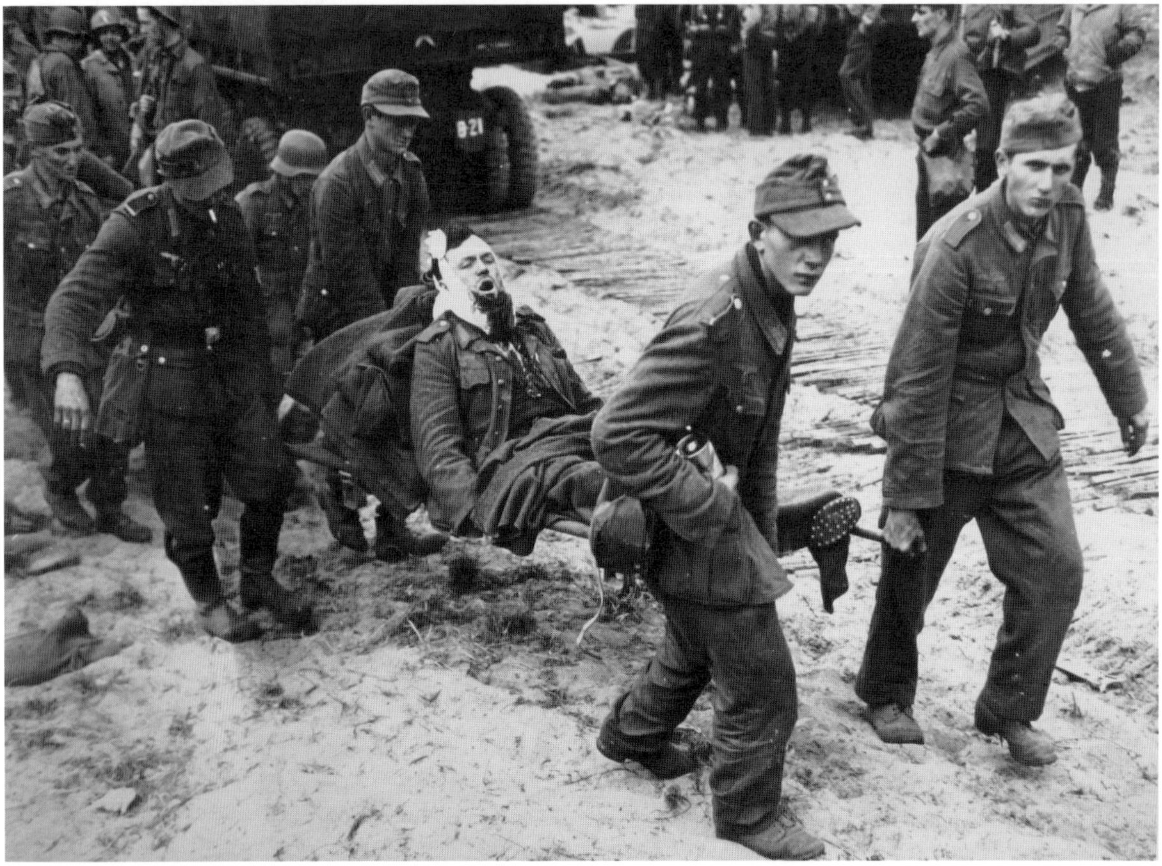
B-21

(**Opposite, above**) US Army medics tend to wounded 8th IR soldiers on Utah Beach at Les Dunes de Madeleine on 6 June 1944. The US 4th Infantry Division had 21,000 troops arriving that day at Utah, and suffered only 197 casualties, due to southeasterly tides serendipitously shifting the amphibious assault landing craft away from the heavier German troop concentrations at Les Dunes de Varreville, the planned landing area. *(NARA)*

(**Opposite, below**) American shore-party soldiers watch captured German troops carry their wounded across the sand for evacuation by LCVPs from Omaha Beach, after this contentious locale was secured at a high cost to both sides. Sections of the German 352nd Division suffered 1,200 casualties on 6 June 1944, while the Americans suffered 2,400 casualties by the end of the day after landing 34,000 troops. Note that fabric matting has been placed by American engineers to facilitate the movement of their vehicles in the soft sand. *(NARA)*

(**Above**) A British MP ('Red Cap') probably of the Field Security Police Wing is seen escorting German POWs into a stockade, along a dirt track with secure barbed wire fencing on either side and above the path. The MP is armed with a 9mm Sten SMG that was relatively easy and inexpensive to manufacture compared to a 0.45in calibre Thompson SMG. *(NARA)*

(**Above**) The Normandy lodgment area a few days after the initial beach assaults. LSTs are unloading their vehicles while other transports and destroyers are off shore and barrage balloons discourage low-flying Luftwaffe sorties. At a higher altitude are twin-engined medium bombers of the 9th TAF attacking Nazi concentration areas, railroads, marshalling yards, and bridges to hinder FM Rommel from reinforcing his German forces that were trying to contain the expanding Allied beachhead. (*NARA*)

(**Opposite, above**) Liberty ships were deliberately scuttled to make artificial breakwaters. However, a larger 'Mulberry' B (not shown) at Arromanches, which was part of the Gold Beach landing area, had a British-built prefabricated artificial port as large as Dover, constructed in Great Britain and towed across the Channel, then mounted piece by piece, which was vital to the Allies to funnel troops and machinery into France. It was 2 miles wide between the outer breakwaters and nearly a mile from the outer breakwater to the shore. The 'Mulberries' consisted of several unique elements, including floating steel pier heads and roadways and massive hollow concrete breakwaters for the inner harbour. These structures consumed over 600,000 tons of concrete, 100,000 tons of steel and took 45,000 men eight months to construct. A strong storm on 19 June 1944, which raged for three days, destroyed Mulberry A at St. Laurent, dedicated to the Americans at Omaha Beach. Mulberry B also suffered damage but was easy to repair and continued to discharge 10,000 tons of equipment per day. During the Normandy battle, 400,000 troops and 500,000 vehicles transited through Mulberries A and B. (*NARA*)

(**Below**) A tangled mass of crossed steel underwater obstacles is seen after the immense seaborne invasion occurred on 6 June 1944. FM Rommel's steel beach obstacles would be cut apart by American engineers and then welded onto the hulls of US M4 and M5 tanks as 'Culin blades' turning them into 'Rhino tanks' to cut paths through the obstructing Normandy hedgerows of the *bocage*. (NARA)

The wreck of a German fighter, once the pride of the vaunted Luftwaffe, after it was shot down over one of the American sectors by a P-51 Mustang fighter of the US 9th TAF soon after the invasion, during one of the few enemy sorties. *(NARA)*

Chapter Three

Commanders and Combatants

The Western Allies were successful in establishing their lodgment on the European Continent on 6 June 1944, across the Normandy beaches between the Orne river and the base of the Cotentin Peninsula, under the overall ground force leadership of General Bernard Montgomery (promoted to FM in September 1944). There followed fierce combat in the Normandy hedgerows for LG Omar Bradley's US First Army and before the city of Caen, regional capital of Calvados, for Montgomery's 21st AG, comprised of LG Miles Dempsey's Second British Army, and the later activation of LG Henry Crerar's Canadian First Army, the latter wielding LG Guy Simonds's II Canadian Corps. Montgomery's forces were a conglomeration of Britons, Scots, Welshmen, Irishmen, Canadians, Poles, and Free French forces.

Popularized misconceptions, controversies, and disputes exist about the Normandy campaign against the Wehrmacht forces under FM Gerd von Rundstedt, C-in-C (West) and FM Erwin Rommel's AG B, the latter comprised of the German Seventh Army defending Normandy and Brittany, and the German Fifteenth Army north of the Seine. After overcoming Rommel's 'Atlantic Wall' and beach obstacles, a link-up of the five Allied beaches into one solid lodgment along the Caen–Bayeux–Carentan axis was needed to close gaps between the Allies through which the Germans would attempt to penetrate.

By nightfall on 6 June 1944, the lead elements of the 12th SS-Panzer Division *Hitlerjugend* were in position on the left flank of 21st Panzer Division. Over the next few days, the *Hitlerjugend* made fanatical counter-attacks against the Canadian 3rd Division as the Nazis attempted to drive a wedge between Juno and Sword Beaches through to the sea. Other German divisions reacted with the elite Panzer *Lehr* Division arriving by 9 June to oppose the British 50th Division around Tilly-sur-Seulles, south of Bayeux, on the road to Villers-Bocage. These three Wehrmacht divisions were to comprise the main defence of Caen, and would delay

Montgomery from taking this important Norman city until 19 July. Other fortified villages inland from the beaches became 'choke' points for Rommel's forces to stymie the Allied advance inland.

Speculation exists as to whether a quick Allied advance was jeopardized by the extensive combat frontage along the invasion area, with a wide dispersal of assault troops rather than a concentration of strength at a decisive point. When the Allies failed to advance past their narrow beachhead salient from Utah Beach in the west to Sword Beach to the east, a leadership crisis developed in the Allied High Command, centering around the post-D-Day plan of Montgomery, the Allied Ground Forces C-in-C. LG Bradley wrote after the battle, 'By 10 July 1944, we faced a real danger of a World War I-type stalemate.'

British political and military leaders meet at General Montgomery's temporary HQ in Bayeux on 12 June 1944, five days after the town's capture by elements of the British 50th (Northumbrian) Division. From left to right are LG Sir Miles Dempsey, CG Second British Army; General Sir Alan Brooke, CIGS; Prime Minister Winston Churchill; General Sir Bernard Montgomery, CG 21st AG and Allied Ground Forces commander; and South African Prime Minister Jan Smuts, a confidant of Churchill's. Dempsey, having served with Montgomery since after Alamein, always questioned his autonomy as an Army commander because of the 21st AG commander's meddling during the battle. Nonetheless, he was a loyal subordinate to Montgomery. Dempsey wanted to limit infantry casualties by utilizing his growing armoured forces (in 3 armoured divisions, 5 independent armoured brigades, and 3 independent tank brigades) of over 2,000 medium and 400 light tanks, to break into the good tank country of the Caen-Falaise Plain. (NARA)

US JCOS are briefed on 14 June 1944 in Normandy inland from the beaches, by General Dwight Eisenhower, Supreme Commander SHAEF (*second from left*) standing between General Henry Arnold, CG USAAF and General George Marshall, US Army COs. Next to Marshal, pointing, is LG Omar Bradley, CG US First Army. At far right is Admiral Ernest King, C-in-C US Fleet and CNO. Behind Eisenhower and Marshall is MG Charles Corlett, CG First Army's XIX Corps. (*NARA*)

General Sir Bernard Montgomery, CG 21st AG (*left*), confers with LG Henry D.G. Crerar, CG First Canadian Army at a forward HQ. Crerar, like Montgomery, was a First World War veteran in the Field Artillery. He was GOC I Canadian Corps, which participated in the disastrous Dieppe raid in August 1942, although he did not have any role in the operation's planning. Crerar participated in the Sicily campaign during the summer of 1943 and in Italy from September 1943 to March 1944, when he returned to England to help plan Operation *Overlord* as CG First Canadian Army. After the successful Juno Beach assault, Crerar led the 2nd, 3rd, and 4th Canadian Divisions as well as the 1st Polish Armoured, the 49th British and the 51st (Scottish) Divisions. His forces were integrally involved in Caen's siege and the closure of the Falaise-Argentan Pocket. (*NARA*)

General Dwight Eisenhower, Supreme Commander SHAEF (*front row, second from right*) with his principal American generals in France in late August 1944. LG George S. Patton, CG Third Army (*front row, left*), LG Omar Bradley, CG 12th AG (*next to Patton*), LG Courtney Hodges, CG First Army (*front row, far right*). Second row (*left to right*): MG William Kean who in late 1943 was COS to LG Bradley, CG II Corps in North Africa and then assigned as COS to Hodges' First Army. He served in that capacity until the end of the war. Beside him, MG Charles Corlett commanded XIX Corps in the First Army, and previously led the 7th Infantry Division during the Marshall Islands Pacific campaign at Kwajalein. As of 17 June 1944, he led the 29th, 30th, 35th Infantry, along with the 3rd Armoured Division. At the end of July, the 28th Infantry Division was added to his corps. Next to Corlett is MG J. Lawton Collins, CG VII Corps, which captured Cherbourg on 26 June 1944. A former division commander (25th Infantry Division), he fought in the South Pacific at Guadalcanal after 25 November 1942 and in the New Georgia group of islands from 3 July to 6 October 1943. Collins, as of 6 June 1944, led the 4th, 9th, 79th, 90th Infantries along with the 82nd and 101st Airborne Divisions. Next to Collins stands MG Leonard T. Gerow, CG V Corps. Gerow was in the War Plans Division (WPD) in Washington, D.C. with Eisenhower when both were junior officers. On 6 June 1944, Gerow led the 1st and 29th Infantry Divisions and on 17 June the 2nd Armoured Division. His troops struggled but eventually overcame the German defences at Omaha Beach on D-Day. At far right is MG Elwood Quesada, CG 9th TAF, integral in tactical air-ground warfare against the Germans.

Absent from the photograph is VIII Corps CG, MG Troy Middleton. On 1 August, Eisenhower reorganized American forces with Bradley's 12th AG HQ becoming operational. Hodges moved from deputy to command the First Army, and Patton's Third Army was activated. Though Bradley was co-equal with Montgomery, with each AG commander having two armies, Montgomery remained the Allied Ground Forces Commander until Eisenhower could establish his SHAEF on the Continent and assume direct control of the land forces. (*NARA*)

LG Lesley McNair (*right*), CG Army Ground Forces is shown talking with a subordinate officer. On 24 July 1944, 1,600 aircraft set out to bomb the St Lô–Périers road, but the operation was botched. The bombers were hastily recalled but not until 700 tons of bombs had been dropped on the target area, killing 25 soldiers and wounding 131 soldiers of the US 30th Infantry Division. They had bombed the St Lô–Périers road at right angles rather than parallel to the road. Bradley rescheduled another bombing mission for the next day, 25 June, so as to not postpone or cancel Operation *Cobra*. US 9th TAF fighter-bombers were followed by 1,500 heavy bombers of the 8th AF and they dropped 3,400 tons of bombs; however, there was 'short bombing' which again struck the 30th Infantry Division and a unit of the 9th Infantry Division. Casualties were once more severe, with 111 killed and 490 wounded. Among the dead was McNair, the highest ranking Allied officer to be killed in Normandy, who had visited the front lines to observe the bombing, despite advice to remain further back. McNair had taken over Patton's notional army in England as part of Operation *Fortitude* since the Third Army's CG's presence in Normandy could not remain clandestine any longer. He was buried with the strictest secrecy. (*NARA*)

(**Above**) LG Guy Simonds, CG II Canadian Corps, is shown in his command vehicle at the Canadian initial crossing of the Seine river in late August 1944. Simonds, previously a sapper, led Canadian troops during both the Sicily and Italian campaigns from 1943 to 1944, and was a commander whom Montgomery increasingly relied on. In Normandy, he led his II Canadian Corps during Operations *Totalize* and *Tractable*, utilizing innovative tactics such as a night attack with self-propelled gun carriages escorting his infantry against the northern shoulder of the Falaise-Argentan Pocket. Under Simonds's command were the 2nd and 3rd Canadian Infantry, the 4th Canadian and 1st Polish Armoured Divisions. On the night of 7 August 1944, preceded by a massive RAF Bomber Command air attack, Simonds launched his II Canadian Corps on a renewed offensive southwards towards Falaise, Operation *Totalize*. (NARA)

(**Opposite, above**) LG Gerard Bucknall (*left*), CG British XXX Corps, with Brigadier Harold Pyman in a Normandy field. Bucknall was a First World War veteran and in 1941 was appointed GOC 53rd (Welsh) Infantry Division. In August 1943, he became GOC of the 5th Infantry Division in Sicily and this formation invaded the Italian mainland in September as part of Montgomery's Eighth Army, participating in the First Battle of Cassino in January 1944. Having impressed Montgomery, Bucknall took command of XXX Corps on 27 January 1944, but he was deemed to have performed poorly during Operation *Perch* and was replaced in August the same year. Pyman had been second in command of the 6th RTR and was a staff officer in the 7th and 10th Armoured Divisions of the British Eighth Army. (Author's collection)

(**Opposite, below**) LG Brian Horrocks, CG British XXX Corps stands next to Montgomery (*left*) as they and two other officers review maps on the hood of a staff car, on the east bank of the Rhine in March 1945. On 4 August 1944, Montgomery had relieved Bucknall and replaced him with the dynamic Horrocks after Operation *Bluecoat* became bogged down. XXX Corps' performance improved under Horrocks and he served as its CG for the remainder of the war in Europe, notably during Operations *Market Garden* in 1944 and *Plunder* in 1945. Horrocks commanded British XIII Corps as part of Montgomery's Eighth Army at the southern end of the El Alamein line in 1942. (NARA)

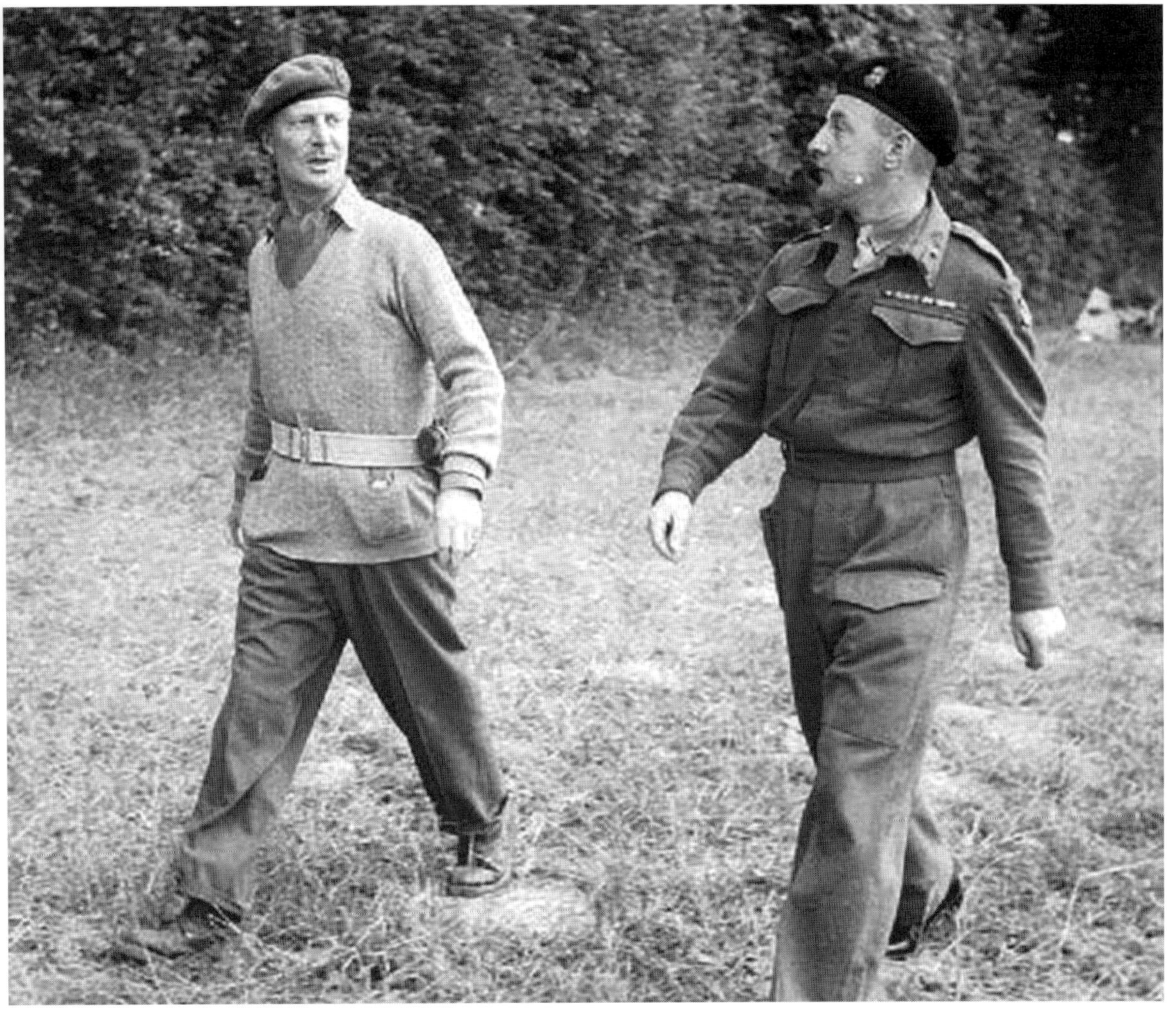

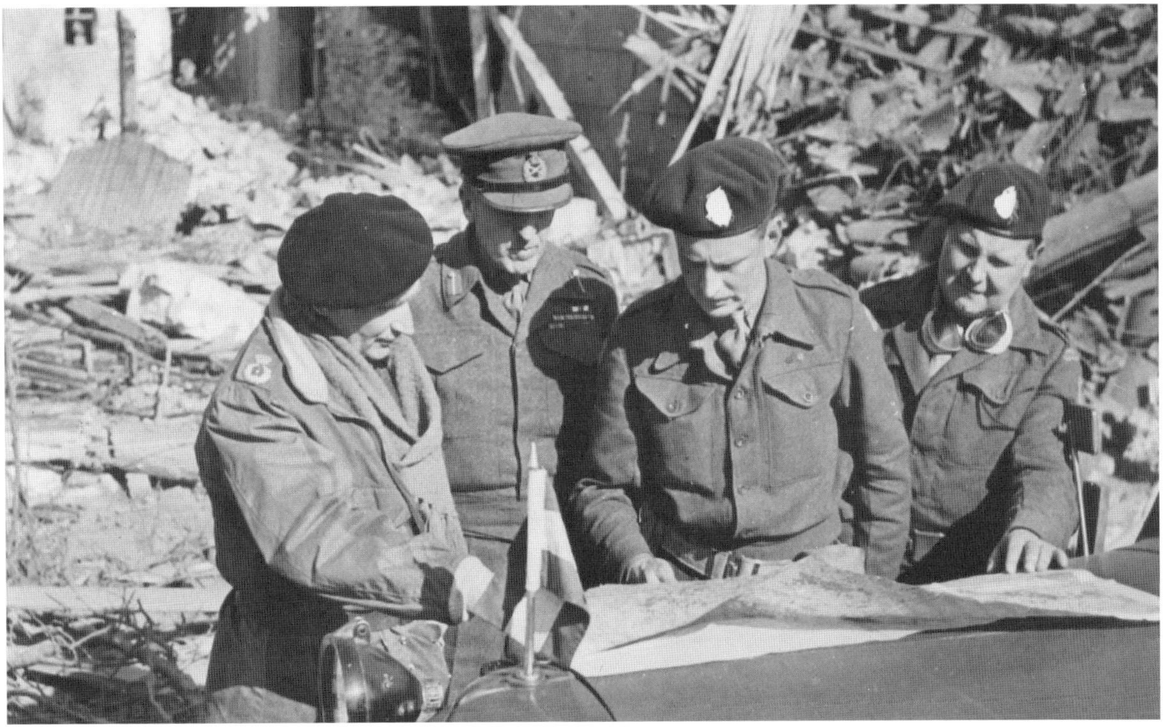

(**Above, left**) LG Sir Richard O'Connor, CG British VIII Corps, in Normandy. O'Connor commanded Western Desert Force (later British XIII Corps), successfully routing the Italian Tenth Army at Beda Fomm during Operation *Compass* in 1940–1. Later in 1941, Rommel launched a 'mirror image' drive against a weakened British XIII Corps line in Cyrenaica and captured O'Connor who was trying to stabilize the disaster. O'Connor escaped from an Italian POW facility after three and a half years, making it back to England to be offered VIII Corps for the Normandy invasion. To reduce the detection of VIII Corps' movement during Operation *Goodwood* by German OPs in the Colombelles Steel Factory towers, O'Connor ordered his three armoured divisions to proceed at night under aerial and artillery bombardment of Caen. Once at the Orne river's west bank, only the British 11th Armoured Division was to cross on the night of 17/18 July 1944, the Guards and the 7th Armoured Divisions being held back until the operation had progressed. Both Montgomery and Dempsey agreed on the need for full RAF air support before the operation. (*Author's collection*)

(**Above, right**) MG Sir Percy Hobart, a British engineer and at Normandy the CG British 79th Armoured Division, RE at his HQ. Hobart was one of Britain's first mechanized force enthusiasts in the late 1930s and experimented with his Mobile Division in the Western Desert. He was dismissed by General Sir Archibald Wavell, C-in-C Middle East in 1940, due to his 'unconventional' views of armoured warfare, which conflicted with those of the War Office. He joined the Home Guard as a lance corporal but Churchill recalled him to train the 11th Armoured Division in England. At Dieppe, the regular Churchill Infantry tanks failed to overcome fortified obstacles in that doomed amphibious landing, so Hobart created specialized armoured vehicles ('Hobart's Funnies'). He developed the specialized Churchill tanks within a new British 79th Armoured Division, RE, that was extremely effective at neutralizing German fortified positions and obstacles, both during the 6 June 1944 amphibious assault and beyond, by being attached to other units. By the war's end, the 79th Armoured Division, RE, had 7,000 specialized vehicles. (*Author's collection*)

MG Douglas Graham, GOC British 50th (Northumbrian) Division, with Montgomery, 20 June 1944. Graham's division landed at Gold Beach on 6 June as part of British XXX Corps. Graham had commanded British 56th Division at Salerno's amphibious assault in September 1943, where he defended against German beach resistance and counterattacks. At Normandy, German strategists considered Gold Beach an unlikely landing beach so its defences were weak. Nonetheless, Graham's 50th Division had to overcome fierce resistance in the area called La Rivière, between the eastern end of Gold Beach and the village of Ver-sur-Mer, near the Gold–Juno Beach boundary. Other 50th Division units landed and moved inland, accomplishing the furthest advance of all the amphibious assault troops on 6 June, enabling the British to take Arromanches that evening and Bayeux the next day almost undamaged. *(Author's collection)*

MG J. Lawton Collins (*left*), CG VII Corps, stands atop the ruins of Fort du Roule, a Nazi final redoubt overlooking Cherbourg Harbour, getting a report from Captain Robert Kirkpatrick as the port-city fell on 26 June 1944. Fort du Roule was the city's highest point, dominating the harbour. Cherbourg's relatively early capture served as a lesson when compared to the Anzio's flawed amphibious assault of 22 January–5 June – that failure to risk aggressive action by competent commanders while the enemy was still off balance was tactically unsound. Collins's forces cleared the Cotentin Peninsula and reached Cherbourg on 22 June, but the German defenders were well dug-in on the heights around the city, especially in the vicinity of the nineteenth-century Fort du Roule, built deep into rock and pointed seaward. It could be defended from the land, since the Germans had reinforced it with concrete pillboxes, mortar and MG emplacements, also barbed wire and AT ditches. (*NARA*)

BG Theodore 'Ted' Roosevelt, Jr stands in front of his CP in Sainte-Mère-Église on 12 July 1944 – he died later that day from a heart attack. He was a First World War veteran, eventually leading the 26th IR, 1st Infantry Division as LC and had been wounded in the leg in the summer of 1918, near Soissons. Roosevelt was the assistant division commander in the 1st Infantry Division for the Operation *Torch* landings at Oran, in northwest Africa, on 8 November 1942, and was awarded a French Croix de Guerre. He served in that same capacity under MG Terry de la Mesa Allen for the Sicily invasion on 10 July 1943. When Allen was relieved of command by LG Omar Bradley towards the end of the Sicily campaign, Roosevelt was re-assigned as a commander of Allied Forces on Sardinia and as liaison to the French Army in Italy for Eisenhower.

Roosevelt received a posthumous Congressional Medal of Honor on 28 September 1944 for valour during the Normandy invasion. He was the only general to land with the first wave of troops by sea on 6 June. He led the 4th Infantry Division's 8th IR and 70th TB at Utah Beach. When Roosevelt was informed that the landing craft had drifted more than a mile south of their objective, and the first wave was a mile off course, he reconnoitred the area to locate the causeways inland and told his subordinate officers, 'We'll start the war from right here.' At the time of Roosevelt's death, Eisenhower had selected him for promotion to MG and had cut orders for him to be CG 90th Infantry Division. (NARA)

BG Norman 'Dutch' Cota, assistant CG of the 29th Infantry Division, receives the DSC from General Montgomery for his gallantry at Omaha Beach on 6 June 1944. Cota was in the second assault wave that morning becoming the senior ranking officer at Omaha. There, he rallied his troops and US Ranger units to breach the seawall with Bangalore torpedoes under intense enemy fire and then advance inland against further German gunfire and obstacles. On 14 August 1944, Cota became CG 28th Infantry Division with a promotion to MG on 4 September. *(NARA)*

MG Matthew B. Ridgway, a 1917 West Point graduate, was the Assistant Division Commander of the 82nd Infantry Division at its activation in March 1942, just before it was turned into one of the Army's new elite airborne divisions. He was promoted to commander on 26 June 1942, before the 10 November invasion of northwest Africa. After overcoming logistical hurdles of aerial drops on enemy positions while passing over nervous, 'trigger-happy' Allied shipping AA crews during the Sicily invasion, he led the 82nd Airborne Division into action in Italy and Normandy, before taking command of the newly-formed XVIII Airborne Corps in August 1944. He commanded that corps in the Battle of the Bulge and in Operation *Varsity*, the airborne component of Montgomery's Rhine crossing in March 1945. Ridgway commanded US Eighth Army in 1950 and in April 1951, when he succeeded MacArthur as both supreme commander of the United Nations forces in Korea and the US Far East Command. He rose to become the Army Chief of Staff from August 1953 to June 1955. (NARA)

MG Manton Eddy, CG 9th Infantry Division, speaks with a German officer at the surrender of Nazi forces in Cherbourg on 27 June 1944. Eddy's 9th Infantry Division was part of MG J. Lawton Collins' VII Corps. Eddy was a First World War veteran. In May 1943, his 9th Infantry Division defeated the German defenders of Bizerte, Tunisia, involving much urban combat. Later, Eddy led the 9th in Sicily in August 1943. After that his formation was sent to England to prepare for the Normandy invasion and the 9th Infantry Division landed on Utah Beach four days after the initial 6 June landings. In August 1944, Eddy became CG XII Corps, as part of Patton's recently activated Third Army. (NARA)

General Philippe Leclerc, CG French 2nd Armoured Division, arrives at Normandy on 31 July 1944, greeted by US MG Walton H. Walker, Patton's Third Army XX Corps CG. After France's fall in 1940, Leclerc had left for Britain, defying a Vichy French directive. Sent to Africa, he rallied Free French sympathizers in Chad and then in Libya, where his L Force covered the British Eighth Army's flank into Tunisia for participation in the Mareth Line offensive. L Force was transformed into French 2nd Armoured Division for the Normandy 'breakout' offensive. Within weeks of his arrival, the Seine was crossed en masse by four Allied armies, from Elbeuf near the mouth of the river to the area of Fontainebleau below Paris. On 25 August, Paris was liberated by Leclerc's French 2nd Armoured Division. (NARA)

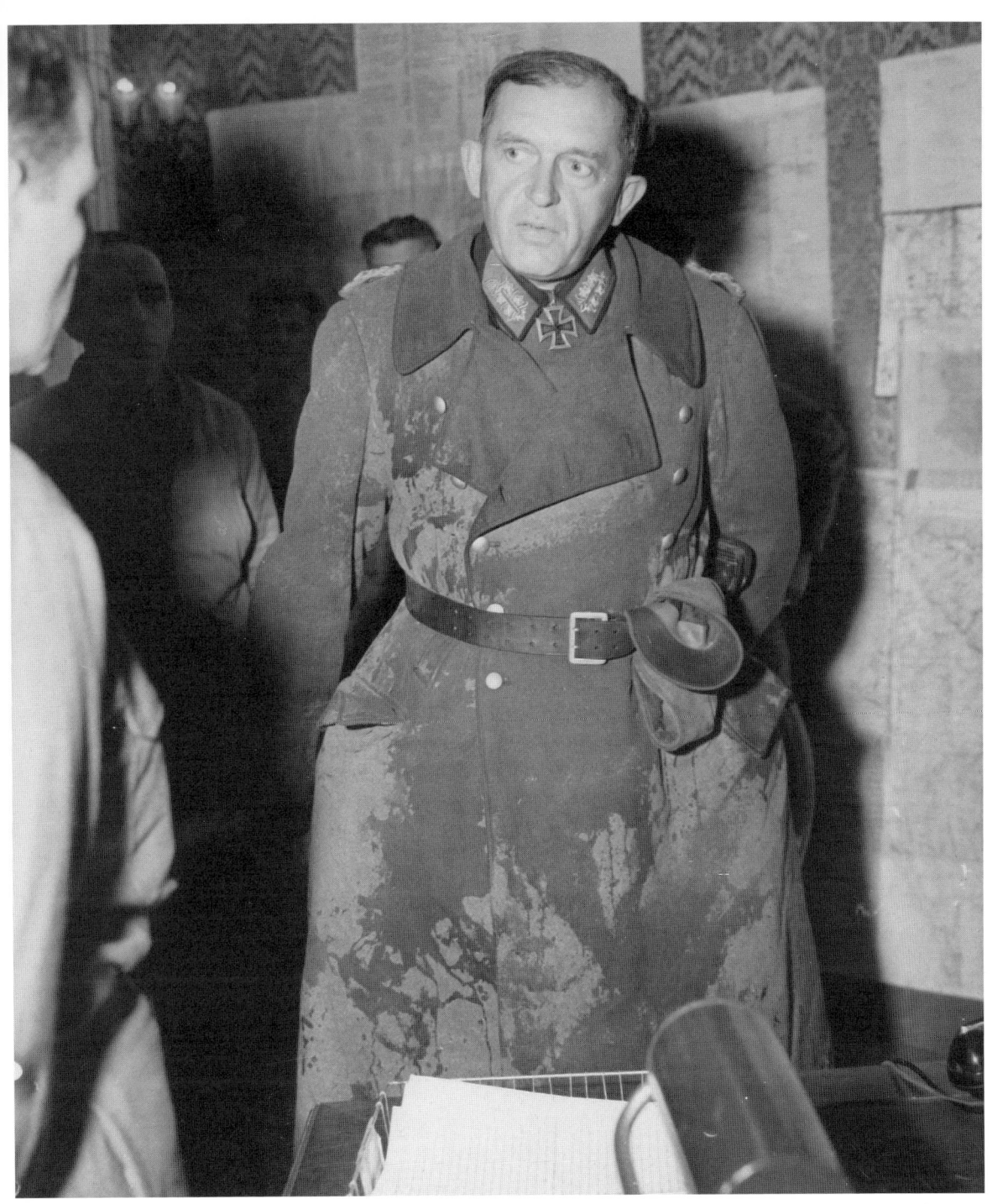

German LG Karl-Wilhelm von Schlieben, CG of the Cherbourg garrison, at MG Collins's VII Corps HQ after surrendering the port-city and fortress on 26 June 1944. Hitler ordered von Schlieben to fight to the death and he initially refused Collins's 21 June surrender demand. But within a day of a massive air, naval and artillery bombardment Cherbourg's resistance ended, with the fortifications and arsenal capitulating. Final pockets of German resistance were neutralized by 1 July. Cherbourg's port facilities were so devastated that it would be a month before they were made functional for Allied shipping. (NARA)

(**Above, left**) LG Fritz Bayerlein, CG Panzer *Lehr* Division, one of the Wehrmacht's best armoured formations, joined 12th SS-Panzer Division *Hitlerjugend* and 21st Panzer Division around Caen, to halt Montgomery's thrust to occupy the city. Bayerlein was Rommel's DAK COS during the Desert War, culminating at El Alamein from July to November 1942. In Normandy, the Panzer *Lehr* was initially harassed and suffered serious losses from Allied air forces during its daylight move (which Bayerlein objected to) on 7 June, from Chartres to the Seulles River valley to block British XXX Corps' advance from Bayeux towards Tilly-sur-Seulles and Villers-Bocage. The inability of British I Corps to take Caen and Carpiquet airfield to the west had given Rommel time to mount a defence. Later in the campaign, Bayerlein, with Panzer *Lehr* dug in along the edge of the Operation *Cobra* target area, described the US 8th and 9th AFs along the St Lô–Périers road on 24 and 25 July as 'hellacious', with bomb carpeting producing a moonscape and at least 70 per cent of his forces dead, wounded, or crazed. (*Author's collection*)

(**Above, right**) SS MG Kurt Meyer of 12th SS-Panzer Division *Hitlerjugend* is shown near Caen, with some of his troops. Meyer was exceptional and battle-hardened from his campaigning in Romania and the Soviet Union. Although still a colonel in command of a regiment on 6 June, Meyer was promoted within days to MG, taking over command of the 12th SS-Panzer. When his division moved, late on 6 June, the cloud cover had cleared and they took a pounding by Allied air units as they began the trek from Lisieux to the battlefield. Meyer entered the SS in 1933 as a member of Hitler's elite bodyguard. In 1939–40, he fought in Poland, Holland, and France. He played a major role as a regimental commander during the Greek campaign and he fought in the Soviet Union for three years, reaching deep into the Caucasus and fighting his way out from encirclement a few times with a handful of survivors.

On 3 July, the 3rd Canadian Division approached Caen from the west capturing Carpiquet village, but Carpiquet Airfield was heavily fortified and defended by elements of Meyer's 12th SS-Panzer Division *Hitlerjugend*. The Canadians were able to secure only a portion of the airfield against Meyer's defences, during a two-day battle with high casualty lists on both sides. During the closure of the Falaise-Argentan Pocket Meyer personally escaped, but his division lost over 75 per cent of its tanks and soldiers along with more than half the personnel carriers and artillery. About a hundred German armoured vehicles managed to escape across the Seine. The Canadian government convicted Meyer of war crimes after the war and sentenced him to death, but that was later commuted to life imprisonment as there was no proof that he had ordered the shooting of Allied POWs against stone walls in Le Mesnil Patry and Audrieu, northeast of Tilly-sur-Seulles. (*Author's collection*)

A heavily kitted Canadian infantryman waits for an artillery and armour barrage to lift before advancing at Verrières Ridge on 25 July 1944 during Operation *Spring*, which took place along with US First Army's Operation *Cobra*, after Caen was captured. The infantryman is equipped with a small pack, a shovel, respirator, a half-sheet, a water bottle, and his SMLE 0.303in calibre rifle among other items. The Canadian troops in France were all volunteers, as conscripts were raised for national defence and were exempt from overseas service unless they volunteered. The Canadian 2nd Division, commanded by MG C. Foulkes, joined the Canadian 3rd Division, the Canadian 2nd Armoured Brigade, and the Canadian 4th Armoured Division in Normandy in early July, to form II Canadian Corps under LG Guy Simonds. Montgomery's 21st AG which included the First Canadian Army fought a hard campaign for possession of Caen. On 19 July, attacking out of the centre of Caen, Canadian 2nd Division pushed across the Orne river to link up with the Canadian 3rd Division, completing the encirclement of Caen. The Norman city was completely in Allied hands after several weeks of bitter fighting with the best of the Nazi panzer units. *(NARA)*

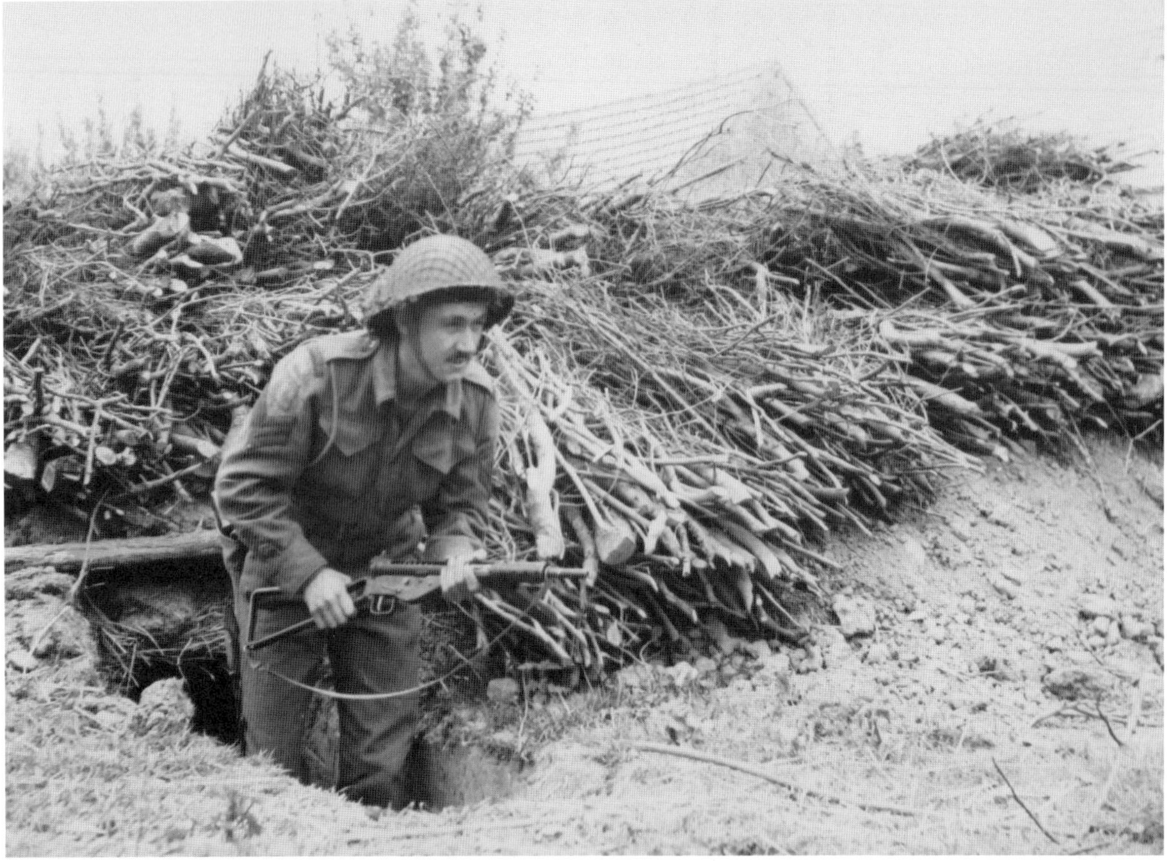

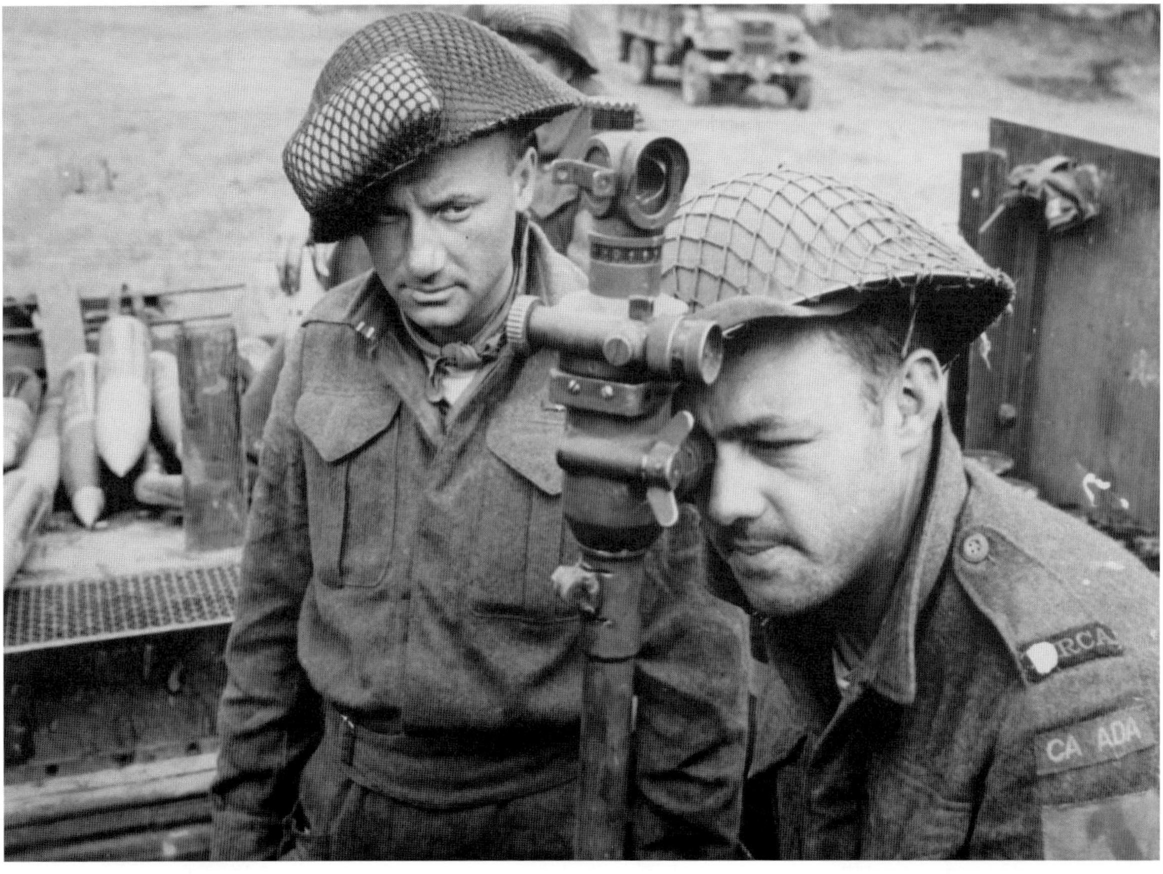
RCA
CA ADA

(**Opposite, above**) A Canadian infantry sergeant emerges from his camouflage netted, fascine-covered dugout carrying his 9mm Parabellum Mk II Sten SMG, a gun with a simple design and very low production cost. The Sten gun was designed in 1940 and manufactured by half a dozen different contractors. It had an effective firing range of 100 metres and a 32-round detachable box magazine. 'Sten' is an acronym for the designers, Major Reginald Shepherd and Harold Turpin at the Enfield factory. Over 4 million Sten SMGs were produced in various versions in the 1940s. (*NARA*)

(**Opposite, below**) Two Canadian artillerymen in the Caen sector site in their 105mm howitzer, in a SPA known as a 'Priest' due to the pulpit-like MG ring. The British-named vehicles followed the same tradition with the 'Bishop' and 'Deacon' SPAs. The Priest was used in the ETO, the Pacific theatre, and in Asia. It carried 69 rounds of 105mm M1/M2 artillery shells and an M2 Browning MG. Over 4,000 M7 SPA vehicles were made. After the Normandy invasion, the artillery regiments of the British 3rd and 50th Divisions, and the Canadian 3rd Division were equipped with the M7; however, these were replaced by other towed guns in early August 1944. (*NARA*)

(**Above**) A Canadian 105mm howitzer SPA gun, 'Priest' is stationary for a firing mission on Caen, the capital of Calvados, in the summer of 1944. Stacks of artillery shells are behind the vehicle, which has a clear field of fire. The predecessor of the M7 Priest was the T19 half-track, which was used in North Africa and Sicily, but it lacked the necessary protection and off-road capabilities of the M7. In 1941, the M3 Lee chassis was chosen to house the 105mm artillery piece. The M7B1 variant was based on the M4 Sherman chassis. The British created a 'Defrocked Priest' where the M7 was converted into armoured personnel carriers for the British 2nd Army's Operation *Goodwood*, from 18 July to 20 July 1944. A Canadian version of the M7 was converted as a dedicated armoured personnel carrier, the 'Kangaroo', for operations in Holland and the crossing of the Rhine from October 1944 to April 1945. (*NARA*)

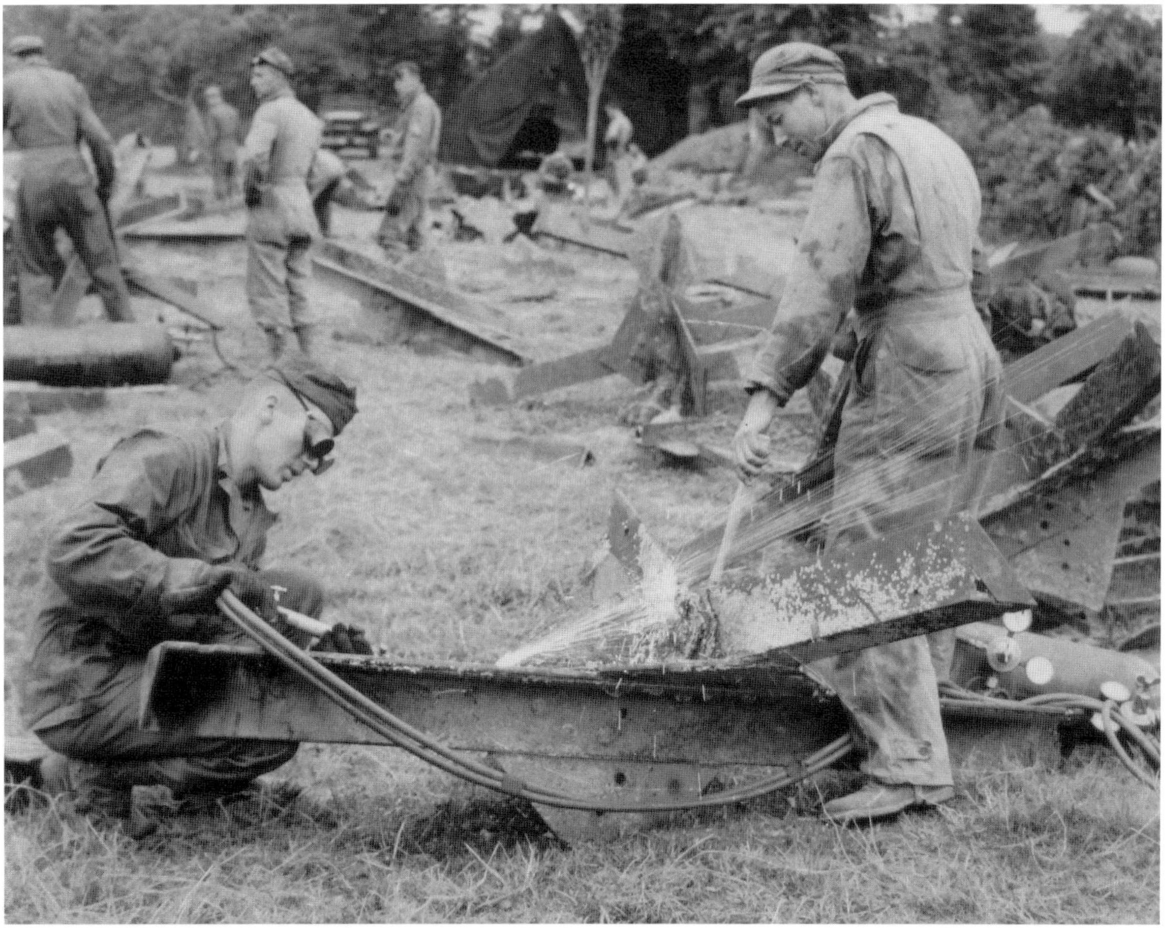

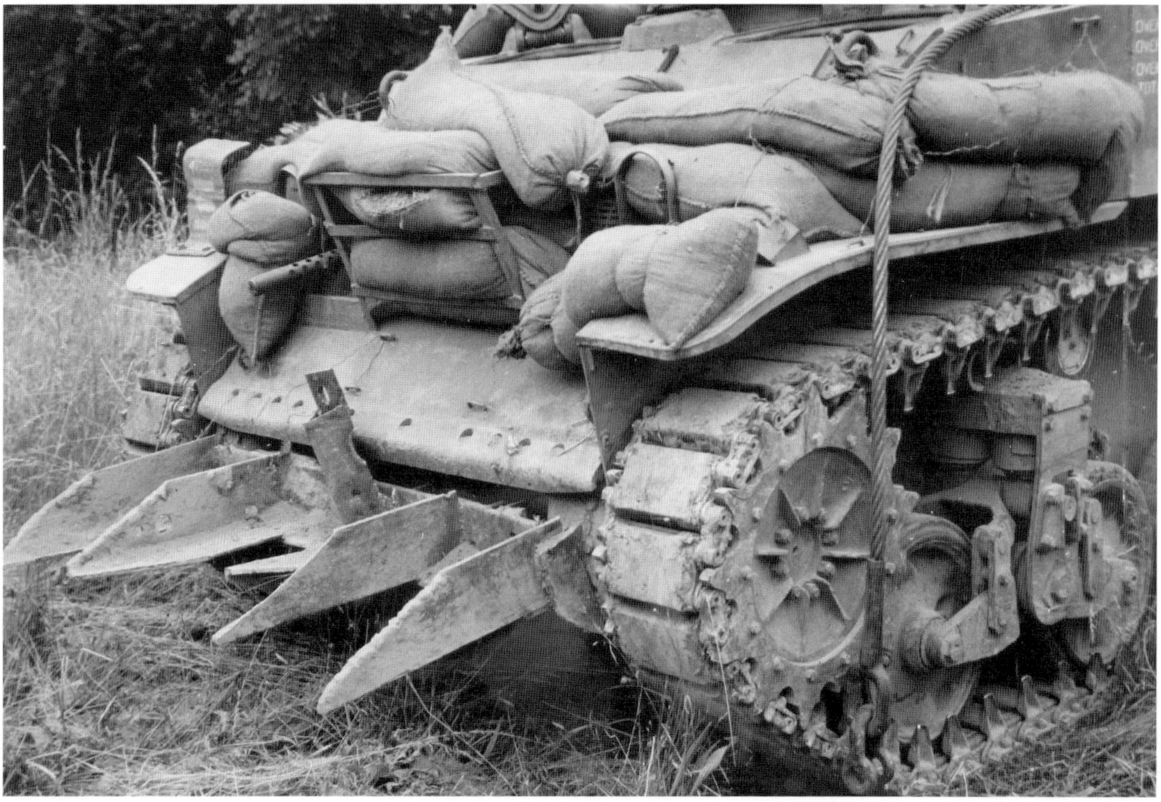

(**Opposite, above**) American engineers use acetylene torches to cut up German steel hedgehog beach obstacles into smaller pieces. Sergeant Curtis G. Culin, US 102nd Cavalry Reconnaissance Squadron, 2nd Armoured Division, was credited with using the steel to invent this hedgerow-breaking blade that could be fitted to Allied armoured vehicles. Thus armed they were able to break through the *bocage* by rapidly creating gaps in the hedgerows rather than riding over them as before, a manoeuvre which exposed the thin underside of American tanks to German AT weapons while the armoured vehicle was unable to bring its own guns to bear. Some hedges were so entangled with foliage and small trees that Allied tanks could be trapped while attempting to push through, or lose a tread becoming immobilized. Culin received the Legion of Merit for his hedgerow cutter innovation. He lost a leg to an enemy land mine in the Huertgen Forest after the Normandy battle was over. (NARA)

(**Opposite, below**) An American M5 tank with Culin hedgerow cutters made from German steel hedgehog beach obstacles fitted to the bottom front of the vehicle. They were called Rhino tanks and when General Bradley, CG First Army, saw a demonstration of Culin's device while visiting 2nd Armoured Division on 14 July 1944, he ordered First Army Ordnance Section to begin construction of the hedgerow cutters on an emergency basis. Between 15 and 25 July, when Operation *Cobra* started, over 500 Rhino tanks were fitted up. (NARA)

(**Above**) American engineers lay steel wire matting for vehicles to exit one of the US landing beaches. At Utah Beach, initial units of the 1st Engineer Special Brigade to land were the 1st and 2nd Battalions, 531st Shore Regiment. At Omaha Beach, the 6th Engineer Special Brigade accompanied the 116th IR, 29th Infantry Division and the 5th Engineer Special Brigade was attached to the 16th IR, of the 1st Infantry Division. The engineers laid out rudimentary roads for vehicles to move inland, widened gaps that combat engineers created in the seawall, searched for mines, improved exits for infantry movement, set up supply dumps and reconnoitred. (NARA)

(**Above**) An M4 medium tank disabled by a mine detonation under the left rear tread is assisted by a US Army Engineer in ARV (*right background*). ARVs were designed to tow tanks needing battle damage repair in rear echelon areas or simply to extricate tanks stuck in water, shellholes, road or other terrain impediments and to expeditiously get them back into combat. The ARVs possessed motorized tracks to operate on uneven ground and were essentially repurposed tanks with the turret and armament removed and replaced with a winch system. (*NARA*)

(**Opposite, above**) An American Engineer Special Brigade lieutenant proceeds carefully through a German minefield with a metal detector, not too far from the beach on 13 June 1944. An American soldier had been killed by a mine going off, to the right of the tape. A helmet and destroyed walkie-talkie lie on the ground in front of the warning sign for mines. (*NARA*)

(**Opposite, below**) US Army engineers and signalmen string communications wire along an ancient sunken narrow lane, the hedgerows' tall earthen walls covered with vegetation concealing it, in the St Lô sector on 13 July 1944. The hedges created a network of inverted trenches, forming a natural, layered fortification system that favoured the defenders. The earthen bases shielded them from the enemy and were thick enough to protect against small arms and MG fire. The top vegetation provided camouflage and restricted the observation of the attacking force. The hedgerows also provided a solid base for infantry to be shielded from mortar and artillery fire. (*NARA*)

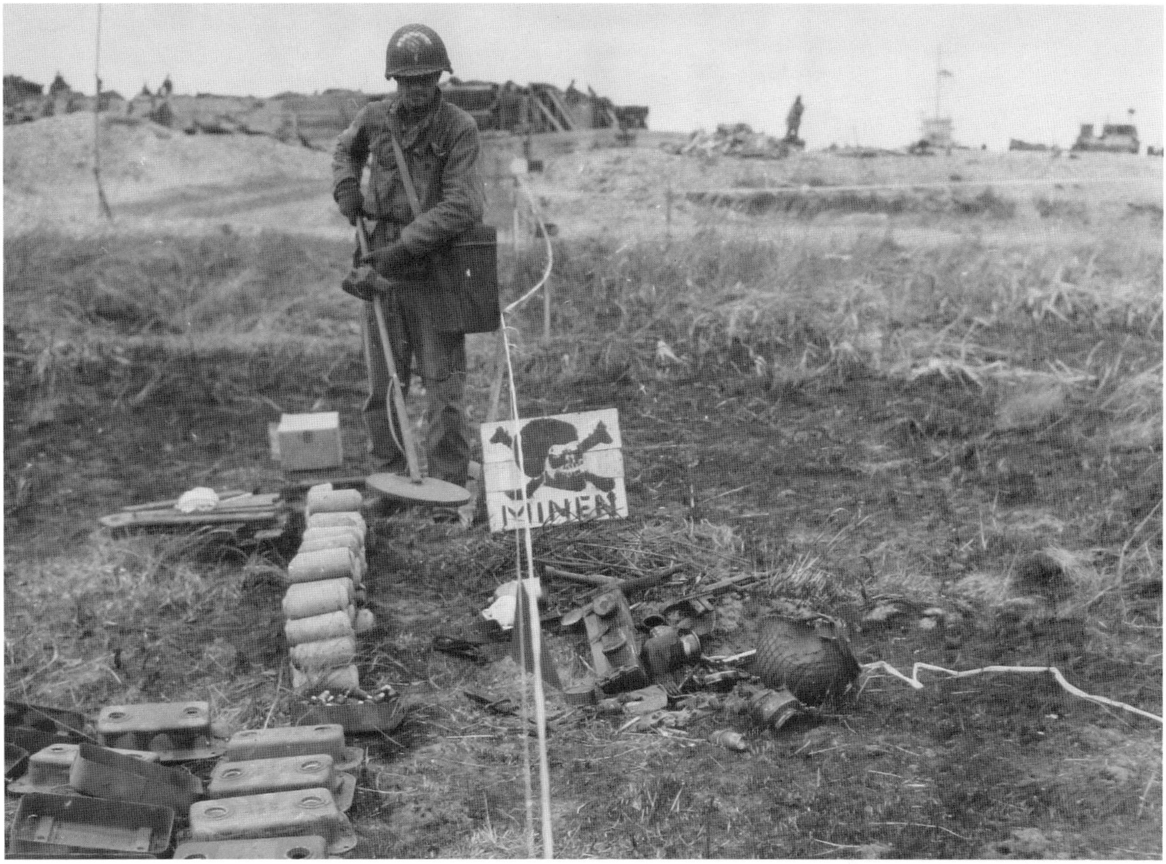
MINEN

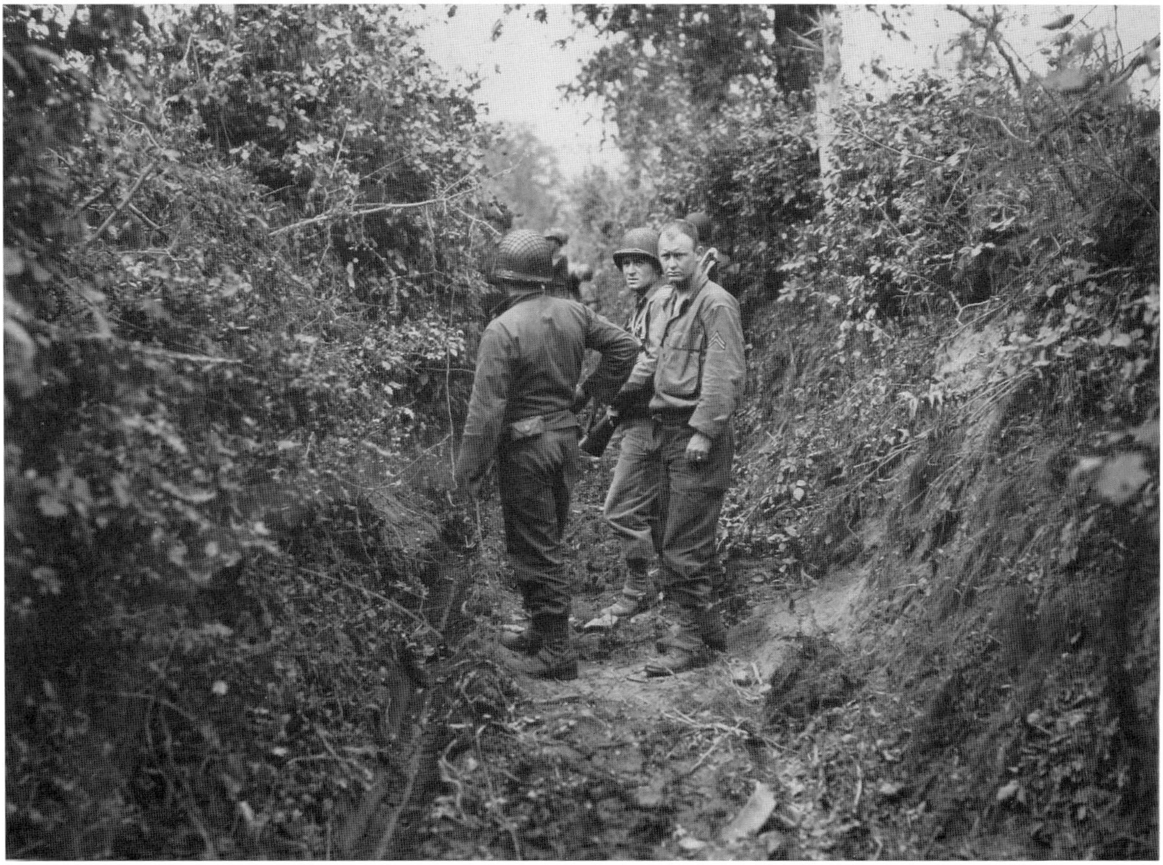

(**Above**) Two US First Army officers examine an operations map at a division HQ inland on 14 July 1944. On 3 July, a week after the port-city of Cherbourg was captured, four US First Army corps, V, VII, VIII and XIX, began to attack southwards towards St Lô. The *bocage* made for very slow progress and heavy casualties. On 14 July, the situation map showed the First Army frontlines stretching from just south of La Haye-du-Puits in the west to just north of St Lô to the east, with the latter locale captured by the Americans on 18 July. The Americans faced the German Seventh Army, commanded by SS-*Oberstgruppenführer* Paul Hausser, the replacement for *Generaloberst* Friedrich Dollmann, who died mysteriously on 29 June after being dismissed by Hitler within days of Cherbourg's fall. The German Seventh Army was comprised of infantry, parachute and armoured divisions of the Wehrmacht's 84th Corps, under General Dietrich von Choltitz, which included the Panzer *Lehr* Division, the 2nd SS-Panzer Division *Das Reich*, the 17th SS-*Panzergrenadier* Division 'Götz von Berlichingen' (named after a legendary German knight), the Luftwaffe's II Parachute Corps (3rd and 5th Divisions), along with three infantry divisions. Panzer *Lehr* Division was situated northeast of St Lô while German II Parachute Corps defended the area west of St Lô. (*NARA*)

(**Opposite, above**) A USN Beachmaster CP points to someone on Utah Beach late on 6 June 1944. They were facetiously called the 'traffic cops of invasion' with the difficult responsibility of establishing and maintaining order. Their rigorous training made them specialists in beach reconnaissance, shore-to-ship radio communication, boat repair, and supervision of US naval beach battalions to render combat first aid, evacuate casualties and move the dead. These groups gave target locations to USN destroyers running parallel to the beach 200 yards offshore, to provide 5-inch gunfire onto the bluffs beyond the beach due to the absence of adequate American armour early on 6 June. The Beachmaster used a power megaphone, flags, blinkers, and walkie-talkies to direct landing craft, men and supplies. His naval beach battalions, comprised of three companies each with three platoons, also had a boat repair section which could make temporary repairs to disabled landing craft. (*NARA*)

(**Below**) A USN Shore Fire Control Party (SFCP) sets up in a shellhole near Les Dunes de Varreville, some time after the initial assault waves landed, to immediately direct naval gunfire to support the American ground forces near Utah Beach. The SFCP is shown using a radio to communicate with ships' gunners — it is powered by a hand-cranked generator and a walkie-talkie is used at the same time to obtain target bearings and accuracy of gunfire from troops inland. (*NARA*)

Paratroopers of the 101st Airborne Division (identified by the Screaming Eagle emblem on the left shoulder patch) meet local French citizens in Sainte-Marie-du-Mont on 7 June 1944, after rounding up German POWs. This commune is inland from Utah Beach and between the villages of La Galle to the north and Vierville to the south, on the road running perpendicular to the Douve river. Enemy forces in the vicinity included the 6th Parachute Regiment between Carentan and Isigny and the Wehrmacht's 91st Infantry Division near the Merderet river, west of Sainte-Mère-Église.

The 101st Airborne Division initially mustered only 1,100 men out of 6,000 after the 5 June overnight parachute drop, which was spread over an area 25 miles long by 15 miles wide and with small isolated elements even further spread out. However, by the evening of 6 June its strength had risen to 2,500 men. Sainte-Mère-Église, the target of the US 82nd Airborne Division, was astride the Merderet, which paralleled the Carentan–Mountebourg–Valognes–Cherbourg road in the Cotentin Peninsula. The 82nd had only one regiment land on its objective and only 4 per cent dropped in their zones west of the Merderet. Both divisions lost large amounts of equipment and almost all glider-borne artillery, much of it in the floods of the Merderet and Douve rivers. Neither division was able to prepare adequately for the next wave of glider landings with troops and equipment. (NARA)

Wounded American paratroopers and infantrymen on 7 June 1944 await evacuation to an LST bound for an English port. The first Army field hospitals came ashore on 7–8 June. They included the 13th and 51st Field Hospital Units at Omaha Beach and the 42nd and 45th Field Hospital Units at Utah Beach. Parenthetically, in the 82nd Airborne Division, 50 per cent of the medical officers were unaccounted for during the first 72 hours of combat. In the 101st Airborne Division, only two members of a sixteen-man medical detachment maintained contact with its paratroopers, as the division lost 20 per cent of its medical personnel, most of them in the first few days. The 101st Airborne Division recovered only 30 per cent of its air-dropped supply containers due to inaccurate dispersal and sinking in the flooded fields by the Douve river. A surgeon in the 101st Airborne Division concluded later that it had been a mistake to drop so much materiel in the early hours of the invasion, when the accompanying field surgeons did not yet need it and darkness made it almost impossible to find. During the first hours on the ground, MOs and medics gave first aid to men injured in the jump or in glider crashes as well as in the first firefights with German defenders, and those medical personnel that reached their battalion assembly areas established field aid stations, usually near their battalion CPs. (NARA)

A captain, the executive officer of Company A, 134th IR, 35th Division, XIX Corps, is stretchered by medics to a jeep ambulance during combat north of St Lô. The officer had previously sustained shrapnel injuries but came back to duty to replace his badly wounded company commander. He had been leading his company for two days when he was wounded in the leg by a German sniper. The tall hedgerow not only interfered with combat but meant the medics had to negotiate a steep slope to remove the wounded man. It took some time to climb up the bank, over the top, and bring him down to the jeep, all the while offering a target for enemy gunfire. *(NARA)*

A US Army bugler blows 'Taps' at a special mass celebrating the American cemetery at Sainte-Mère-Église on Bastille Day, 14 July 1944. The 82nd Airborne Division was sent to seize Sainte-Mère-Église and prevent German counterattacks against the seaborne forces moving inland. In total, 4,000 glider men and over 6,000 paratroops of the 82nd participated in the 5–6 June aerial assault. Since Roman times, the ancient system of roads had been dominated by Sainte-Mère-Église. It was also an essential element of the German landline cable system of communication between Cherbourg, in the northern Cotentin Peninsula, and to the south in the direction of Paris. In May 1944, the Germans moved their 91st Infantry Division to the eastern part of the Cotentin Peninsula.

In addition to the American paratroopers that perished on 5/6 June, General Wilhelm Falley, the CG of the Wehrmacht's 91st Infantry Division, was killed on 6 June near Picauville, to the south of Sainte-Mère-Église, while returning to his HQ. Other targets of the 82nd Airborne Division were the seizure of the area north of Sainte-Mère-Église between Neuville-au-Plain and Beuzeville-au-Plain and two bridges over the Merderet river near Chef-du-Pont and La Fière; also the destruction of the bridges over the Douve river further to the south, thus cutting off the possible German counterattack from this direction. (NARA)

(**Above**) British REs ('sappers') remove road bombs in August 1944, after the breakout from Caen and on to the excellent tank terrain of the Falaise Plain. The REs in the Second World War had newer roles including bomb disposal, mine clearance, airfield construction, building Bailey bridges, and the use of AVRE for battlefield engineering. Engineers also helped design, build and operate the 'Mulberry' Harbour at Arromanches after the initial landing at Gold Beach. (NARA)

(**Opposite, above**) A British ambulance jeep carries two medics and three wounded soldiers in a double-decker of stretchers over a pontoon bridge across a stream. This took place after an assault across the Orne river near Caen that enabled Anglo-Canadian forces to capture the Calvados capital city on 19 July 1944, after combat siege against fanatical Nazi resistance. Accounts by British MOs upon entering Caen after its capture described the city as completely flattened, including the city centre, many of the churches and the university quarter. (NARA)

(**Opposite, below**) A Canadian armoured car ('Staghound') crosses over a Bailey bridge constructed by engineers across a Normandy waterway. These bridges, devised by a British War Office civil servant, Donald Bailey, were pre-fabricated steel truss structures that were transported to previously demolished bridge sites in 10ft sections. After rapid assembly with simple tools, the temporary bridge could be pushed across the waterway. A wood-planking road surface was added to support a minimum of 20 tons of materiel. (NARA)

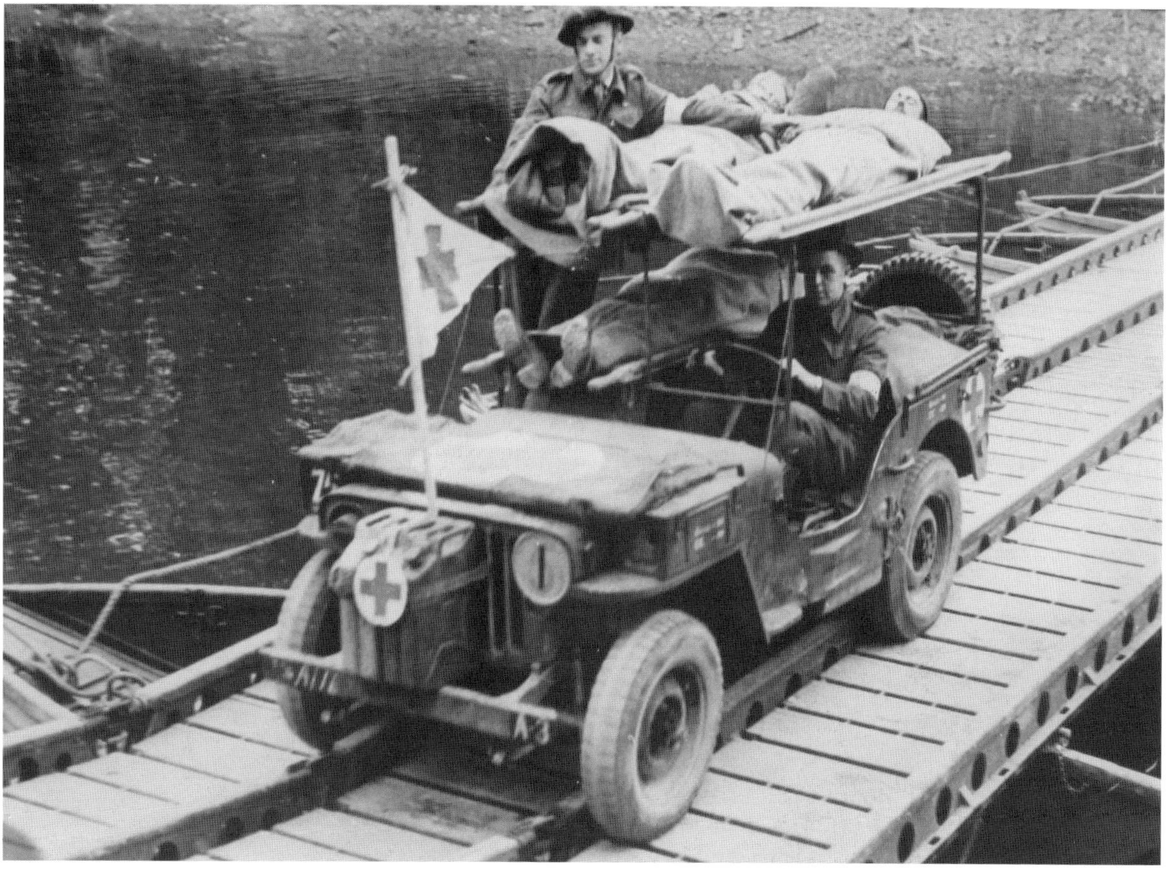

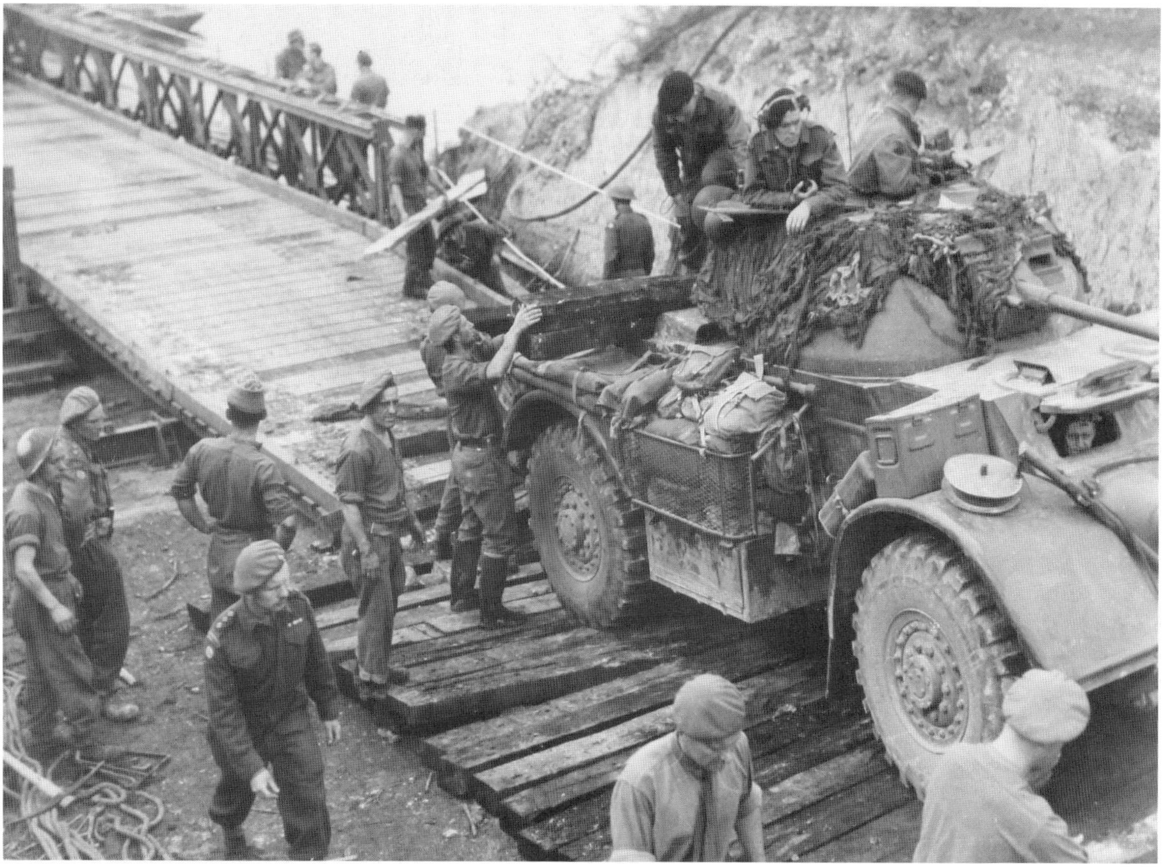

(**Above**) British REs, as signified by the white band over the brim of the helmets with unit shoulder insignia censored out, examine three small German remote-control tracked mines called Goliaths, in a Normandy field. These were disposable, single-use, unmanned demolition vehicles that had electric (Sd.kfz.302) or gasoline-powered (Sd.kfz.303a and 303b) engines. They had a maximum speed of under 4 miles per hour and an operational range of 0.9 miles on-road and 0.5 miles off-road, and could carry 130–220lbs of HE. They were known as 'beetle tanks' by the Allies and were used on all fronts where the Wehrmacht fought, from early 1942. They were used principally by panzer and combat engineer units. A few Goliaths were seen on the Normandy beaches, but most were rendered inoperative after artillery blasts severed their command cables. A total of 7,500 were produced. Three disabled Allied vehicles appear in the background. At left is a damaged Allied amphibious 6-wheeled modification of a General Motors Corporation (GMC) 2.5-ton truck (DUKW), while a British Associated Equipment Company (AEC) Matador artillery 4 × 4 tractor is off to the right. The destroyed vehicle in the middle is unidentifiable. (*NARA*)

(**Opposite, above**) An American MP in camouflage uniform (*left*) and a British Dispatch Rider are seen at the junction of Allied lines in the French village of Pacy-sur-Eure on 27 August 1944. Some American soldiers and French civilians are looking on, with a sign for Paris in the background. The village is on the Rouen to Paris road. During the Second World War, the Royal Corps of Signals soldiers carried out the role as dispatch riders using Triumph, Norton, BSA, Matchless and Ariel motorbikes. The US 17th Armoured Engineer Battalion moved to Pacy-sur-Eure on 27 August for re-equipping. Company E of the 17th, in conjunction with the 82nd Engineer Battalion, constructed a 720ft floating treadway bridge across the Seine at Meulan-en-Yvelines on 29 August. The newly constructed bridge provided US XIX Corps with a supply route into northern France. (*NARA*)

(**Below**) A Canadian Ordnance ML 4.2in mortar crew in action next to their Universal Carrier, outside Gruchy to Caen's west on 7 July 1944. This mortar was a smooth-bore weapon of the Stokes pattern. It entered widespread British use in 1942, equipping chemical warfare companies of the RE; but its combat debut was with the Australian 24th Infantry Brigade at the Second Battle of El Alamein. After the heavy saturation bombing of Operation *Charnwood* early on 7 July, the Canadians that day attacked the villages of Buron and Gruchy, the site of their bloody defeat a month earlier at the hands of 12th SS-Panzer Division *Hitlerjugend*. The teenage *Hitlerjugend Panzergrenadiers* still put up fierce resistance as the SS troops withdrew into Caen. (*NARA*)

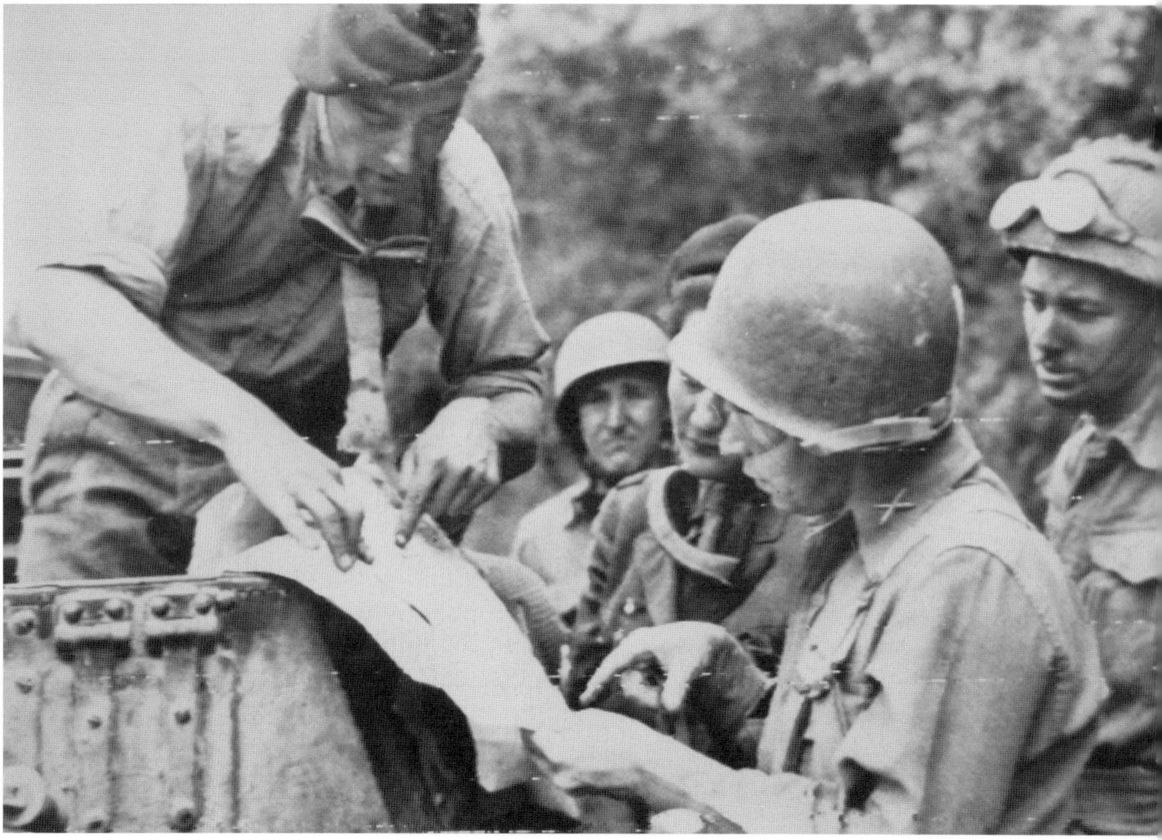

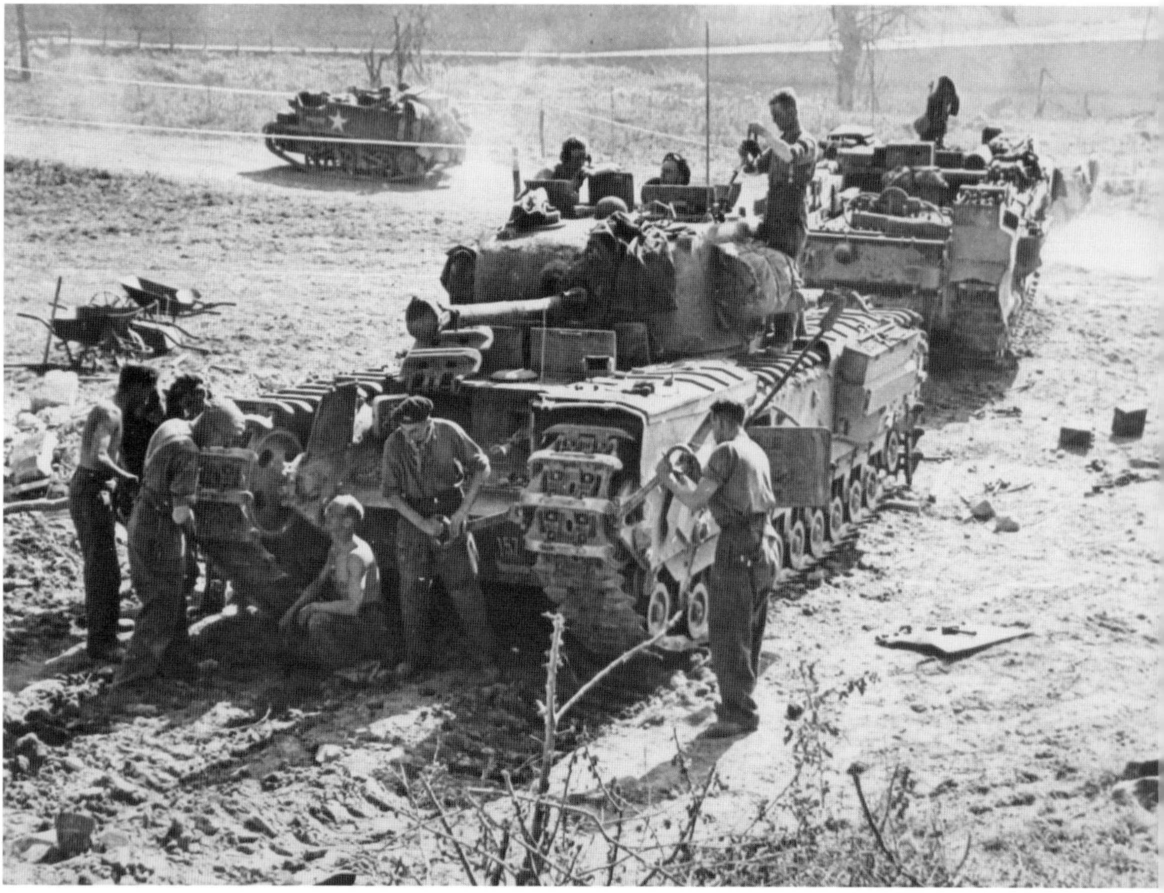

(**Opposite, above**) A Polish tanker (*left*) goes over plans with a US Army infantry officer to close the Falaise-Argentan 'Gap' on 22 August 1944. On 19 August, Polish and American forces combined to close the gap and trap 50,000 soldiers of the German Seventh and Fifth Panzer Armies. However, two main escape routes existed: at the footbridge at St Lambert and the ford at Moissy, both across the river Dives. On 20/21 August the remnants of the German Seventh and Fifth made a last attempt to get across the waterway before the gap was completely sealed. On 21 August, additional Canadian and American troops arrived to strengthen the cordon between Trun, captured by the 4th Canadian Armoured Division on 18 August, and Chambois, captured by the Polish 10th Mounted Rifles on 19 August, to link up with elements of the US 90th Infantry Division's 359th IR. (*NARA*)

(**Opposite, below**) British sappers repair a damaged tread (*foreground*) on a Churchill Mk IV Infantry (I) Tank to get it back into action. This Churchill Mk IV had a QF 6-pounder main turret gun and as an I tank, it had a maximum speed of 15mph. Over 1,600 of the Mk IVs were built. The vehicle behind the Mk IV is a Churchill ARV, which transported the sappers to the required site and gave protection. It was a turretless tank with a stripped interior, giving extra storage space for the engineers' equipment. In the background a Universal Carrier moves between white tape boundaries signifying that the road has been cleared of mines. (*NARA*)

(**Above**) Members of the 834th Engineer Aviation Battalion, 9th TAF use magnetic detectors to clear a grassy field of German mines at St-Pierre-du-Mont, which is located 1km east of the Pointe du Hoc battery between Omaha and Utah beaches. The furious fighting that took place in this area delayed the start of the airfield's installation until 7 June and it was completed by the evening of 8 June. This site became an Advanced Landing Ground (ALG) or airfield used by the 9th TAF. (*NARA*)

(**Above**) Sappers of the 834th Engineer Aviation Battalion, 9th TAF lay down steel matting during the four-day construction of the airfield at St-Pierre-du-Mont. The airfield's length was eventually 5,000 feet and was constructed with square-mesh track. Then, pierced steel plating was added. This airfield became the main base of the 366th Fighter Group's 389th, 390th, 391st Squadrons using P-47 Thunderbolts, until 25 August 1944. It was also used by the 370th Fighter Group's 401st Squadron of P-38 Lightnings. (*NARA*)

(**Opposite, above**) A P-38 Lightning, with its twin boom and tricycle landing gear, uses the uncovered runway at St-Pierre-du-Mont on 10 June 1944, and there is a Piper L-4 reconnaissance plane at the side of the runway. The airfield was extremely close to the invasion beaches and was pressed into service initially as an Emergency Landing Strip 1 (ELS A-1) – an untracked runway serving only small reconnaissance aircraft. The next day it was upgraded from a Refuelling and Rearming Strip (RRS A-1) to one capable of handling heavier aircraft. Eventually five airfields became operational in proximity to the Normandy beaches. (*NARA*)

(**Opposite, below**) C-4 Waco gliders loaded with essential supplies land at an airstrip, within several days of the amphibious assault landings. The partially completed airfield is situated outside Sainte-Mère-Église near the La Londe farm. It was built by the 819th Engineer Aviation Battalion of the 9th TAF Engineering Command. The missions started on 10 June 1944. Despite the steady stream of gliders bringing in men and equipment from England, the work on the airfield proceeded uninterrupted. The glider pilots were from the 80th and 81st Troop Carrier Squadrons of the 436th Troop Carrier Group. Additional glider pilots were detached from the US 82nd Airborne Division on 12 June. Piles of square-mesh track are situated to the left side of the runway. This picture has been used as the banner photograph of the National WWII Glider Pilots Association. (*NARA*)

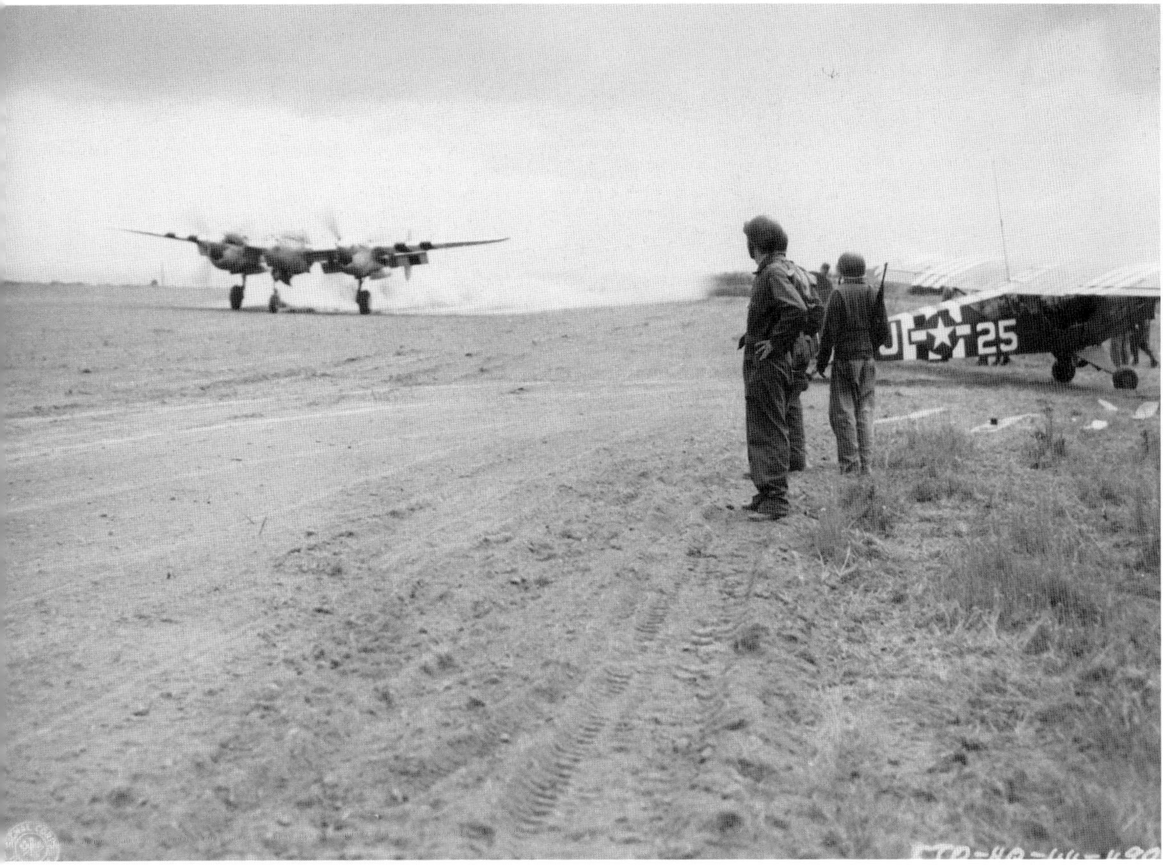
J 25

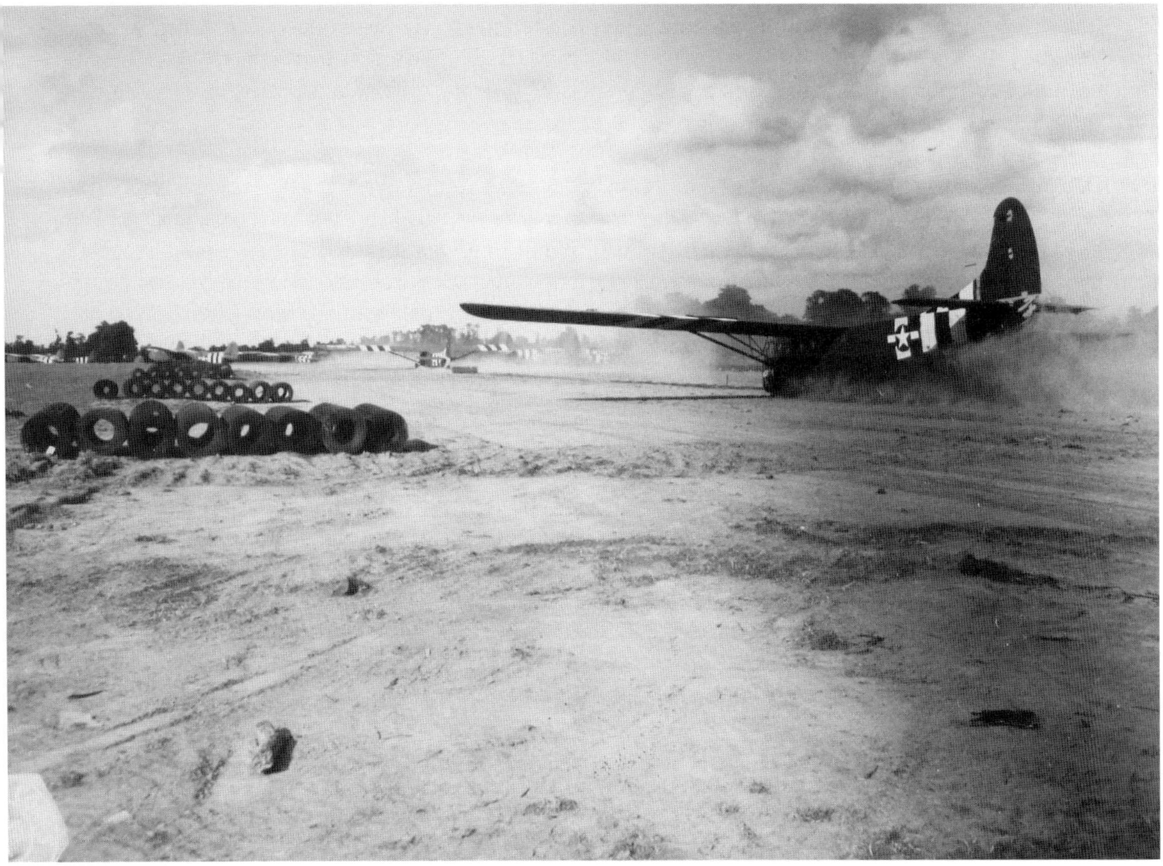

(**Above**) P-47 Thunderbolt pilots fly from a new Allied landing strip in Normandy. On 17 June 1944, the 366th Fighter Group arrived from England flying P-47s. They were joined by the 401st Fighter Group. Last to arrive at the airfield was the 390th Fighter Squadron on 20 June. The P-47 was armed with eight 0.5in calibre Browning MGs and could carry a bombload of 2,500lbs of various explosives. It could also carry 5in rockets as a fighter-bomber in a ground-attack role. The aircraft had a maximum speed of 426mph at 30,000 feet and an operational range of 800 miles at 10,000 feet. Its maximum ceiling was close to 40,000 feet. (NARA)

(**Opposite, above**) An American M2 Chemical 4.2in (or 107mm) rifled mortar unit gets two of its weapons ready to fire the large bullet-shaped shells, in support of ground forces moving inland from the invasion beaches against a German pillbox, on 10 June 1944. The HE rounds were aimed at part of the Nazi defensive works near Utah Beach at Les Dunes de Varreville, defended by elements of the Wehrmacht's 709th Infantry Division. The M2 could be disassembled into three parts and carried by its crew, and first saw action during the Sicilian campaign of 1943. An M29 'Weasel' (*right*) served as an ammunition hauler. The M29 tracked vehicle was originally designed to operate in snow, in support of American raiders of the First Special Services Force in Norway, but that mission never came to fruition. The Weasels were useful over sandy, muddy, and desert terrains in all theatres, performing a variety of functions including evacuating wounded, as a mobile command centre, and signal line layer. In Normandy, they could get to places even jeeps could not negotiate. The M29 was also able to cross some minefields as its ground pressure was often too low to set off German AT Teller mines. (NARA)

(**Opposite, below**) A US 90mm M1 AA gun goes into action as a ground artillery weapon at an American beachhead, as the Luftwaffe's presence was minimal. A later M2 was designed in 1943 with a gun shield for both AT and AA fire. The intensity of fire from this particular AA gun is indicated by the pile of empty shell cases tossed outside of the sand-bagged gun pit. (NARA)

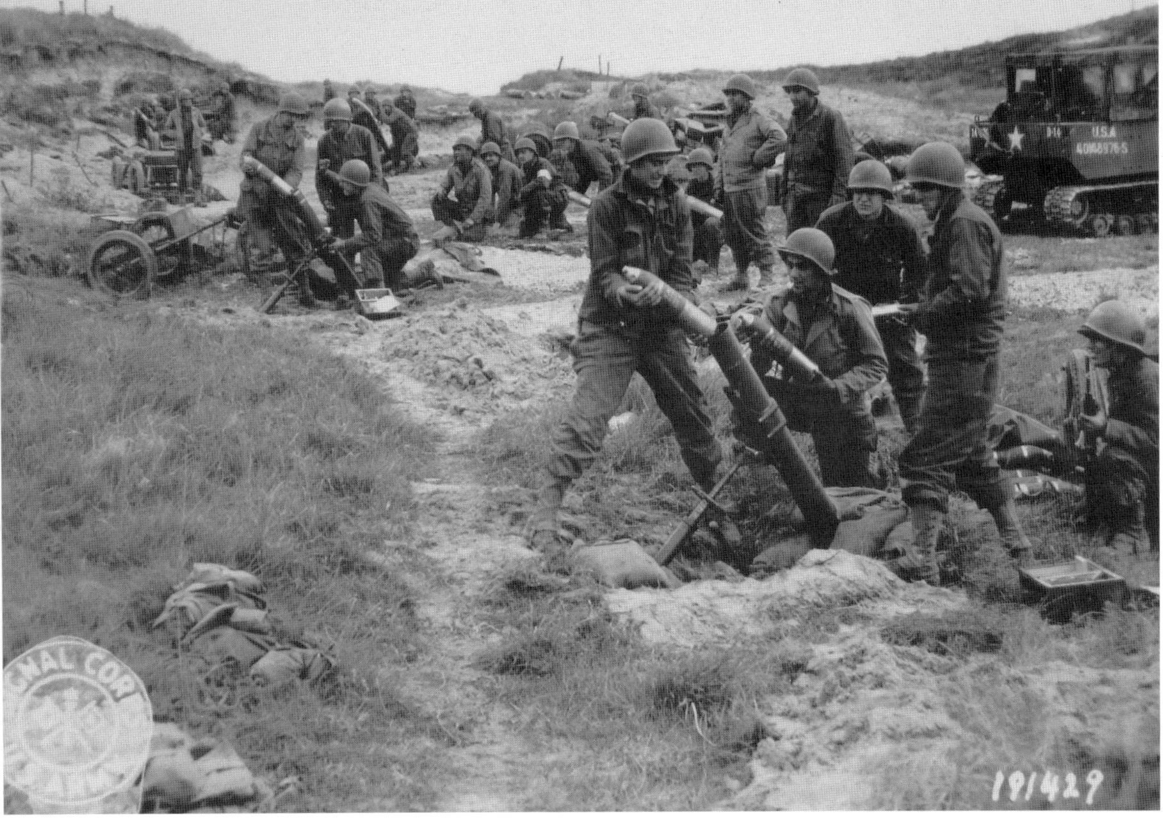
U.S.A
191429

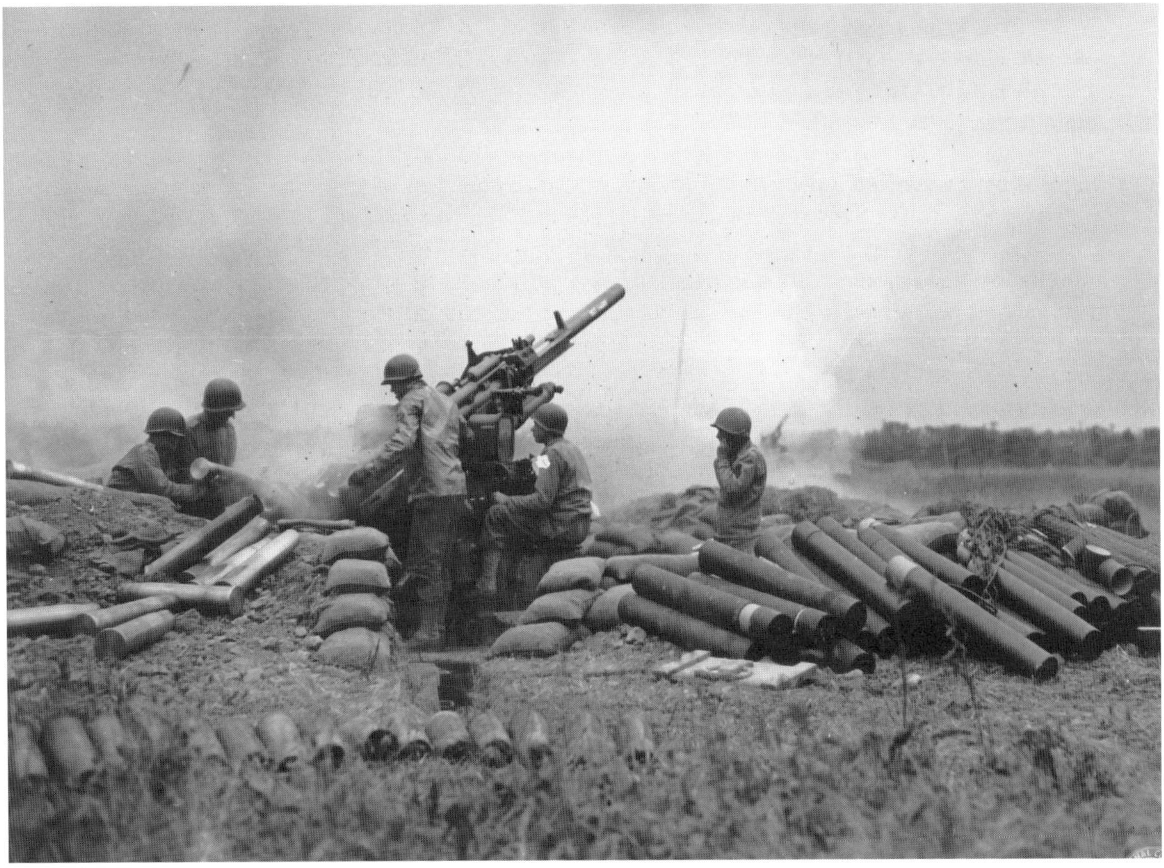

(**Above**) Two American ordnance officers inspect a German 30cm *Nebelwerfer* 42 ('Moaning Minnie'), a six-barrelled mortar. It was one of the most formidable weapons in Normandy, useful in generating heavy defensive fire when the shortage of German infantry and artillery had become severe. It could fire six rockets, each with a 45kg warhead, with a range of more than 3 miles. Its German name suggests that this weapon was designed to lay down smokescreens but it proved very effective as a mortar. A very high proportion of Allied casualties were due to German mortaring. (*NARA*)

(**Opposite, above**) Three RN seamen are shown resting on Omaha Beach after coming ashore from an overfilled LCA as the vessel was badly shot up, 6 June 1944. Many RN-crewed LCAs brought elements of the US 116th IR, 29th Infantry Division to the Omaha assault beaches. Also at Omaha, other battalions of American troops were landed from seven British transport ships and LCA flotillas on 6 June; including both the 2nd and 5th US Ranger Battalions and the 1st Battalion of the US 16th IR, 1st Infantry Division. Other British-crewed LCA flotillas participated in the US 4th Infantry Division landings at Utah Beach on 6 June. (*NARA*)

(**Opposite, below**) A well-camouflaged German 3.7cm *Panzerabwehrkanone* (Pak) 36 AT gun, poised for action in Normandy, July 1944. Although this AT weapon was the main gun until 1942 it then began to be replaced by the 5cm Pak 38 – however, it was still being used in Normandy in 1944 because of its easier mobility and suitability for hedgerow concealment, having a barrel length of only 5ft 5in. Its crew comprised a commander, gunner, loader, and two ammunition bearers. A good crew could fire thirteen 3.7cm calibre rounds per minute. (*NARA*)

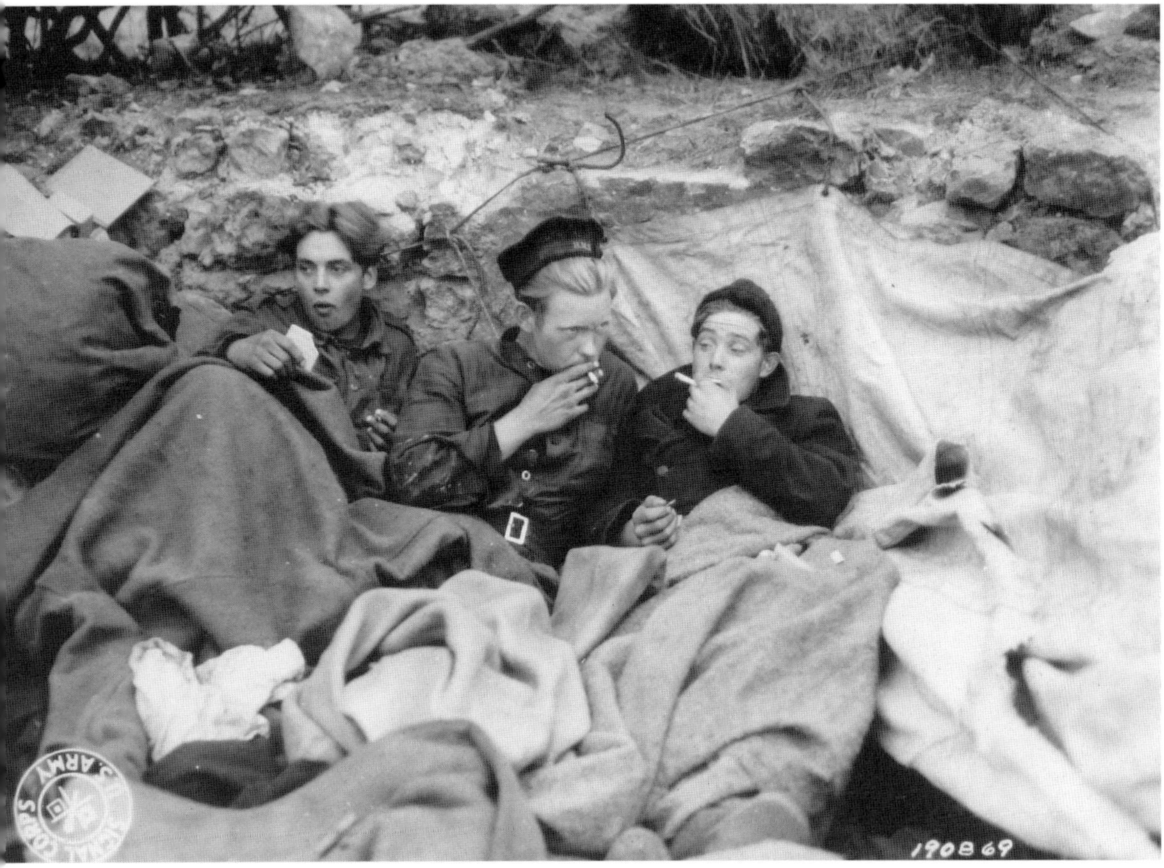
190869

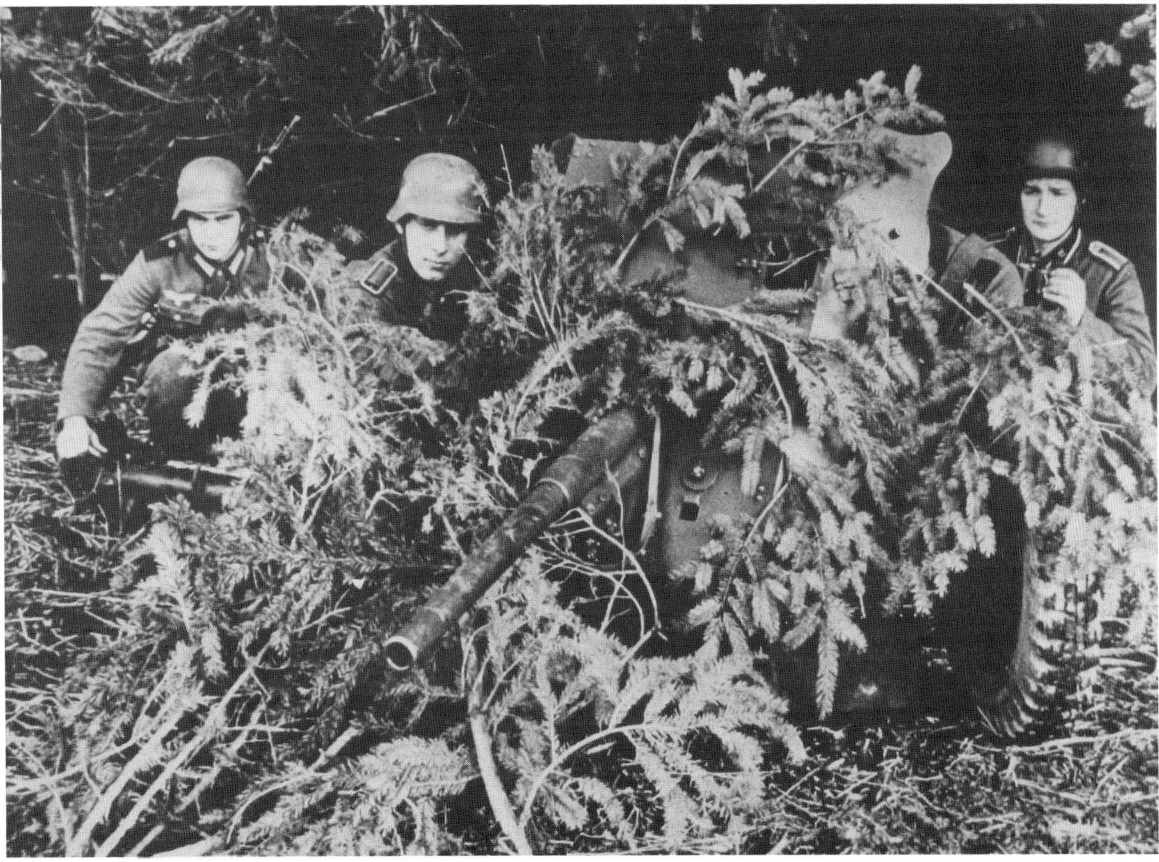

(**Above**) German paratroops take cover behind a disabled Allied M4 medium tank awaiting another one coming up the road. This patrol is armed with a *Panzerfaust* and a *Panzerschreck*, both extremely effective in Normandy. *Panzerfaust* means 'tank fist' and was introduced into combat in July 1943, with a total of 8 million being produced during the final two years of the war. They were simple in design and inexpensive to manufacture as well as easy to operate and not requiring specialized crews. Weighing less than 3lb, it comprised a thin disposable preloaded launch-tube fitted with an explosive warhead. It had a range of 60 metres and could penetrate up to 200mm of tank armour. The *Panzerschreck* was designed as a lightweight, reusable 88mm rocket launcher for German infantry as an effective AT weapon and its name means 'tank fright'. It weighed 24lb and had an effective firing range of 150 metres. It was an enlarged facsimile of the American 'bazooka', using a fin-stabilized rocket with a shaped charge warhead and was made in smaller numbers than the *Panzerfaust*. (*Author's collection*)

(**Opposite, above**) Nazi SS-*Panzergrenadiers*, in camouflage smocks, seek shelter from Allied artillery behind a stone wall. As the combat raged in Normandy, Hitler stripped units from other areas of France, the Netherlands, and the Eastern Front including four SS-Panzer Divisions with their motorized *Panzergrenadiers* and powerful Panzer V ('Panther') and Panzer VI (Tiger) tanks. (*NARA*)

(**Opposite, below**) German parachutists are shown setting up their 8cm *Granatwerfer* 34 or mortar in a concealed position amid Normandy's dense vegetation, making it very difficult to spot and destroy. It was the standard German infantry mortar throughout the war and was known for its accuracy and rapid firing rate of 15–25 rounds per minute. The 8cm calibre shell had an effective firing range of 400–1,200 metres. Luftwaffe parachutists fought with unrivalled ferocity when used as infantry. (*NARA*)

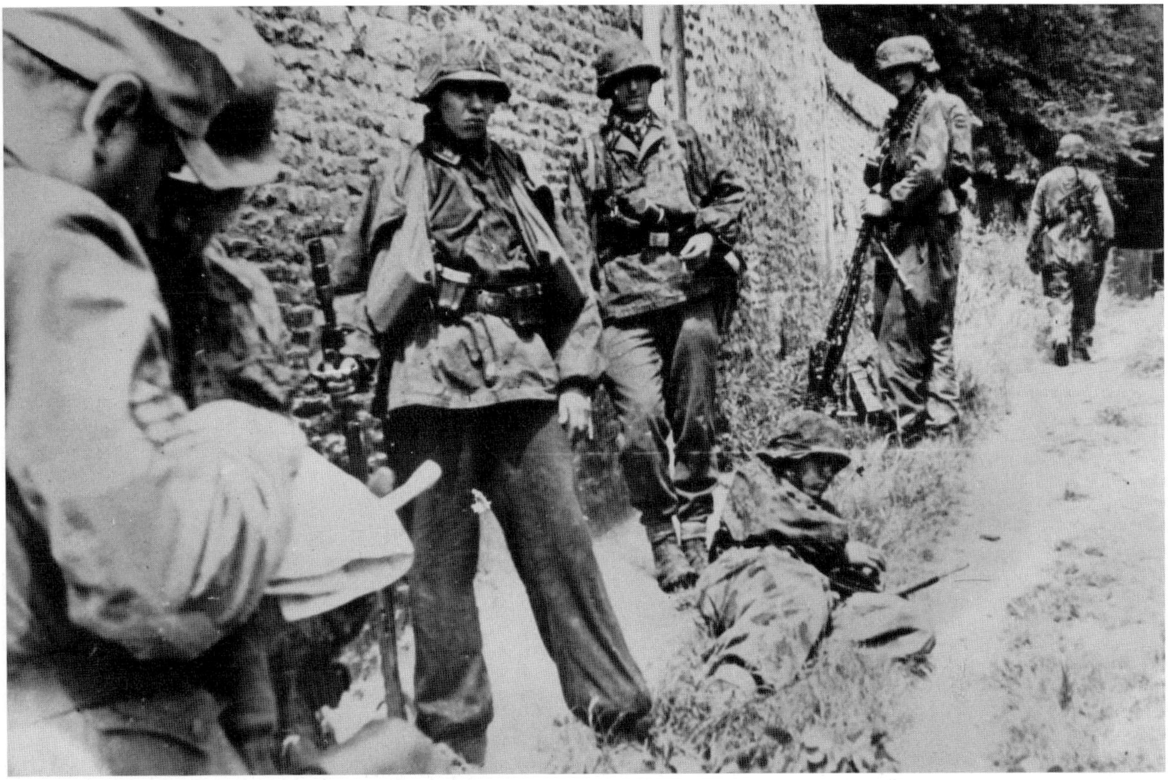

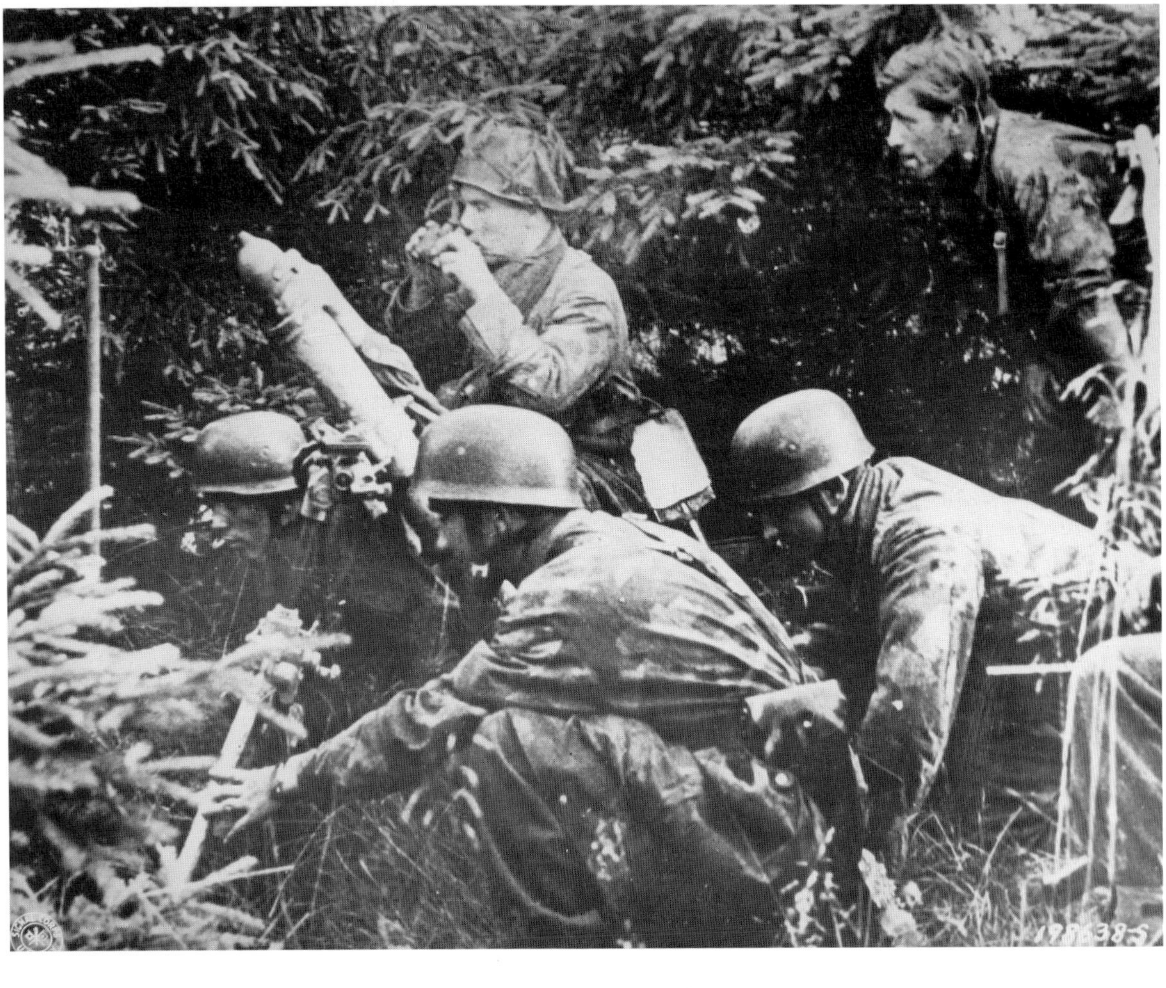

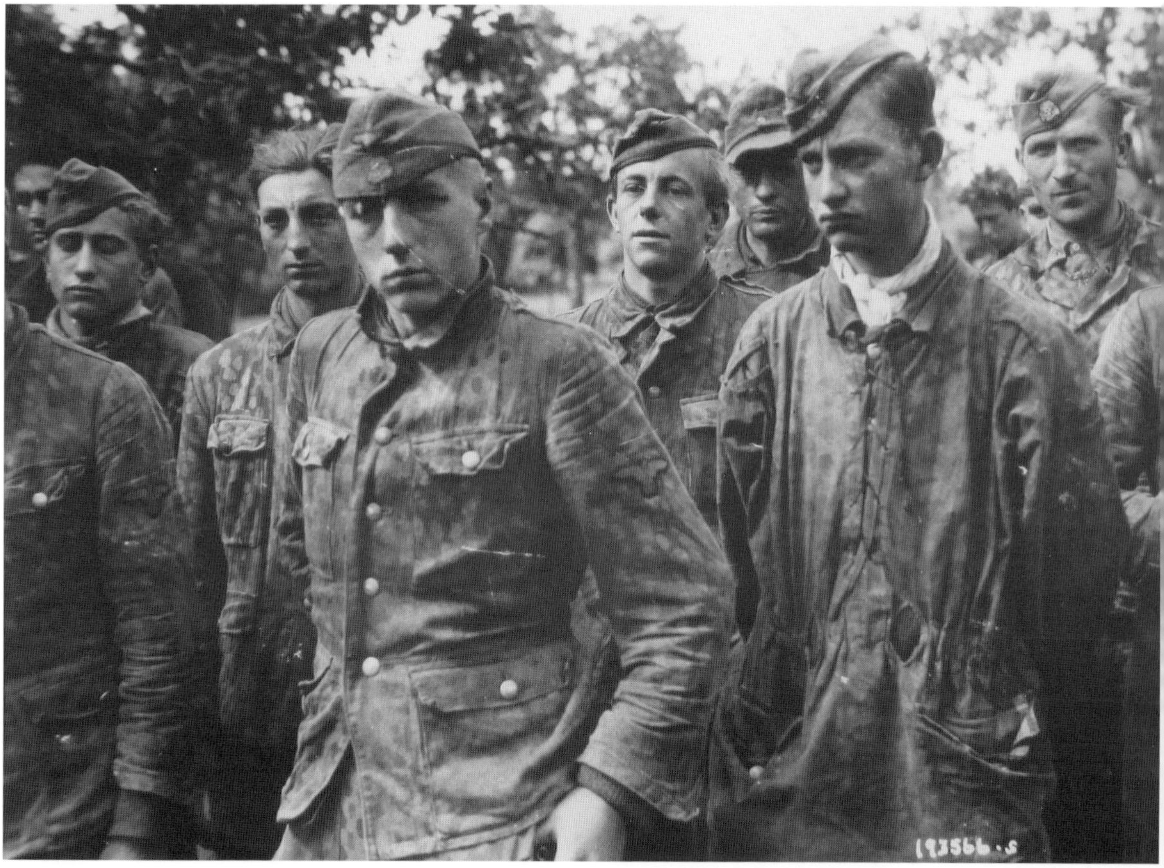
193566.S

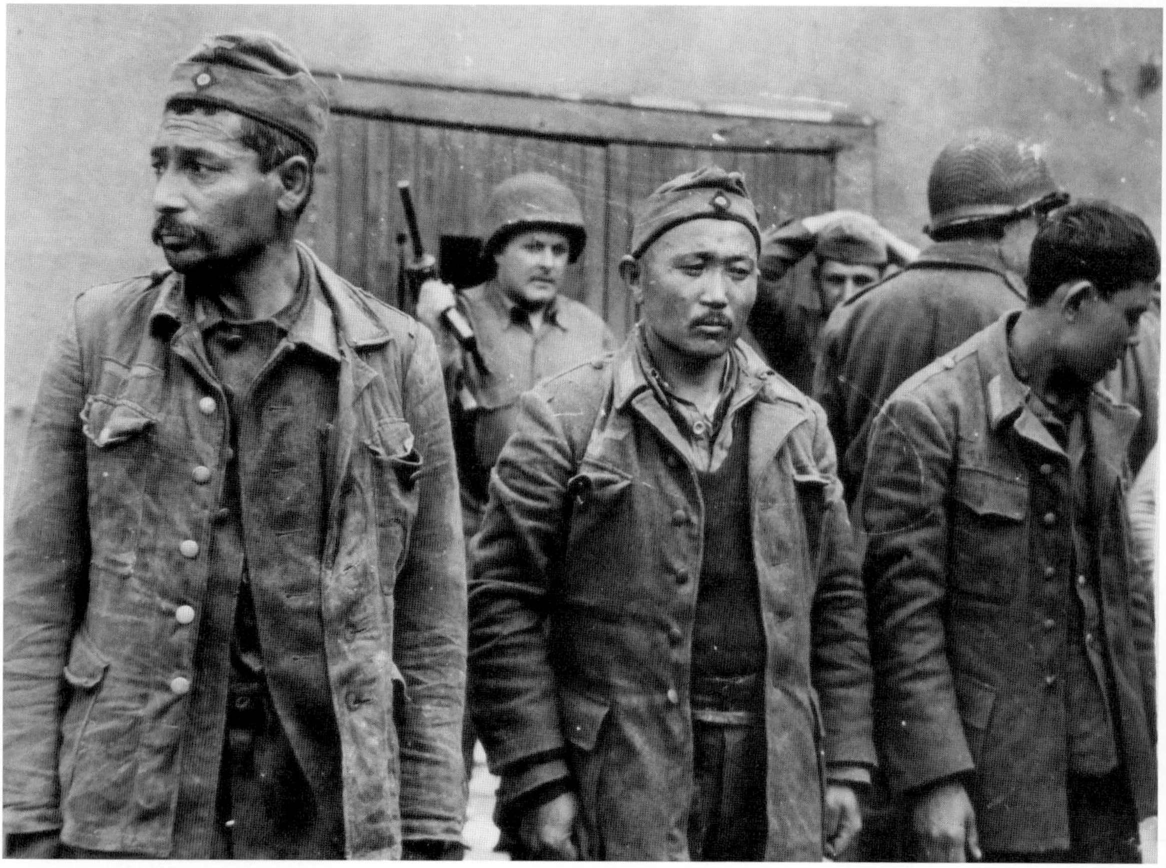

(**Opposite, above**) Elite Waffen-SS infantrymen are shown after capture, not demonstrating any sign of defeat, after the closure of the Falaise-Argentan Gap and retreat to Belgium in late August–early September 1944. The Anglo-Canadians in the Caen sector faced the most SS troops, such as the 12th SS-Panzer Division *Hitlerjugend*, as early as 7 July 1944; however, the Americans were confronted by the 2nd SS-Panzer Division and the 17th SS-*Panzergrenadier* Division 'Götz von Berlichingen', which saw action against US forces in Normandy from 10 June and suffered heavy losses. The Waffen-SS divisions fought with tenacity, many of its young soldiers preferring to die rather than surrender. (*NARA*)

(**Opposite, below**) German POWs are guarded by an American MP armed with an M3 or 'Grease Gun' SMG in Bréhal, France, on 2 August 1944. These POWs were previously Soviet soldiers of Georgian, Volga Tatar or Mongolian ethnicities. *Hiwi* is the German abbreviation of the word *Hilfswilliger* or 'auxiliary volunteer'. By 1944, there were more than 600,000 such auxiliary volunteers on all German fronts. After Operation *Cobra* on 25 July, US infantry divisions (4th, 8th and 79th) attacked to the east and were supported by the 3rd, 4th and 6th US Armoured Divisions. During the American advance, Bréhal and Avranches among other French villages and towns were liberated. (*NARA*)

(**Above**) Combat photographer Robert Capa (*left*), who took iconic images of the 6 June 1944 bloody assault at Omaha Beach, of which eleven have survived, as well as other battle photographs including 'The Falling Soldier' during the Spanish Civil War. Capa stands with author Ernest Hemingway (*right*), at this date a war correspondent for *Collier's* magazine, with their jeep driver, Private Olin Tompkins (*middle*). Capa and Hemingway were at a crossroads next to their US 2nd Armoured Division jeeps, waiting for a signal to move forward on 30 July 1944 from Pont Brocard, Normandy, towards Paris. Capa was killed by a land mine in Indochina in 1954 at the age of 40. Hemingway committed suicide in 1961, aged 61. (*NARA*)

Chapter Four

Initial Inland Movements from the Beaches

Following the successful landings of 6 June 1944, combat for the American forces developed into almost two months of intense fighting in the *bocage* just inland from the Bay of Seine beaches, terrain consisting of centuries-old 3–15ft tall hedgerows and sunken lanes. For the Anglo-Canadian troops around Caen, their struggle was to defeat the increasingly fanatical Nazi armoured resistance in heavily-fortified villages, and at locales such as Carpiquet Airfield and the Colombelles steelworks, before waging urban warfare amid the rubble of Caen, the capital of the Calvados department, after its destruction by saturation bombing.

The *bocage* was compartmentalized into small orchards or cultivated fields bordered with hedgerows, several feet thick and topped with bramble, thorns, vines and trees – excellent to enclose and protect crops and cattle from harsh ocean winds but also providing natural enclosures for German troops dug in there, camouflaged by the vegetation. Each field thus became its own small battleground, with observation limited to yards. The conditions did not favour the American attackers as the hedgerows hid the enemy's lines of fire, while their impassable structure restricted the US combat troop movements to nothing greater than platoon-size. Elsewhere, the *bocage* was characterized by broken ground, low ridges, narrow valleys, marshy depressions, sluggish streams and drainage ditches, all of which discouraged offensive warfare.

American armour and weapons were held up by the *bocage* until bulldozers or tanks fitted with Culin blades, cut from German beach obstacles and welded to the hulls of US M4s and M5s, could punch holes in the banks of vegetation. Even after getting through the hedgerow wall, Allied vehicles still had to negotiate the sunken lanes, like a labyrinth, ideal for Nazi ambushes with MGs, mortars, or artillery such as the deadly dual purpose 88mm piece. These improvised German defences made the conflict beyond the landing beaches a nightmare for the American forces. The separate battles within the individual enclosed fields were eventually won by junior officers, NCOs and private soldiers' initiative; however success came at a high price in casualties, with limited advances made.

The Caen region, at the eastern end of the Allied front and inland from Juno and Sword beaches, was where the Anglo-Canadian forces made slow progress, amid terrain characterized by numerous defended villages, with vast plains and fields that favoured Nazi panzer movement and combat. The importance of Caen and the Falaise plain beyond centred on terrain suitable for massed Allied armour operations for a thrust to the Seine and Paris, as well as topography fit for airfield construction.

Allied intelligence on Normandy's coastal regions was vast, but little attention was given to conditions beyond the landing beaches, thereby overlooking the difficulties of an inland advance. They were preoccupied with smashing the German beach defences, getting ashore on 6 June 1944, and building and reinforcing a secure and replete lodgment. Fighting in these vastly different arenas of Normandy would continue until the American breakout from hedgerow country following Operation *Cobra* on 25 July and the Anglo-Canadian capture of Caen on 19 July.

A USN-crewed LCVP carries wounded from one of the American beaches to a transport for more intensive medical care on 8 June 1944. The most forward wounded soldier on the left has a German helmet on his chest and appears to have a rolled up German camouflage smock as a pillow. *(NARA)*

Wounded Allied soldiers are escorted down an LST ramp in an English port – the repatriations of injured men began on the day of the landings, 6 June 1944. The cost in terms of those killed in action that day was under 2,500 men, of whom 1,000 were lost at Omaha Beach. Eisenhower stated in an after-action report that the comparatively light casualties sustained on all beaches except Omaha, were in large measure due to the success of MG Percy Hobart's 79th Armoured Division, RE, with its diverse array of novel armoured weapons, which landed among the leading waves of the British and Canadian assault forces at Gold, Juno and Sword beaches. *(NARA)*

(**Above**) US Army glider pilots, some of the first Allied soldiers who arrived in Normandy on 5/6 June 1944, are evacuated from beaches in a USN LCVP through the rough surf of the Bay of the Seine to offshore transports, for transit to England. The first American gliders to arrive during the early hours of 6 June came in two lifts; the first flown by the 434th Troop Carrier Group and the second by the 437th Troop Carrier Group. For these initial missions, American CG-4A Waco gliders were used. Later in the day, more missions were flown by the 434th and 437th Troop Carrier Groups piloting British Horsa gliders. They were met with stiff German AA fire and the small Norman fields and hedgerows caused numerous problems. The wooden Horsas cracked up in the hedges and trees and, with a heavier load than the CG-4A Wacos, the numbers of casualties were greater. On 7 June, two further glider missions flown by the 434th and 437th brought in elements of the US 82nd Airborne Division via both CG-4A Waco and Horsa gliders. This was the last time that the Americans used Horsas in a combat operation. These glider pilots pictured flew subsequent resupply missions to Normandy without significant casualties, days after the initial landings made on airfields that were still under construction. (*NARA*)

(**Opposite, above**) Engineers attached to the 3rd Canadian Infantry Division lay out matting to enable units of the Canadian 2nd Armoured Brigade to exit Juno Beach on 6 June 1944. They needed to get inland between Creully and Douvres in order to head for Carpiquet Airfield and the northwestern sector of Caen, which were two of Montgomery's goals for seizure that day. The Canadian infantry was assisted by the 41 and 48 RM Commandos. This sector was defended by the Wehrmacht's 716th Infantry Division and the 736th IR. Also, elements of the German 21st Panzer Division attacked during the afternoon of 6 June in an attempt to drive a wedge between Juno and Sword beaches. (*NARA*)

(**Below**) A British Matilda II flail tank variant called the Baron (evolved from the Scorpion flail tank) clears mines from a beach during a manoeuvre – it was initially designed for use in the North African desert sands in 1942. The mine flail consists of a number of heavy chains ending in fist-sized steel balls, attached to a horizontal, rapidly rotating rotor mounted on two arms at the front of the armoured vehicle. The rotation caused the flails to spin wildly and strike the ground violently. The force of a flail strike above a buried mine mimics the weight of a person or vehicle so that the mine detonates, but in a safe manner that does little damage to the flails or the armoured vehicle. The Baron was never used operationally; however, MG Percy Hobart's M4 Sherman Crab flail tank was an improvement in Normandy, as the flails were driven from the main tank engine. There was also a revised flail for the M3 Grant tank. The flail tanks were urgently needed on the Anglo-Canadian beaches, to carve clear lanes through to the exits for the mass of armour and vehicles building up. (*NARA*)

Canadian infantry reinforcements march past a disabled German fortification at Juno Beach on 7 June 1944, following the valiant efforts of the assault infantry and armour the day before. East of the Seulles river, Allied progress from 6 June was good as flail tanks had opened the exits from Juno before 0930 hours, with Hobart's AVRE fascine and bridging tanks filling in the worst of the craters and culverts. At Bernières, between Courseulles-sur-Mer and Saint-Aubin-sur-Mer, Crab flails and AVRE petards smashed exits through the 12ft-high sea wall, and cleared lanes and laterals in time to work in with the infantry against pillboxes and strongpoints. Before noon on 6 June, elements of the Canadian 2nd Armoured Brigade were advancing inland. (NARA)

Men of 46 RM Commando, 4th Special Service Brigade, attached to the British 3rd Infantry Division, move through the village of Douvres-la-Délivrande on 8 June 1944 watched by French civilians. The RM mission was to secure two German radar stations north and southwest of the village, defended by 230 members of a Luftwaffe unit, with both sites surrounded by barbed wire, minefields and AT guns. However, even though the village was secured on 8 June, the radar stations were still inaccessible to the RM Commandos, who bypassed the position. Days later, British 79th Armoured Division, RE tanks advanced with the 41 RM Commando and the 5th Battalion, the Black Watch, and forced 200 Germans to surrender. Nevertheless, several Allied tanks were destroyed. (*NARA*)

(**Above**) An American Heavy Weapons squad of assault troops from the 3rd Battalion, 16th IR, 1st Infantry Division, move inland late on 6 June 1944 around a chalk cliff at Omaha Beach. One soldier shoulders an M1917A 0.3in water-cooled Browning MG barrel, while another at the rear carries ammunition boxes. A considerable quantity of combat gear and kit are apparent on the shingle, alongside wounded or dead infantrymen from the hard-won and bloody initial assault. Omaha was between the outcropping rocks of Pointe de la Percée in the west, and Port-en-Bessin in the east, a shallow arc of sand and shingle enclosed inland by bluffs rising 150ft to a plateau of hedge-enclosed fields, deep lanes and scattered hamlets built of stone. This was the terrain that greeted the infantry of the 1st and 29th Infantry Divisions of V Corps as they exited Omaha Beach. The deepest penetration by V Corps, by 7 June, was less than a mile. (*NARA*)

(**Opposite, above**) American soldiers of the 2nd Infantry ('Indianhead') Division move off from Omaha Beach in the vicinity of Saint-Laurent-sur-Mer, on 7 June 1944. They wear their distinctive Indianhead left-shoulder patches. From the beach they climbed up the Omaha bluff at the E-1 draw, past the *Widerstandsnest* ('nest of resistance') 65, behind the column that defended the route up the Ruquet Valley, to Saint-Laurent-sur-Mer. Attacking across the Aure river on 10 June, this division captured Trévières and on 11 July participated in the assault on Hill 192, a key enemy strongpoint at Lessay, on the road to St Lô. After exploiting the St Lô breakout, the 2nd Division advanced across the Vire to take Tinchebray on 15 August 1944, before moving against the port-fortress of Brest in Brittany. (*NARA*)

(**Below**) A British M4 Sherman tank and AEC Matador artillery tractors disembark from an LST hull on to a flat deck at Arromanches at the western end of Gold Beach sector, 6 June 1944. By 1100hrs, with the aid of Hobart's specialized tanks of British 79th Armoured Division, RE, seven lanes had been cleared on Gold Beach for the British 50th Infantry Division aided by the 47 RM Commando, as the bridgehead was soon 3 miles in depth. The objectives at Gold were to capture Arromanches, future site of one of the artificial 'Mulberry' harbours; to contact American forces at Omaha; to capture Bayeux and the small port at Port-en-Bessin; and link up with the Canadian forces at Juno to the east. Although they stopped about 4 miles short of Bayeux on 6 June, the town became the first French locale to be captured the next day. By the close of 6 June, 25,000 men had been landed at Gold, along with 2,100 vehicles. *(NARA)*

(**Above**) British and American soldiers are seen walking past the intact shopfronts of Bayeux, which was liberated by the British 50th Northumbrian Division and 151st Brigade reconnaissance patrols of XXX Corps, at 0900 hours on 7 June 1944. German soldiers of the SS had left the town on 6 June so it was not bombed. Bayeux became the French capital during the summer of 1944, until Paris was liberated on 25 August. (NARA)

(**Opposite, above**) Soldiers of the US 8th IR, 4th Infantry Division, enter an inland Normandy village after their relatively unopposed 6 June 1944 amphibious landings. Only a few roads ran inland from Utah Beach via which the American troops advanced. There were initially few American casualties but the number increased as the German artillery became active. The 8th IR's mission was to contact the 82nd and 101st Airborne Divisions, which had dropped west of the flooded area from Vierville to Sainte-Mère-Église. Elements of the 4th Infantry Division and units of the German 709th and 91st Infantry Divisions fought at the towns of Emondeville and Azeville, two German strongpoints which, once overcome, enabled other US VII Corps infantry divisions (the 9th and 79th) to join the 4th in cutting off the Cotentin Peninsula. The Germans in the peninsula, realizing the situation's gravity, withdrew to Cherbourg to make a stand in the fortress-port city. MG J. Lawton Collins, the VII Corps CG, wrote to the 4th Infantry Division CG, MG Raymond Barton, 'The 4th Infantry Division made the initial landing on Utah Beach, broke through the stiff German resistance there, and, in conjunction with the 82nd and 101st Airborne Divisions, succeeded in establishing a firm beachhead which was the basis for future operations.' The 4th Infantry Division was in continuous action from 6 to 28 June, when the last resistance east of Cherbourg was eliminated, incurring 5,000 casualties; 800 men were killed in action during this interval. (NARA)

(**Below**) An American paratrooper from the 82nd Airborne's 505th PIR runs towards the door of the Sainte-Mère-Église church, while another keeps watch for any of the 300–400 German defenders from the 3rd Battalion, 1058th Grenadier Regiment, 91st Infantry Division and artillerymen of the 4th battery of the 191st Artillery Regiment, 6 June 1944. On the night of 5/6 June, the 82nd Airborne Division had difficulty destroying the Douve river bridges and establishing a line of defence. At 0500hrs on 6 June, LC Edward Krause's 505th PIR took the town with little resistance; however, German counterattacks began in earnest later that day. At noon on 7 June, American infantry from Utah Beach landings arrived to help completely clear Sainte-Mère-Église. (*NARA*)

(**Above**) A destroyed German SPA litters the N13 road from Neuville-au-Plain to Sainte-Mère-Église on 7 June 1944, a day after the US 4th Infantry Division's amphibious assault at Utah Beach. The SPA was destroyed by H Company of the 82nd Airborne's 505th PIR with a 57mm AT gun (*background, right*). Sainte-Mère-Église is located along a national road connecting Cherbourg to Paris, at a junction between five departmental roads, which the Germans would have used for any counterattack on the troops landing at Utah and Omaha. (*NARA*)

(**Opposite, above**) Paratroopers of the US 82nd Airborne Division patrol the streets of Sainte-Mère-Église on foot and on horseback on 7 June 1944. Only one of the 82nd Airborne's missions went according to plan – the capture of Sainte-Mère-Église, due to the accurate drop of the 505th PIR to the city's northwest which lacked a major enemy formation. Local German units were caught off guard and before dawn on 6 June the town was in American hands. (*NARA*)

(**Opposite, below**) French citizens and a gendarme line the western part of the main square in Sainte-Mère-Église to greet the arriving Americans. The famous church is off to the left behind the trees beyond the frame. A US M10 3in GMC TD followed by an M4 medium tank come down the street as a jeep moves away in the opposite direction on 7 June 1944. (*NARA*)

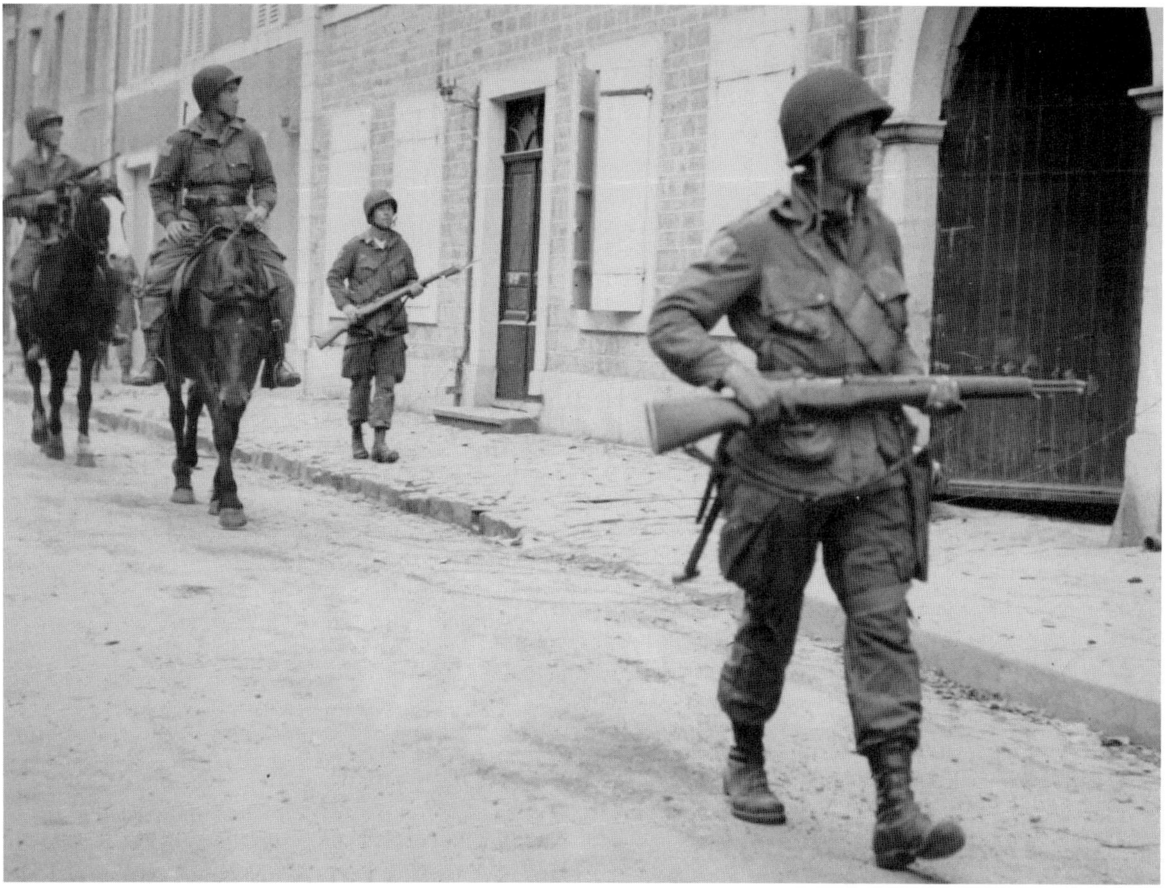

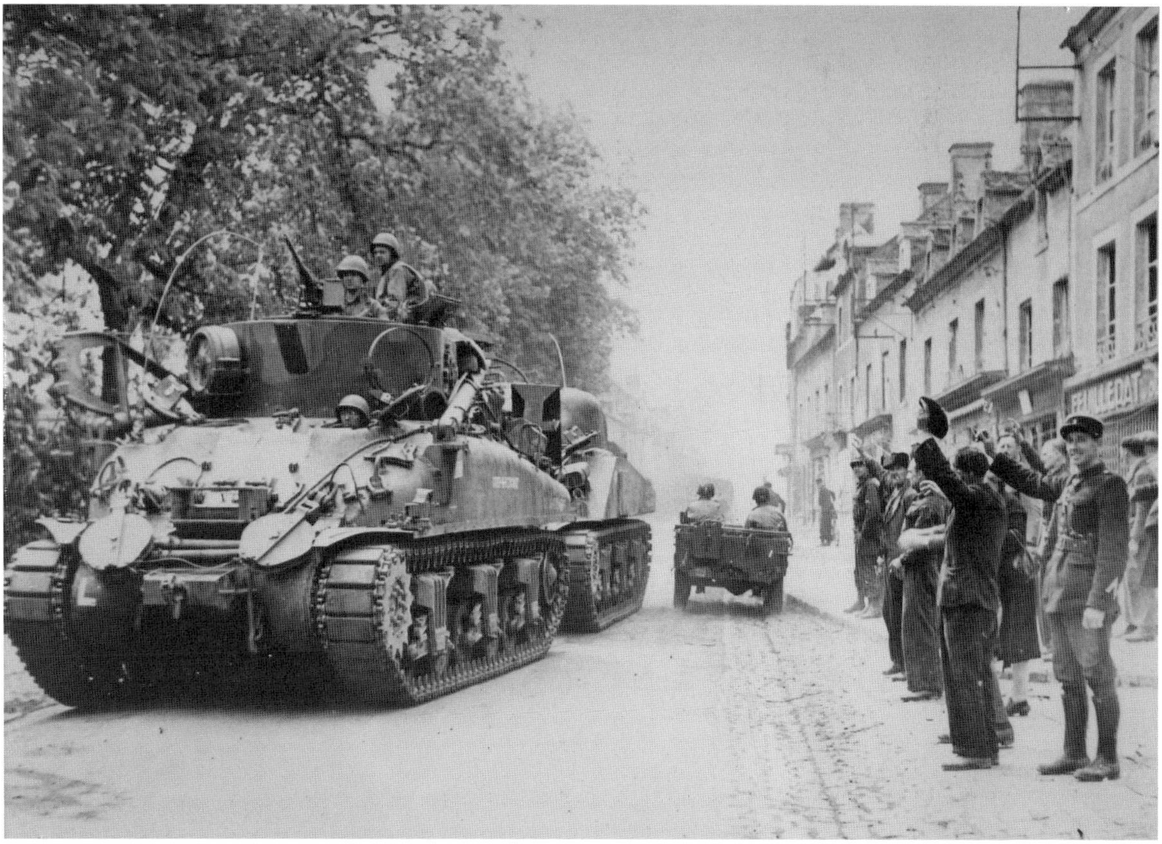

Paratroopers of the US 82nd Airborne Division pose with a captured Nazi flag and helmet in Sainte-Mère-Église on 7 June 1944. The 505th PIR of the 82nd Airborne arrived reasonably intact at its objective to capture the town early on 6 June. However, the tasks of the division west of the Merderet river and the crossings of the Merderet and Douve rivers could not be fulfilled, as the remainder of the division was scattered. Much of the 82nd Airborne Division had dropped on the assembly area of the German 91st Infantry Division, who were trained in the role of defence against airborne attack. However, the commander of the German 91st was ambushed and killed by a small group of American paratroopers, hampering that Wehrmacht division's effectiveness. *(NARA)*

US 90th Division (indicated by the kneeling sergeant's left shoulder patch) riflemen attached to a Heavy Weapons Unit take a break to reconnoitre the road ahead, as they advance inland from Uncle Red Beach at Utah on 10 June 1944. A German mine warning sign is off to the right. Initial elements of the 90th Division saw action on 6 June at Utah Beach, the remainder entering combat on 10 June, cutting across the Merderet river to take Pont l'Abbé in heavy fighting. Next the division saw heavy fighting along the Douve river, attacking the Forêt de Mont-Castre (Hill 122) and clearing it by 11 July despite fierce resistance. During this action, the 90th suffered 5,000 killed, wounded or captured, one of the highest divisional casualty rates of the war. On 12 August, the division drove across the Sarthe river, north and east of Le Mans, and took part in the closing of the Falaise-Argentan Pocket, reaching the 1st Polish Armoured Division in Chambois on 19 August. (NARA)

(**Above**) British 6th Airborne paratroopers move a captured German AT gun into Bréville-les-Monts near the Ranville jump zone, combating the German 346th Infantry Division from 8 to 13 June, between the Orne and Dives rivers. British paratroopers and glidermen of the 9th and 12th Parachute Battalions, along with units of the 6th Airlanding Brigade and 22nd Independent Parachute Company fought with units from the German 346th, 711th, and 716th Infantry Divisions. On 11 June, the 5th Battalion, the Black Watch, was tasked with taking Bréville-les-Monts, which was still in the hands of the German 858th Grenadier Regiment. The British assault was a complete failure. Subsequently, the capture of Bréville-les-Monts was conducted by the 6th Airborne Division reserve, comprised of the above-mentioned units and supported by a squadron of the 13th/18th Royal Hussars and artillery of the 53rd Airlanding Regiment, RA. During the action on 12 June, Brigadier Lord Lovat, CO 1st Special Service Brigade, was observing an artillery bombardment by the 51st Highland Division when he was seriously wounded by a stray shell, falling short of its target. That 'friendly fire' also killed LC A.P. Johnson, CO, 12th Parachute Battalion and seriously wounded Brigadier Hugh Kindersley of the 6th Airlanding Brigade. By 13 June, after much fighting, the municipality was in Allied hands, but with staggering losses – only 32 paratroopers of the 12th Parachute Battalion were still able to fight as nearly 130 had been killed or wounded. The Germans lost 418 out of 564 men of the 858th Grenadier Regiment. (NARA)

(**Opposite, above**) Elements of the 327th Glider Infantry, 101st Airborne Division, get directions from American MPs with two intact Horsa gliders (*background*). This was near Vierville, between St-Côme-du-Mont and Sainte-Marie-du-Mont on the road emanating from La Madeleine at Utah Beach, 9 June 1944. Vierville was directly north of Carentan, which was south of a bend in the Douve river and Carentan was defended by the German 6th Parachute Regiment, commanded by Major von der Heydte, the finest enemy troops in the area. Without being able to get orders from his senior commanders, von der Heydte sent his three battalions into battle: one to the north to attack Sainte-Mère-Église on the Carentan–Mountebourg road, another to the northeast to protect the seaward flank in the area of Sainte-Marie-du-Mont between Vierville and La Madeleine, and the third battalion back to Carentan. (NARA)

(**Below**) An American jeep tows a 57mm AT gun through the streets of Carentan on 12 June 1944. Signs indicating the direction to Cherbourg and Valognes along the N13 road are on the wall of the corner cafe, while another for Saint-Lô and Paris along the N13 in the other direction are just visible on another building (*right*). Some of the buildings have suffered extensive battle damage. Non-censored left shoulder patches on some of the Americans standing off from the road identify them as belonging to the 101st Airborne, which captured Carentan. The battle for this Norman town on the N13 road raged from 10 to 13 June 1944, defended by two battalions of the German 6th Parachute Regiment, as a lack of ammunition forced the Nazis to withdraw. The 17th SS-*Panzergrenadier* Division 'Götz von Berlichingen' counterattacked the 101st Airborne on 13 June, but though initially successful the Germans were repelled by elements of the US 2nd Armoured Division. (*NARA*)

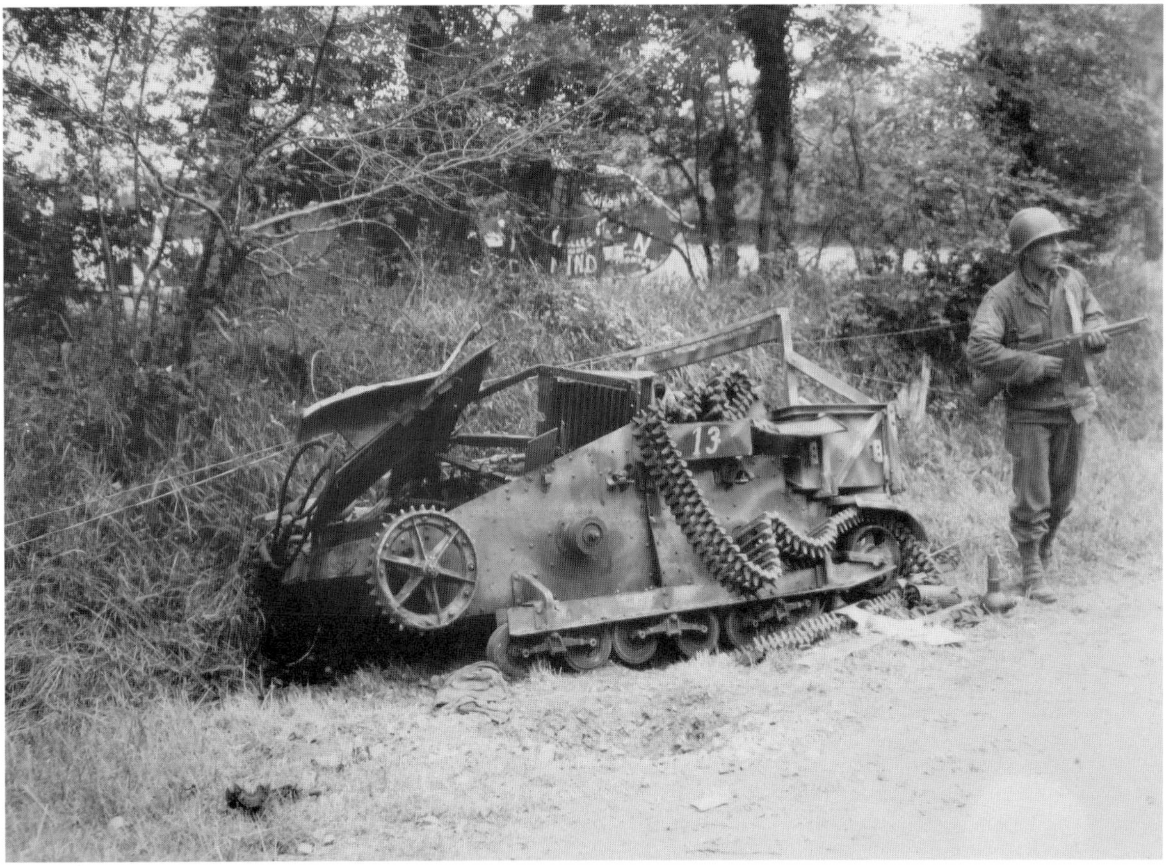
13

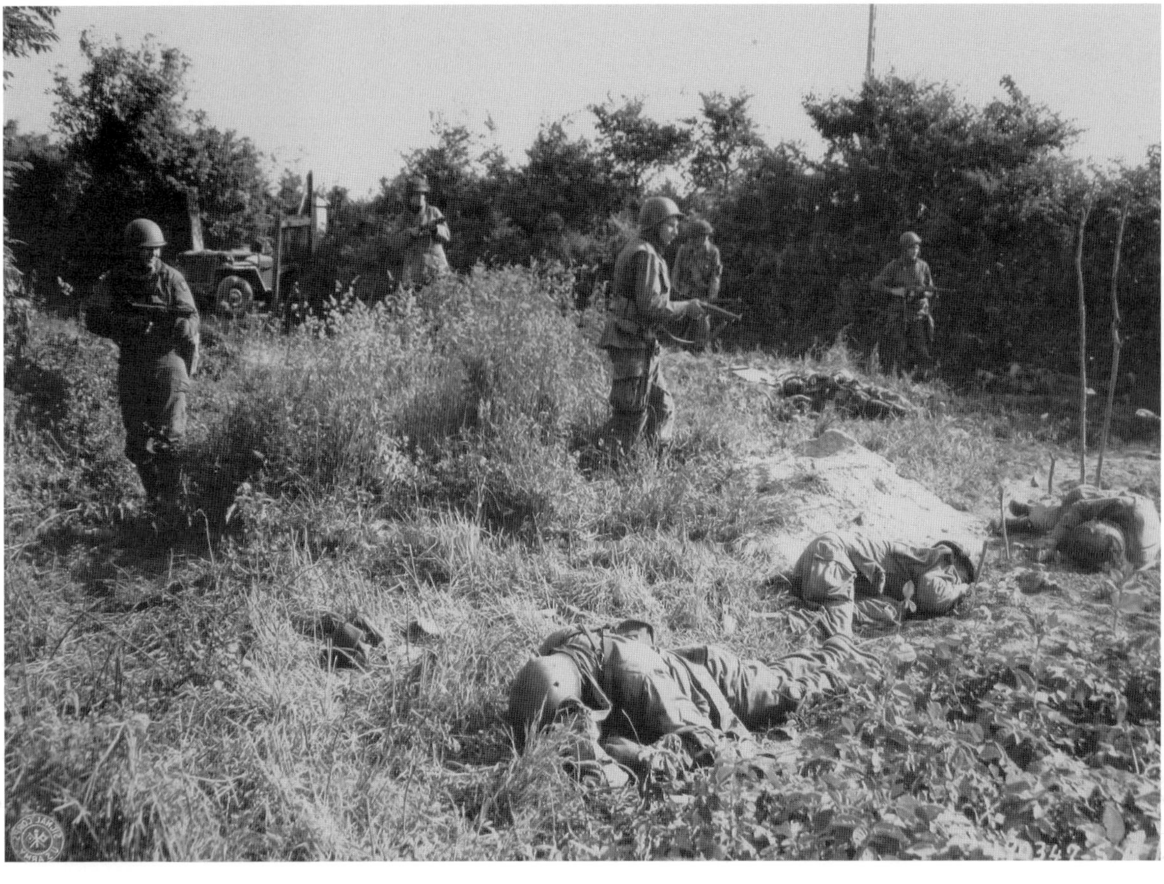

(**Opposite, above**) An American soldier armed with a 0.45in Thompson SMG guards a destroyed German light armoured vehicle near Carentan on 14 June 1944. A CG-4 Waco glider is in the field behind the trees. Carentan was taken by the 101st Airborne Division's 502nd PIR and the 327th GIR, 10–12 June. The final capture on 12 June was assisted by the 101st Airborne's 506th PIR and units of the 401st GIR, after a massive American artillery bombardment supported by naval gunfire. On 13 June, two battalions of the 37th SS-*Panzergrenadier* Regiment, with armoured support by a battalion from the 17th SS-*Panzergrenadier* Division 'Götz von Berlichingen', attacked the American lines held by the 506th PIR's Dog, Fox, and Easy Companies, the latter making a heroic stand against a railroad embankment while the first two gave way. Company E (Easy), reinforced by the 2nd Battalion, 502nd PIR resisted the German spearhead until the arrival of tanks of CCA, 2nd Armoured Division, arriving from Isigny to Carentan's east. (*NARA*)

(**Opposite, below**) American paratroopers from the 101st Airborne Division on 14 June 1944 come across the dead bodies of fellow paratroopers killed by German snipers. The standing paratroopers carry M1 Garand, M1 carbine and a Thompson SMG at the ready. The man on the left has the Screaming Eagle shoulder patch. A US jeep (*background*) is unoccupied at the gate leading to the field. (*NARA*)

(**Above**) German paratroops fire their 7.5cm *Panzerabwehrkanone* (Pak) 40 AT cannon at American forces in Normandy in June 1944. The German 6th Parachute Regiment was situated between Isigny to the east and Carentan to the west and mounted a counterattack against the 101st Airborne to contest the latter locale on 6 June. The Pak 40 AT gun, after the Flak 88mm dual purpose AT/AT gun, emerged as one of the best cannons in Normandy, after its initial service on the Soviet front in November 1941 against the T-24 and KV-1 Soviet tanks. The Pak 40 had an effective firing range of 2,000 yards and a maximum rate of fire of 14 rounds per minute. It became the standard German AT gun from 1943 until the end of the war. (*Author's collection*)

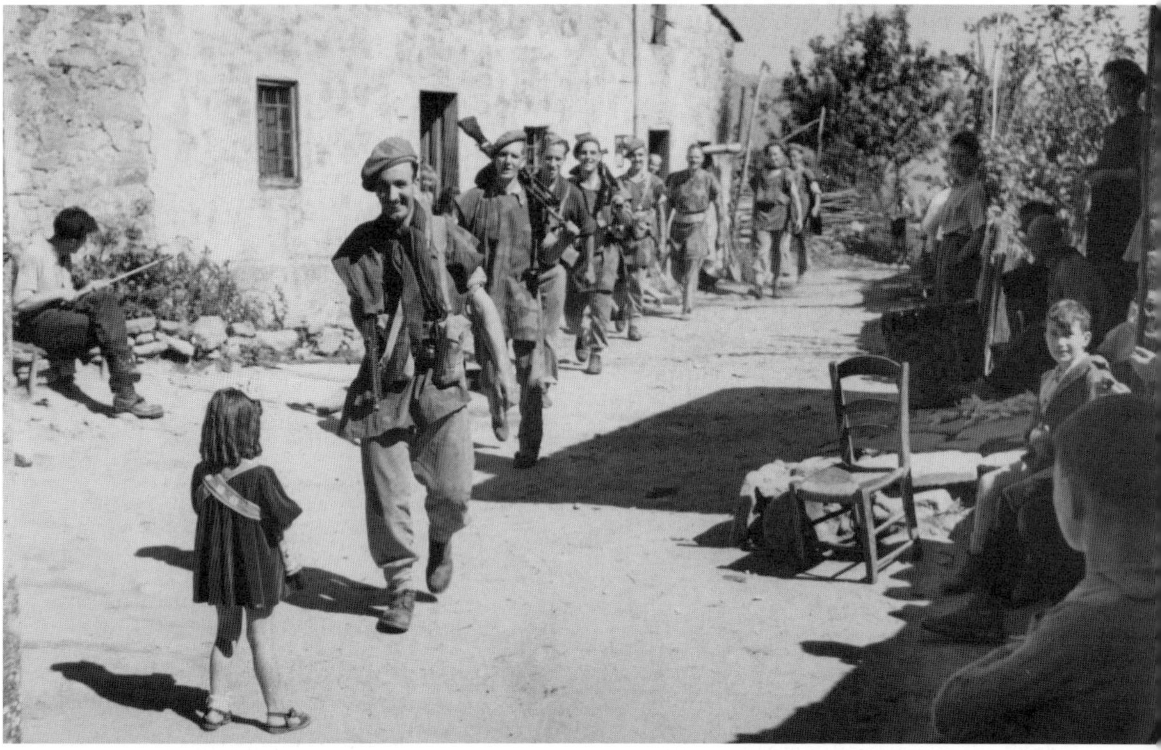

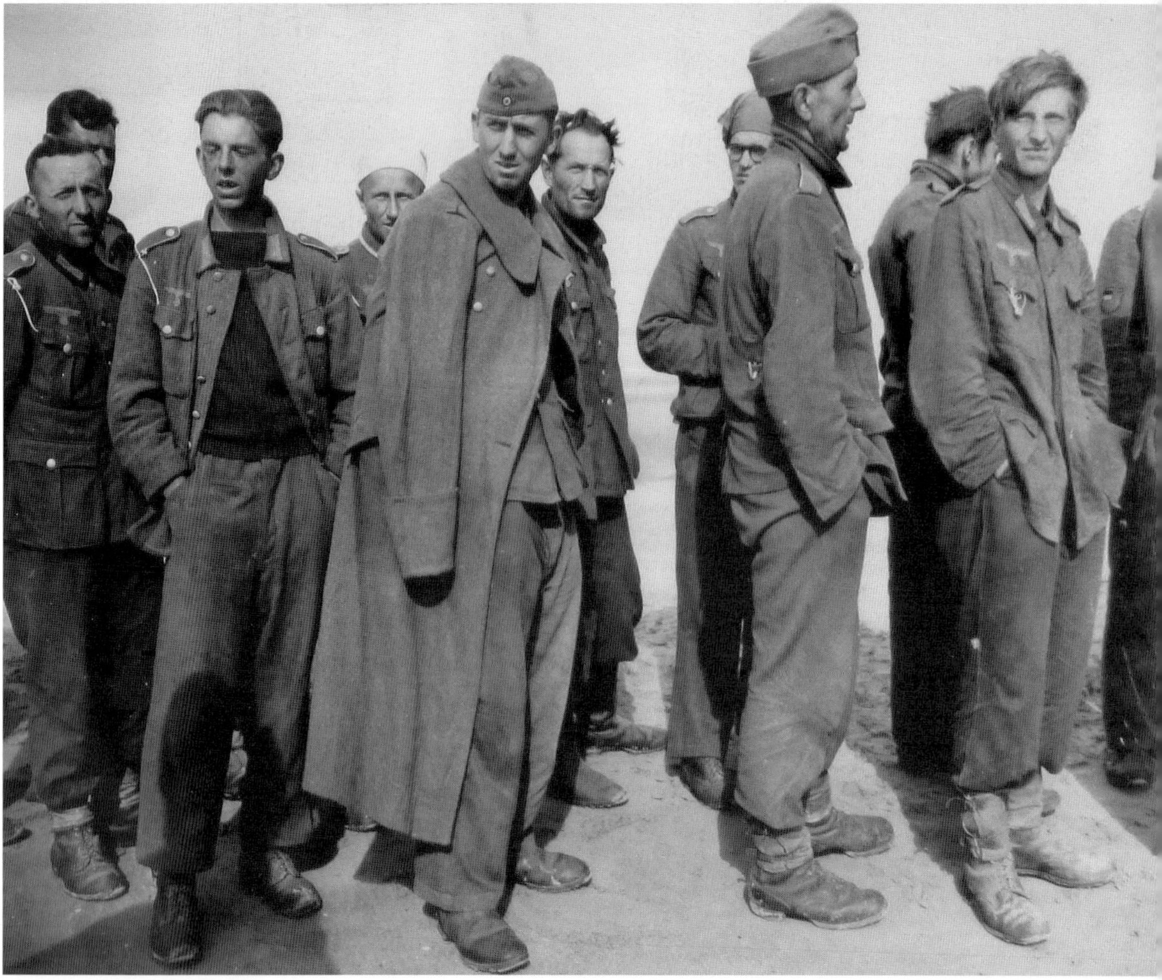

(**Opposite, above**) An eight-man British Commando section wearing camouflage smocks and berets files through a Normandy village, smiling at the residents, after conducting a reconnaissance mission in a thickly-wooded area well inland from the assault beaches. The group is armed with at least a 0.45in Thompson SMG and two 0.303in Bren LMGs. Commando-led reconnaissance missions were common in the Orne estuary prior to larger unit attacks, in the struggle for this key locale that went on from 6 June to 19 July 1944. (NARA)

(**Opposite, below**) German POWs line up at an American landing beach to be taken by LCVPs to Allied transports, for evacuation to English stockades. These German soldiers varied in age and their absence of wounds suggests that they readily surrendered once the immediate Nazi beach defences were breached on 6 June 1944. (NARA)

(**Above**) A temporary Allied Emergency Landing Strip (ELS-1) situated among fields, orchards and hedgerows not far inland from the landing beaches in Normandy, 13 June 1944. American bulldozers and engineers of the 9th Engineer Command of the 9th TAF built the airstrip for Allied fighter-bomber pilots to refuel and re-arm closer to the battlefield targets, while more substantive airfields were under construction. (NARA)

Chapter Five

US First Army's Capture of Cherbourg and Movement Towards St Lô

Two US VII Corps infantrymen attempt to reduce a German position on the outskirts of Cherbourg during the last week of June 1944; the soldier on the left is preparing to fire a rifle grenade. After the Allied beachheads were continuous and secure, General Bradley's first task for the VII Corps was to cut off the Cotentin Peninsula and capture Cherbourg, as a major port was needed for the Allied buildup. Without a port for the increase of ground forces in western Normandy, Bradley's offensive to enlarge the American lodgment south of the Cotentin would be delayed. The approaches to Cherbourg provided a natural defensive barrier in the marshlands of the Merderet river, at the neck of the Cotentin Peninsula. In late June, Bradley reported that the fortress of Cherbourg, its fortifications and arsenal had finally fallen to Collins's VII Corps; however, the port was in ruins. (NARA)

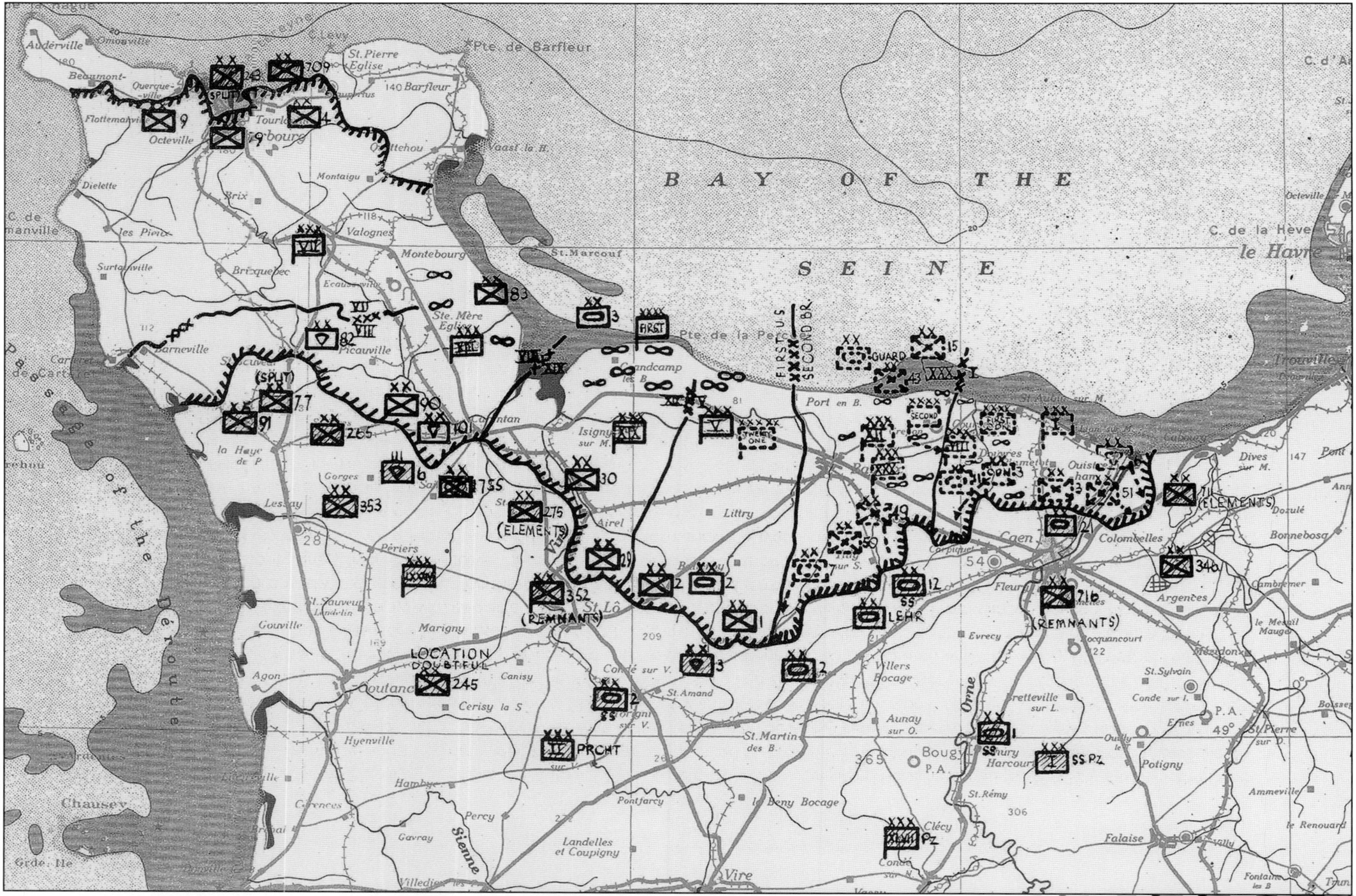
BAY OF THE SEINE
Passage of the Déroute
FIRST U.S.
SECOND BR.
GUARD
FIRST
SECOND
TWENTY ONE
LOCATION DOUBTFUL
(ELEMENTS)
(REMNANTS)
(SPLIT)
LEHR
PRCHT
SS PZ
Pte. de Barfleur
St. Pierre Eglise
Barfleur
Auderville
Omonville
Beaumont-
Querqueville
Flottemanville
Octeville
Dielette
Les Pieux
Surtainville
Brix
Valognes
Montebourg
Montaigu
Bricquebec
Barneville
Ste. Mère Eglise
Picauville
St. Marcouf
Carentan
Isigny sur M.
Grandcamp les B.
Pte de la Percée
Port en B.
Littry
Airel
St. Lô
la Haye du P
Lessay
Gorges
Périers
Marigny
Gouville
Agon
Coutances
Canisy
Cerisy la S
Hyenville
Hambye
Percy
Gavray
Sienne
Villedieu les
Vire
Pontfarcy
le Beny Bocage
St. Martin des B.
St. Amand
Condé sur V.
Torigni sur V.
Landelles et Coupigny
Villers Bocage
Aunay sur O.
Bougy
Evrecy
Caen
Carpiquet
Fleury
Thury Harcourt
St. Rémy
Clécy
Condé sur N.
Falaise
Potigny
Bretteville sur L.
Orne
Colombelles
Dozulé
Dives sur M.
Argences
Bonnebosq
Cambremer
St. Sylvain
Conde sur I.
Ammeville
le Renouard
Trouville
le Havre
C. de la Hève
Chausey
Grde. Ile

A US First Army HQ Situation Map from 2400hrs on 25 June 1944 is shown. The Allied line inland became continuous by 12 June 1944, the same day US XIX Corps was activated and three days later, US VIII Corps. A sustained push by the 29th Division of XIX Corps towards St Lô began on 15 June, but was halted within 5 miles of the city after three days of heavy fighting. The one Allied success was the attack by Collins's VII Corps on 14 June, westward across the Cotentin Peninsula, led by the 9th Infantry and 82nd Airborne Divisions. The VII Corps drive reached the west coast of the Cotentin at Barneville on 17 June, isolating the Wehrmacht's 243rd and 709th Infantry Divisions in the northern part of the peninsula. Now Collins's 9th, 79th and 4th Infantry Divisions would fight their way up the peninsula to Cherbourg, while MG Troy Middleton's VIII Corps took over the Cotentin Peninsula facing south with the 83rd, 90th, and the two US Airborne divisions. To the eastern end of the Allied lodgment, LG Miles Dempsey's 2nd British Army, with two armoured, five infantry and one airborne division duelled with Panzer Group West, comprised of four armoured and one static division; thus far the city of Caen remained in German hands.

On 18 June, Montgomery issued a directive for the capture of Cherbourg and Caen before 23 June. However, the 'Great Storm' of 19–22 June – the worst in 40 years – that unexpectedly lashed Normandy, delayed both the operations and Allied reinforcements (notably Middleton's VIII Corps) and supplies coming ashore, as the American 'Mulberry' artificial harbour at Omaha Beach was destroyed and abandoned, while the British 'Mulberry' artificial harbour at Arromanches on Gold Beach was salvaged. Allied shipping sustained heavy losses, with more than 800 ships of all sizes beached or lost. When the storm ended on 22 June the need to capture Cherbourg became imperative, Bradley's final push for the fortress-harbour having been set back for three days. On 26 June, the fortress of Cherbourg surrendered to Collins's VII Corps and the mopping up continued until 1 July. US First Army divisions had been battered and additional time was needed to receive reinforcements and re-fit in preparation for a new offensive after Cherbourg. The savage fighting in the Cotentin's southwestern *bocage* between the US and German forces would begin after the first week of July at La Haye-du-Puits and then at Lessay. Combat continued until 25 July as Bradley's divisions established themselves along the Lessay–Périers–St Lô road as a jumping off point for the start of Operation *Cobra*. By then, the Germans had strengthened their defences in western Normandy. (NARA)

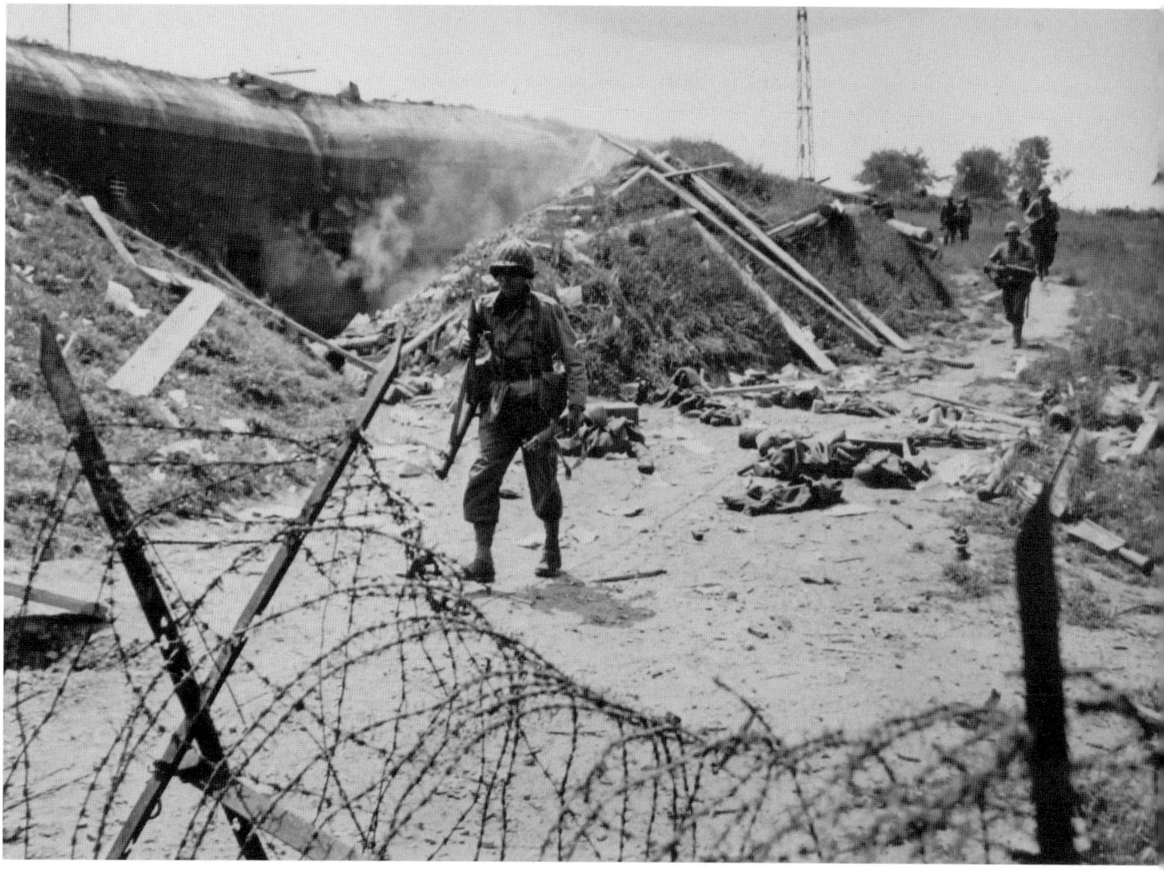

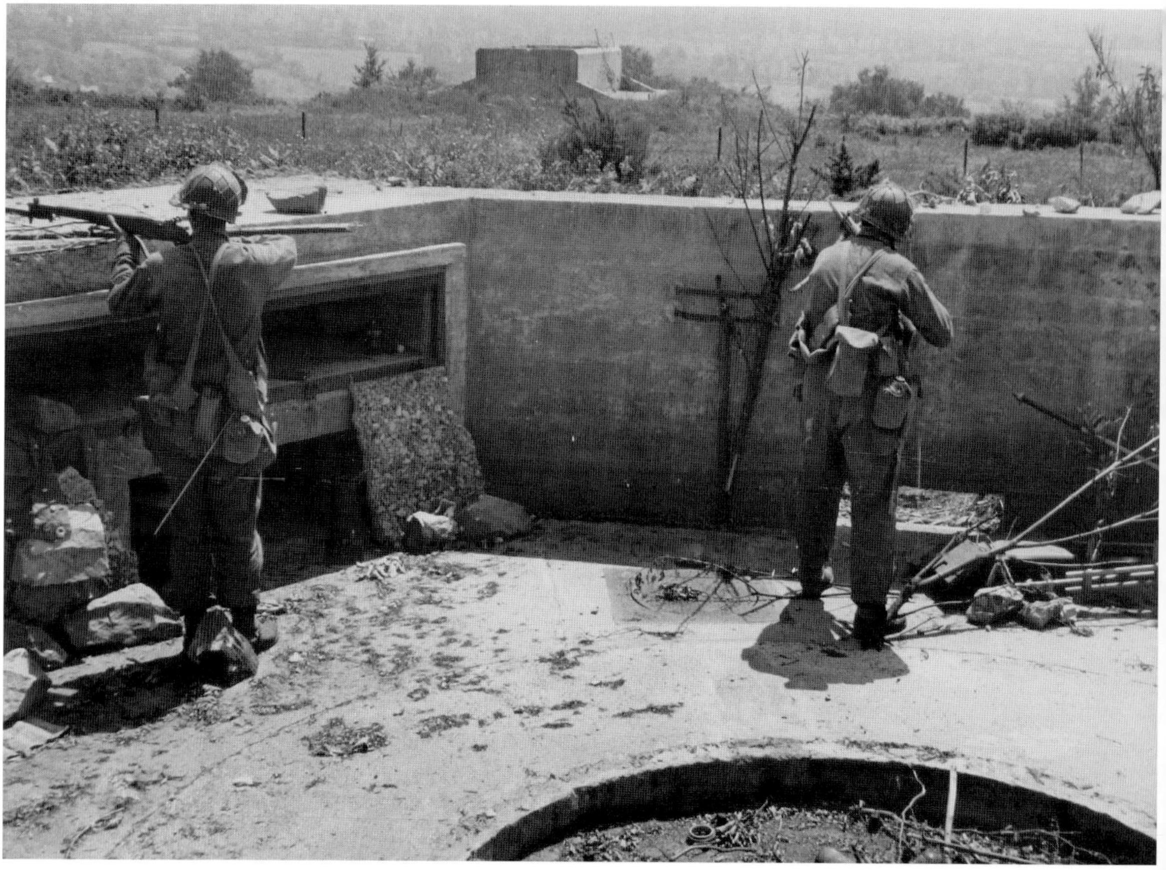

(**Opposite, above**) A US VII Corps infantryman holding a bazooka moves past a still smoking German concrete fortification at Cherbourg. From 23 to 25 June 1944, VII Corps' 4th, 9th, and 79th Infantry Divisions moved slowly forward, taking the German fortified emplacements one by one with fighter-bomber support and artillery, which had to avoid damaging the port facilities. On 25 June Collins ordered the final assault by the 79th Division's 314th IR, with USN seaborne bombardment. Fort du Roule was captured on 26 June. (*NARA*)

(**Opposite, below**) Two American infantrymen from the 79th Division's 314th IR use a former Nazi concrete reinforced fortification as a parapet, to fire on tenacious German defenders in Cherbourg. The 79th Division came under intense small-arms fire. Few German defenders survived the 314th IR's final assault, which began with its 2nd and 3rd Battalions on 25 June 1944. Cherbourg's surrender, due in large part to the capture of Fort du Roule on 26 June, concluded the hard fought VII Corps campaign except for mopping up operations. (*NARA*)

(**Above**) Part of a captured V1 bomb site in the Cherbourg area, with the master control housed under camouflage (*background*), that was never operational but on its way to completion. Several large caches of V1 flying bombs were discovered by the Americans, in addition to a V2 rocket installation at Brix. The power plant, rocket storage and launching pad for this site were reported to occupy 7 acres of land. The site was located on top of a hill overlooking the sea, which the Germans abandoned quickly. On 6 June 1944, German LG Erich Heinemann of the Wehrmacht's 66th Corps, which had a special V-weapons branch, ordered a Colonel Wachtel to prepare for an immediate offensive with the V1 starting 12 June. The first V1 bomb attack hit Clapham in south London on 13 June. In all, 10 missiles were launched that day but only 4 made it across the English Channel. Hitler called them 'revenge weapons' to terrorize British civilians and lower their morale, in light of the successful Normandy assaults and lodgment a week earlier. (*NARA*)

(**Above**) Two US VII Corps infantrymen rout out a German sniper who refused to surrender. The tenacious defender was holed up in a shell- and bullet-ridden building outside the fortress. Each soldier carries the standard issue M1 30.06in Garand semi-automatic rifle. The variability of the weather is evidenced by the two soldiers wearing raincoats over their uniforms. Extremes of terrain also marked the Cotentin-Cherbourg campaign – wet marshlands, rivers to cross, and urban combat with a determined foe often not willing to surrender. (NARA)

(**Opposite, above**) Cherbourg's commanders and 800 other German troops surrender to US VII Corps infantry on 26 June, as they exit from the rocky mountain fortress and arsenal upon which Cherbourg's Fort du Roule overlooked the harbour. LG Karl-Wilhelm von Schlieben, the Cherbourg garrison commander, stands with a German helmet on behind an American soldier/interpreter. Rear Admiral Walter Hennecke, Sea Defence CO of Normandy, stands listening to the right of the interpreter, while a German soldier at the far right holds the admiral's uniform and naval cap. (NARA)

(**Opposite, below**) German POWs march with their hands on their heads, leaving Cherbourg for captivity on 28 June 1944, two days after their commander, LG Karl-Wilhelm von Schlieben surrendered to US VII Corps CG, Collins. They are guarded by VII Corps soldiers holding their personal weapons. The capture of Cherbourg cost the VII Corps 3,000 dead, 3,000 missing and 13,500 wounded. The Germans lost 11,000 killed and 39,000 prisoners in defence of the fortress-port. (NARA)

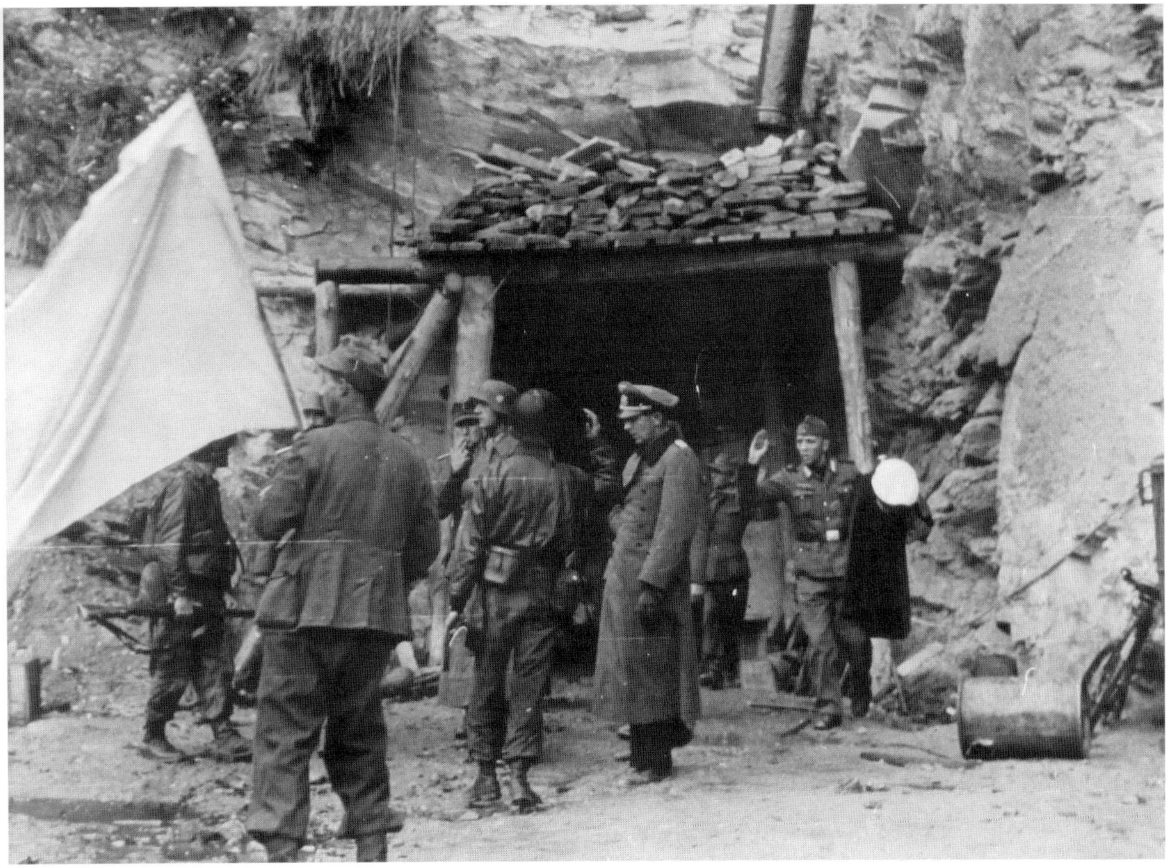

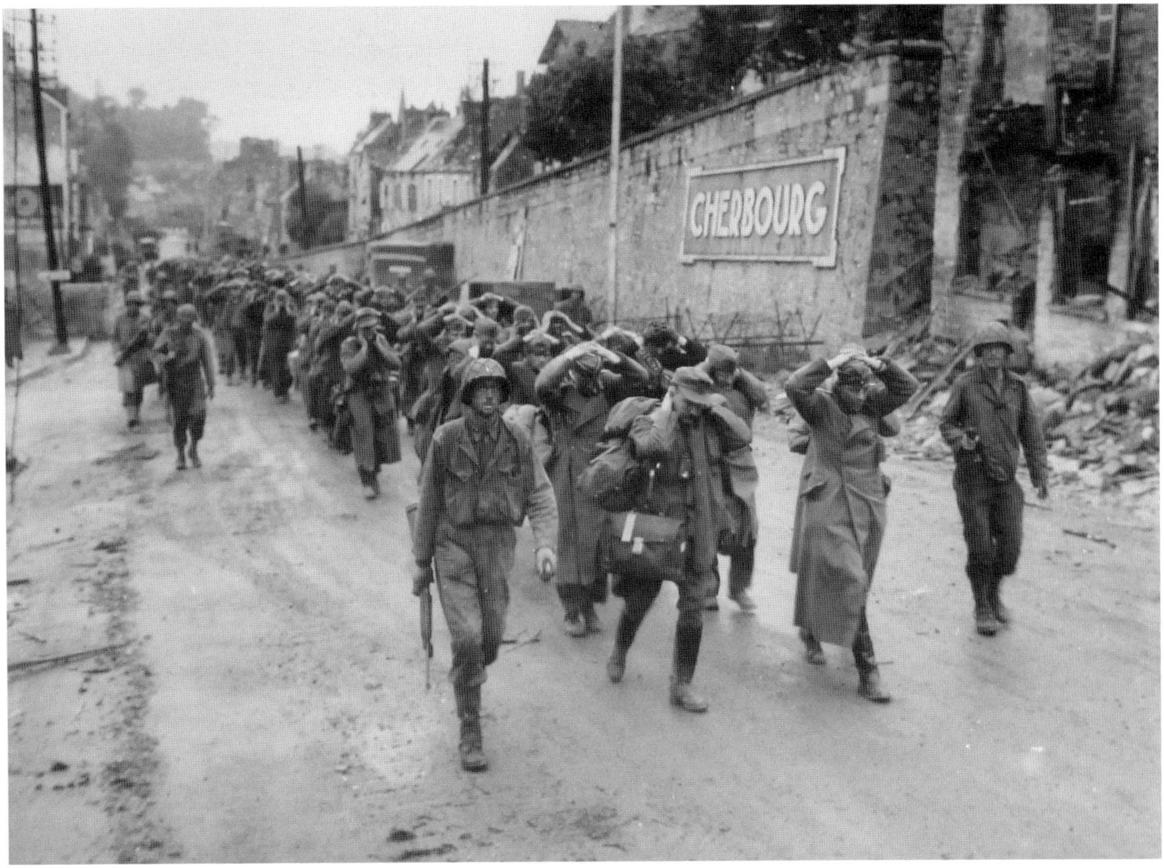
CHERBOURG

American soldiers of the 79th Infantry Division, fresh from their capture of Cherbourg, advance cautiously during house-to-house fighting in the rubble of La Haye-du-Puits, which was liberated on 8/9 July 1944. At the beginning of July American forces had continued to advance in the direction of La Haye-du-Puits. However, the torrential rains slowed their advance due to a lack of air cover and the lanes between the *bocage*'s hedgerows turned into muddy quagmires through which the American vehicles struggled. By 4 July, the 79th Division's 314th IR was only 2km north of La Haye-du-Puits, but facing stout resistance from the Wehrmacht's 243rd and 353rd Infantry Divisions. The advance of the lead companies of the 79th on 5 July was further slowed down by multiple mined obstacles. On 6 July, the US 313th and 314th IRs of the 79th Division gradually encircled the Germans, compelling them to retreat south to maintain their LOC. On 7 July, the Germans counterattacked with the 3rd IR, 2nd SS-Panzer Division '*Das Reich*' (The Realm) and a company of the Luftwaffe's 1st Parachute Regiment, forcing the units of the 79th to withdraw, the Americans losing 1,000 men on that day. On 8 July, the 79th Infantry Division renewed its attack through terrain strewn with German mines, reaching the northwest section of La Haye-du-Puits by early evening. All of 9 July was necessary to seize the remainder of the city, which was largely destroyed by Allied bombings. *(NARA)*

Elements of the US 79th Division finally liberated La Haye-du-Puits on 8/9 July 1944. Shown here is an 81mm mortar team from the division's 315th IR, entering the French town on the Rue de Barneville. The soldier in the right foreground carries the 81mm mortar tube while the two men behind him carry the weapon's bipod and base-plate. Aiding the advance on La Haye-du-Puits on 3/4 July were PIR and GIR units of the 82nd Airborne Division and elements of the 90th Division that attacked a number of German-occupied hills (131, 95, 121), Mont Castré, and the Montgardon Ridge. The 315th IR, early on during the advance, had been ordered to pass by the west in an attempt to encircle the town and meet the 79th Division's 313th and 314th IRs to the south. Upon leaving La Haye-du-Puits, the 79th Infantry Division began its advance to Lessay to the south on the Périers–St Lô road and Portbail to the west at the far end of the Cotentin Peninsula. Allocated to MG Troy Middleton's VIII Corps from 3 July, the 79th participated in the offensive on these locales and during Operation *Cobra*, finally liberating Lessay on 27 July. (NARA)

(**Above**) Troops, armour and mechanized vehicles try to progress in heavy traffic, on the muddy track of a road network to St Fromond near La Vautaire over the Vire river, 9 July 1944. The road bridge across the Vire at St Fromond had been partially destroyed by German artillery and, since it afforded the quickest means of transporting artillery and vehicles, engineers from the 247th Engineer Combat Battalion with trucks spanned the gaps in the bridge with treadway bridging. The Vire was a rapid river, 10 feet deep and 60 feet wide with high, steep banks. The congested traffic to the left side is comprised of M5 light tanks of Company C, 33rd Armoured Regiment, CCB, 3rd Armoured Division, and to the right a column of jeeps, half-tracks, and M8 armoured cars of the 83rd Reconnaissance Battalion. Combat here was between elements of Corlett's US XIX Corps, comprised of the 30th Infantry and 3rd Armoured Divisions with the 113th Cavalry Group, against units of the 17th SS-*Panzergrenadier* Division's *Kampfgruppe* (battle group) Heinze. (*NARA*)

(**Opposite, above**) Two soldiers of the US 2nd Infantry Division man an M1917A 0.3in calibre water-cooled MG from a hedge, with other soldiers dug into a cultivated field behind them, near Hill 192 in the vicinity of Lessay, 11 July 1944. Hill 192 was situated with farmland to the north and the small hill afforded the Germans excellent observation of the Vire river and Caumont. The 2nd Infantry Division attempted to capture the hill in mid-June, losing over 1,000 men. The Germans continued to fortify Hill 192 with the Luftwaffe's 3rd Parachute Division. On 11 July, the 2nd Division's 23rd and 38th IRs attacked two German paratrooper battalions, while American heavy artillery fired 20,000 rounds in support. Companies of the 2nd Division's IRs systematically overcame the Nazi paratrooper defences in each of the hedgerows, reaching and securing the St Lô–Bayeux road on 11/12 July, though 70 men were killed and over 330 wounded or missing in action. The soldier on the left holds a 0.45in calibre M3 SMG, called a 'grease gun' because of the appearance of its barrel. The M3 SMG, which entered service in 1944, was less expensive and easier to produce than the 0.45in calibre Thompson SMG. It had a 30-round detachable box magazine and a range of 300 feet, with a cyclic rate of fire of 450 rounds per minute, making it very suitable for close combat in the Normandy hedgerows. The downsides were its tendency to malfunction due to dust, mud and grime build-up and the difficulty of manually loading the box magazine, particularly under combat conditions. (*NARA*)

(**Below**) Infantrymen of the US 79th Infantry Division engage in combat amid the hedges of the *bocage* near Lessay, in the Manche, 18 June 1944. The soldier on top of the hedgerow is launching a 2.36in rocket from his M1A1 rocket launcher, commonly called a 'bazooka'. Both combatant sides relied heavily on the use of AT rocket launchers while fighting in the *bocage*, in place of artillery that could not be brought to bear in western Normandy's rough terrain, where transport was extremely limited. Almost 53,000 M1A1 2.36in rockets were fired by American forces from late June to early July 1944 – ironically not at armoured vehicle targets. On 27 July, after an artillery barrage, the 79th Infantry Division's 315th IR began its advance towards Lessay. After initially bypassing the city and then attacking back, the Americans seized the locale, despite the resistance of the Wehrmacht's 243rd Infantry Division with reinforcements from the 353rd Infantry Division. (NARA)

In early July 1944 US troops of the 29th Division's 175th IR, on Hill 108 near Villiers-Fossard, search tall hedgerows for snipers on either side of a narrow dirt lane on the way to St Lô, which was liberated 17 July. A dead German soldier lies at the base of the left hedge. The approaches to St Lô were swarming with strongpoints manned by the remnants of the Wehrmacht's 352nd Infantry Division, amid terrain characterized by swampy fields, steep wooded hills and the extensive maze of hedgerows with sunken lanes visible here. At the corners of each cultivated field bordered by hedges, the Germans emplaced heavy MGs to pin down attacking infantrymen in the open. Light MGs were positioned to the front and flanks, to inflict casualties on advancing American soldiers seeking cover and concealment. On 4 July, Bradley shifted his focus from a drive towards Coutances, south of Lessay, to one aimed at St Lô. Bradley's spearhead was Collins's VII Corps, comprised now of the 4th, 9th, and 83rd Infantry Divisions. The objective was to reach the Périers–St Lô road, from where VII Corps' divisions could advance southeast toward St Lô. Exemplifying the strong resistance of the Germans, now augmented by elements of the Luftwaffe's 6th Parachute Regiment and the 17th SS-*Panzergrenadier* Division *Götz von Berlichingen*, the US 83rd Infantry Division lost 1,400 men for just a 200-yard gain on 4 July. On 5 July, the battle recommenced along the Carentan–Périers road, but the 83rd Infantry Division incurred another 750 casualties after advancing only a mile. Even with the more experienced US 4th Infantry Division now in the front line, by 7 July US First Army had advanced less than 3 miles. The *bocage* slowed offensive movement and, along with rain and cloud cover, limited Allied air support. (*NARA*)

Combat in the *bocage* hedgerows near Lessay is exemplified here, on 18 July 1944, as three US 79th Infantry Division soldiers each carry out an assigned task. The soldier in the foreground launches a rifle grenade at the enemy – it had a greater distance than a thrown hand grenade and would not expose that soldier to enemy small-arms fire. The soldier in the centre is observing where the rifle grenade explodes, to note any necessary corrections in its direction or trajectory. The soldier at the right trains his M1 Garand 30.06in calibre semi-automatic rifle on the enemy position, from behind the protection of the hedgerow. New infantry tactics had to be improvised on an ad hoc basis due to the unique conditions of the terrain. During the Occupation, the Germans used the airfield at Lessay. Allied aerial bombardments on 7 and 8 June delayed the advance of German reinforcements towards the landing beaches. The Abbey of Lessay, one of the oldest in Normandy and dating back to the eleventh century, was destroyed and on 11 July, the Germans mined the ruins. *(NARA)*

(**Above**) An American M1 57mm AT gun fires through a thick hedgerow in the Normandy *bocage* as the rest of the crew lie prone to minimize the weapon's blast and recoil. This action took place on the road to Avranches on 31 July 1944. The 57mm AT gun was a direct copy of the successful British 6-pounder AT gun and was widely used in American infantry divisions throughout the war. Its 2.8kg shell was able to pierce 70mm of armour at 1,000 metres. A key objective of the Operation *Cobra* breakthrough on 25 July was the city of Avranches, the gateway to Brittany. By swinging west of St Lô towards Avranches, the US First Army offensive could also trap a large portion of the German Seventh Army. Late on 29 July, VIII Corps CG Middleton gave MG John Wood, CG of the 4th Armoured Division, the assignment of taking Avranches and on 30 July, units of the 4th almost captured SS *Oberstgruppenführer* Paul Hausser and the Wehrmacht's Seventh Army staff. Later that evening, 4th Division tanks entered Avranches, a major action taking place when retreating Germans attempted to break through the thinly-held American lines. (*NARA*)

(**Opposite, above**) American infantrymen take cover behind dead cattle near St Lô on 22 July 1944. Horses and other animal carcasses produced a profound stench from decaying flesh on the battlefield. Despite the smell, in the *bocage* country with its narrow lanes, tall hedges and concealed German defensive positions, American soldiers had to immediately find any cover they could if they came under enemy fire. In western Normandy, the US forces under General Bradley had difficulties in building up a secure starting point for their breakout operations until Operation *Cobra* was unleashed, with a successful massive air bombardment on 25 July. (*NARA*)

(**Opposite, below**) A US M4 medium tank fires at German targets on the way to St Lô in late July 1944. In this country lane there is a dead horse from shelling, a common sight and odour of the battlefield, and wrecked horse-drawn wooden carts near a farmhouse. The Germans used a large number of horses for transport in Normandy among their second line and static infantry divisions. Horse-drawn guns and limbers were also employed by the Wehrmacht. (*NARA*)

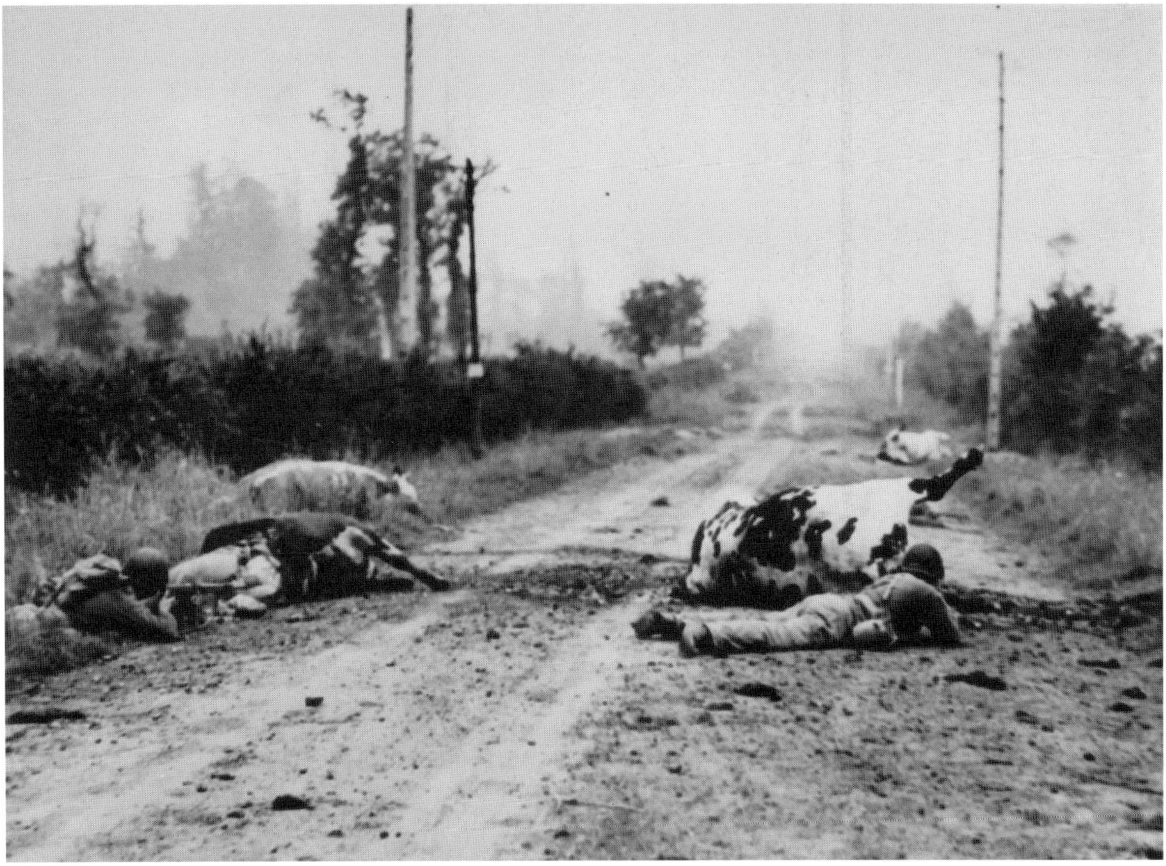

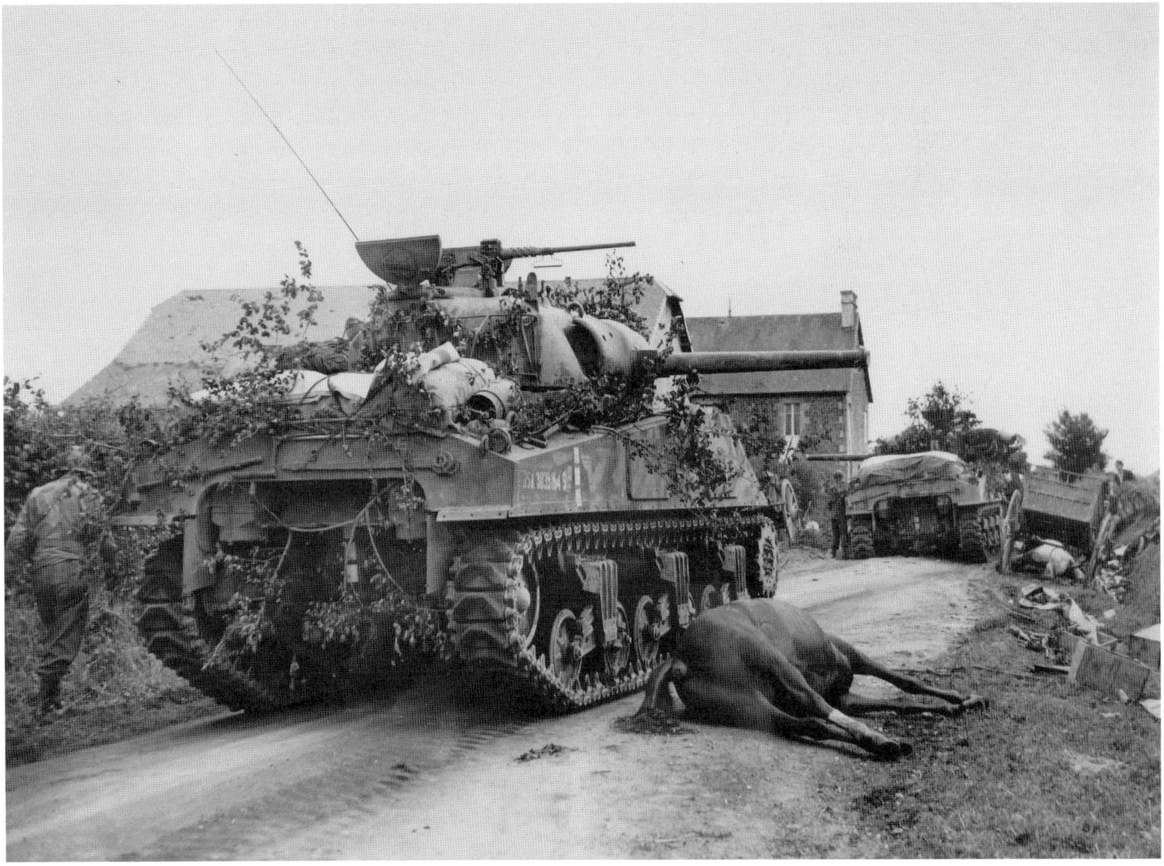

A US M4 medium tank with an M1 dozer blade of the 23rd Armoured Engineer Battalion, 3rd Armoured Division, called 'Here's Dots', ploughs through a densely-wooded area of the *bocage* on 15 July 1944 so that infantry and other vehicles could move forward. In addition, the 'dozer tank' also made pits for artillery and tanks in a 'hull down' position, as well clearing roads and villages of obstacles. The dozer tank was not as widely touted as the Culin 'Rhino' bladed tank, but it was often a more effective means to push through hedgerows. Each TB had four of the dozer tanks. *(NARA)*

American troops of the 3rd Battalion, 47th IR, 9th Infantry Division, move through a breach in a hedgerow created by a dozer tank, 25 July 1944. The 9th, which was instrumental in the late June capture of the port of Cherbourg, suffered significant casualties in the weeks leading up to the breakout after Operation *Cobra* and was often short of armoured support after it. In addition to the urban combat in Cherbourg, MG Manton Eddy's 9th Infantry Division fought the Germans in the Tunisian city of Bizerte, during the closing days of the North African campaign in 1943. *(NARA)*

An M5 light tank with Culin blades advances through a gap made in a Normandy hedgerow into an open field. This photograph demonstrates the *bocage* country that proved such a problem for the US First Army prior to Operation *Cobra* on 25 July and the subsequent breakout. In western Normandy, the fields bordered by hedgerows hid German MGs and small artillery pieces that would pour intense gunfire on American forces entering the open pasture. Many hedgerows were too high to be surmounted by tanks, and even the lower ones made an American tank climbing over the earthen wall vulnerable to an enemy AT round fired at its poorly-armoured underside. Hence, the need for tanks fitted with Culin blades ('Rhino tanks') or tanks fitted with bulldozer blades ('dozer tanks') to cut through the hedge. Aside from limited regional roads between the major towns, individual hedgerows were connected by small openings and footpaths with an occasional sunken dirt lane for farm carts. *(NARA)*

An M4 medium tank of the 3rd Battalion, 33rd Armoured Regiment, CCB, 3rd Armoured Division, passes two Panzer IV Ausf.H tanks of the 2nd Panzer Division *Das Reich*. The German tanks were previously knocked out by an American Tank Destroyer (TD) Battalion, advancing in concert with the US 117th IR, 30th Infantry Division, XIX Corps on 9 July 1944, having crossed the Vire river near St Fromond as MG Corlett's forces made a move toward St Lô. The pace of advance of the CCB, 3rd Armoured Division, was criticized for being slow – it had become wary of using the *bocage* road network as the Germans tended to set up ambushes at crossroads and other key points. The 30th Division commander, MG Leland Hobbs, was comfortable advancing with only his supporting TD Battalion; however, XIX Corps commander, Corlett, wanted CCB, 3rd Armoured Division, to spearhead the advance toward St Lô. Earlier on 7 July, Hobbs' 117th IR was the crux of the 30th Infantry Division's effort to cross the Vire river with its steep banks. While the 30th prepared for a thrust on St Lô, German commanders in Normandy responded to the American crossing of the Vire by ordering troops from the St Lô garrison to temporarily block the XIX Corps' advance until General Fritz Bayerlein's Panzer *Lehr* Division could be pulled from Caen and brought west. FM Rommel also deployed the 2nd SS-Panzer Division in the Vire-Taute region, to slow down Hobbs's advance until Panzer *Lehr* arrived. Rommel and his other commanders knew that if St Lô capitulated, the entire German front line might collapse. In fifteen days of fighting around St Lô, the 30th Division sustained almost 4,000 battle casualties, a loss rate of 25 per cent for the division as a whole but 90 per cent of its rifle platoon strength. (*NARA*)

Two Panzer V Ausf.A 'Panthers' of Panzer Regiment 6 of the *Lehr* Division were knocked out in the vicinity of Le Désert on 11 July 1944. General Fritz Bayerlein, CG Panzer *Lehr* Division, was not pleased with the Panthers' performance, as 10 of his tanks were lost to M10 3in GMC TDs of the US 899th TD Battalion during this engagement. He blamed the loss of 25 per cent of his armour in his counteroffensive to the Panzer V tank's long barrel, which made it difficult to traverse the turret in the *bocage*'s narrow country roads to engage the US TDs. Bayerlein said that his armour had to fight at a maximum range of 200 yards because the hedges concealed everything farther away. German light tanks could have performed better in the terrain, but Bayerlein had not brought them from the Caen sector because his intelligence informed him that the area was suitable for heavier tank operations. (NARA)

An American M29 'Weasel', a tracked, semi-amphibious, lightly armoured carrier capable of performing a variety of tasks, is seen here escorting a line of German POWs to a stockade, 11 July 1944. The road is bordered by a hedgerow typical of the western Normandy *bocage* country, near St-Jean-de-Daye. The M29 was built by Studebaker and developed for an operation against German heavy-water and strategic power plants in snow-covered Norway, to be led by Colonel Robert T. Frederick's 1st Special Service Force. However, as that mission was cancelled, the M29 was reassigned for duties in both Atlantic and Pacific theatres, including ammunition carrier, command centre, ambulance, and as signals vehicle, capable of laying communication lines that could be used in sandy, muddy and desert terrains. Another use for the M29 was crossing minefields, as its ground pressure was often too low to set off AT mines. The M29 was over 10ft long and 5ft wide and could carry a crew of four. It had an operational range of 165 miles and a maximum speed of 36 miles per hour. An M29C Water Weasel was amphibious, with buoyancy cells and twin rudders, but was limited to inland waterways. *(NARA)*

German POWs under an American guard are shown passing an M10 3in GMC TD on a country lane, as US First Army forces move west of St Lô towards Marigny after the 25 July 1944 Operation *Cobra*. Collins's VII Corps exploitation force consisted of the 2nd Armoured and 1st Infantry Divisions, reinforced by CCB, 3rd Armoured Division, with the latter unit leading the attack towards Marigny. The American armoured attacks on 26 July were facilitated by bulldozer tanks clearing roads and 9th TAF P-47 fighter-bombers attacking German 353rd Infantry Division positions in Marigny and St Gilles. By late afternoon on 26 July, CCB, 3rd Armoured Division, was on the outskirts of Marigny where it was attacked by units of the 2nd SS-Panzer Division and remnants of the 353rd Infantry Division. The attack was halted overnight with the US 1st Infantry Division occupying the other side of Marigny. By the third day of Operation *Cobra*, 27 July, German resistance in the Cotentin was melting away. The VII Corps infantry was 7 miles south of the Périers–St Lô road, as it penetrated into the sector of General Dietrich von Choltitz's 84th Corps in the Cotentin.

By 28 July, an American commander proclaimed, 'This thing has busted wide open', as tanks were now moving far ahead of the screening US infantry units. Three mobile columns had taken Marigny and St Gilles, then swung westward toward Coutances. Bradley's G-2 (Intelligence) officer noted that 'the destruction of German 84th Corps is believed at hand and the destruction of the II Parachute Corps is an immediate possibility.' General von Choltitz's HQ had hardly any contact with his divisions. Faced with only shattered remnants of German formations, Bradley looked beyond Coutances, his earlier objective, to Avranches. Bradley oriented his VIII and VII Corps in the Cotentin towards this new objective, as he moved Corlett's XIX Corps westward across the Vire river to further strengthen his attack. Only one US Corps, Gerow's V, remained east of the Vire, linked to the progress of Anglo-Canadian advances. *(NARA)*

Two Americans in a jeep of the 142nd Armoured Signal Company, 2nd Armoured Division navigate through deep mud in the St Lô sector on 23 July 1944. The local flooding was caused by heavy Normandy rains and added another element of harshness to the *bocage* country that the American forces were slogging through. A wire anti-decapitation cutter is vertically mounted on the jeep's front fender to protect the occupants against taut-wire traps. *(NARA)*

(**Above**) Battalion officers of the 175th IR, 29th Infantry Division, XIX Corps plan an attack towards St Lô on 15 July 1944. When the initial attack on St Lô commenced on 11 July, the 29th Division's 175th IR was still in reserve, but was alerted for possible use along the VII–XIX Corps boundary and for movement through the division's 116th IR. After nightfall, the 175th IR relieved the battered 116th IR on the St Lô road. A censor has covered over the distinctive 'blue and gray' shoulder patch of MG Charles Gerhardt's 29th Division. St Lô was defended by the Luftwaffe's 3rd Parachute Division and the Wehrmacht's 352nd Infantry Division, the latter having contested the 29th Infantry Division's landing at Omaha Beach on 6 June. (*NARA*)

(**Opposite, above**) A US VII Corps patrol takes cover along a sunken hedgerow lane just south of St Lô, as a German artillery shell bursts overhead on 23 July 1944, two days before Operation *Cobra*, the massive Allied aerial assault along the Périers–St Lô road. The American troops were attempting to outflank a German position, but combat in these conditions slowed the progress of an infantry advance to the extent that it could be measured in yards. (*NARA*)

(**Opposite, below**) A disabled M10 3in GMC TD, with a dead American tanker lying behind it, offers a reminder of the gruesome combat that took place for St Lô on 19 July 1944. A road sign for Isigny on a bullet-ridden building wall denotes the location of that town in the Omaha Beach sector, well to the north of St Lô. The M10 TD was based on the M4 Sherman tank chassis and utilized an M7 3in AA gun. It was lightly armed, as it was not intended for close-quarter combat and was deemed undergunned against German V (Panther) and VI (Tiger) tanks. Over 5,000 were produced, beginning in the autumn of 1942. It also had one 0.5in calibre MG mounted on its open turret, and a crew of five. Its operational range was 200 miles, with maximum speed of 25–30 miles per hour. In Normandy, the 90mm M3 AA gun was brought into use, replacing the M7 gun as an AA weapon, and the British QF 17-pounder was soon recognized to be a capable AT gun against the German Panzer VI Tiger Mk 1 and Mk 2 tanks. (*NARA*)

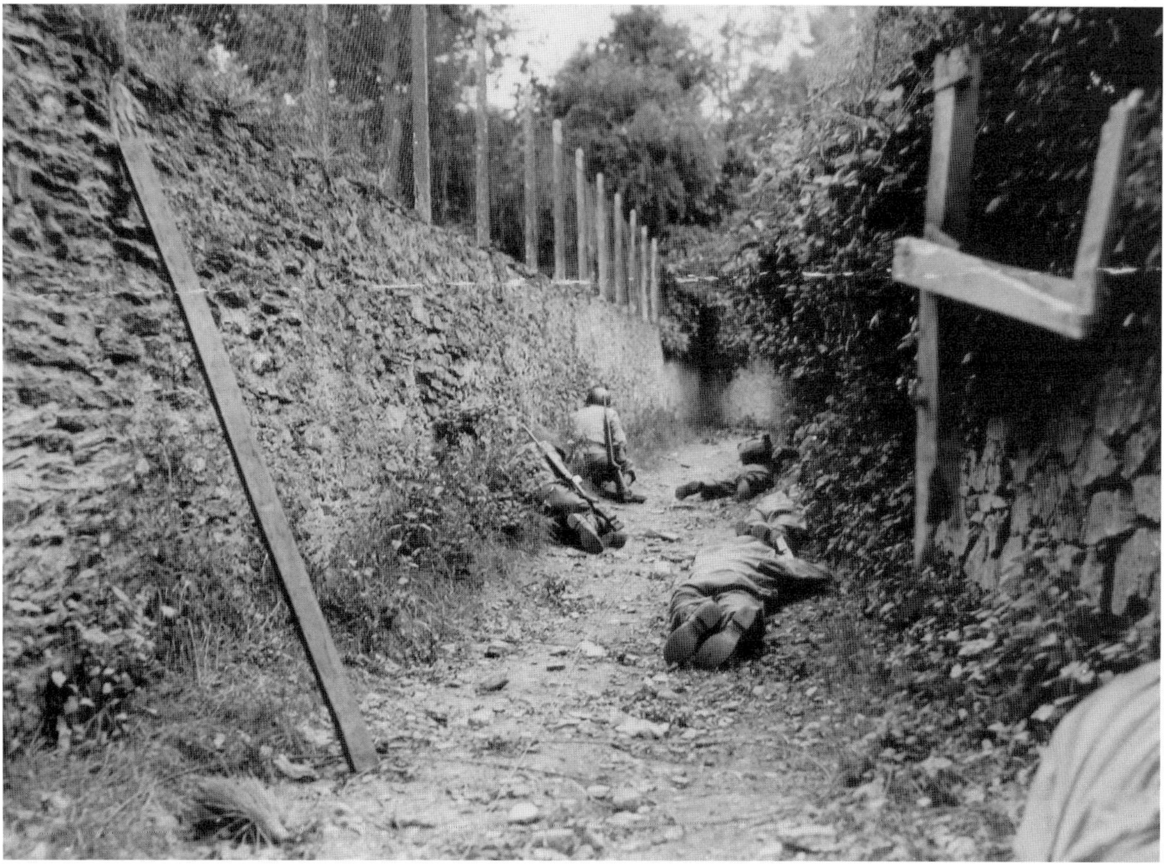

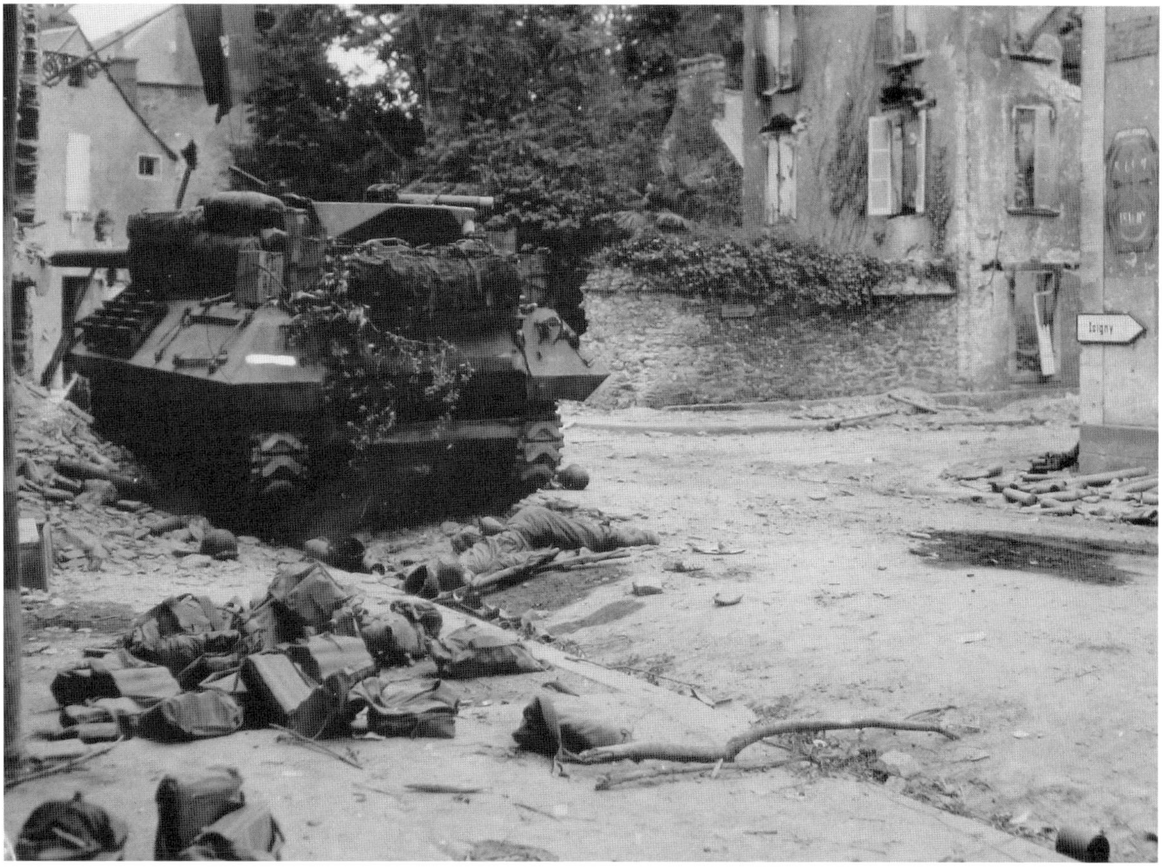
Isigny

American M8 armoured cars of the 113th Cavalry Group, XIX Corps, jam a St Lô street known as '88 Alley' on 19 July 1944, having driven the German garrison from the city. At a cemetery on the outskirts of the town, advancing 29th Infantry Division forces of XIX Corps were met by heavy MG fire and 88mm AT/AA guns among a maze of gravestones. The battle for St Lô turned each block of buildings into a miniature battlefield. German snipers, positioned in two- and three-storey buildings, fired from behind windows, while other Nazi forces made last stands in the city's rubble. On 18 July, Luftwaffe General Eugen Meindl, CG II Parachute Corps, saw that further defence was futile and requested permission to evacuate the city. The Wehrmacht's Seventh Army commander, SS *Oberstgruppenführer* Paul Hausser, who took over from *Generaloberst* Friedrich Dollmann on 28 June, permitted Meindl to withdraw his men southward, except for a delaying force to hold off the Americans as long as possible. On 19 July, the 113th Cavalry Group was sent through St Lô probing for the Germans' new main line of resistance outside the city. They soon found that elements of the Wehrmacht's 352nd Infantry Division had set up a new defence line on the hills immediately south of the town. Units from the 115th IR, 29th Infantry Division entered St Lô and began mopping up German stragglers. The next morning, after eighteen days of hedgerow fighting, St Lô finally fell and Bradley had secured a starting point for a major breakout offensive into the French heartland, after Operation *Cobra* commenced on 25 July. The battle for the hedgerows cost US First Army over 15,000 casualties, among whom a total of 3,700 were from the 29th Infantry Division. Total XIX Corps casualties numbered 11,000 and 3,000 of those were killed. (*NARA*)

US Army medics and soldiers dig out frontline infantrymen who were buried alive during a faulty bombing run along the Périers–St Lô road during Operation *Cobra*. The inception of this plan came to Bradley on 8 July 1944, when he was briefed on the German Seventh Army utilizing much of its reserve units. To penetrate the frontage of German resistance, Bradley developed a carpet-bombing initial attack plan, after which he planned to send two heavy armoured divisions through for a breakout. On 24 July, the Allied carpet-bombing attack scheduled to begin at 1300 hours was cancelled. Some of the aircraft did not receive the message to abort, and released their bombloads. The 30th Infantry Division, XIX Corps, incurred more than 150 casualties from bombs that were dropped short. On 25 July, the aerial carpet-bombing was repeated, and more than 1,500 B-17s and B-24s, along with over 380 medium bombers, accompanied by 550 fighter-bombers, released a total of 4,150 tons of ordnance, wreaking utter devastation. Because great clouds of dust obscured terrain features, some bombs again landed 'short' to the north of the Périers–St Lô road, killing 111 US soldiers and wounding 490, plus inflicting casualties on observers and newspaper reporters. Among the dead was the US Army Ground Forces Commander, General Lesley J. McNair, who had trained the combat troops at home and was visiting the front to check the results of his training programmes. Across the highway that marked the American line of departure, bombs had buried men and equipment, overturned vehicles, cut telephone wires and produced a lunar landscape.

As for the Germans targeted, no fewer than 1,000 Germans died and any enemy survivors in the carpet-bombed areas were stunned. Three German command posts were demolished, a regiment virtually destroyed and a *Kampfgruppe* (battle group) wiped out. The effect on German General Fritz Bayerlein's Panzer *Lehr* Division was devastating. Immediately after the aerial assault, VII Corps ground forces only moved forward a mile toward their immediate objective of seizing Marigny, as pockets of enemy resistance persisted and forward American companies were also stunned by the aerial assault. However, by 26 July German defences began to collapse as CCB, 3rd Armoured Division and the 1st Infantry Division captured Marigny, to the west of St Lô, and the 2nd Armoured Division advanced 7 miles. (NARA)

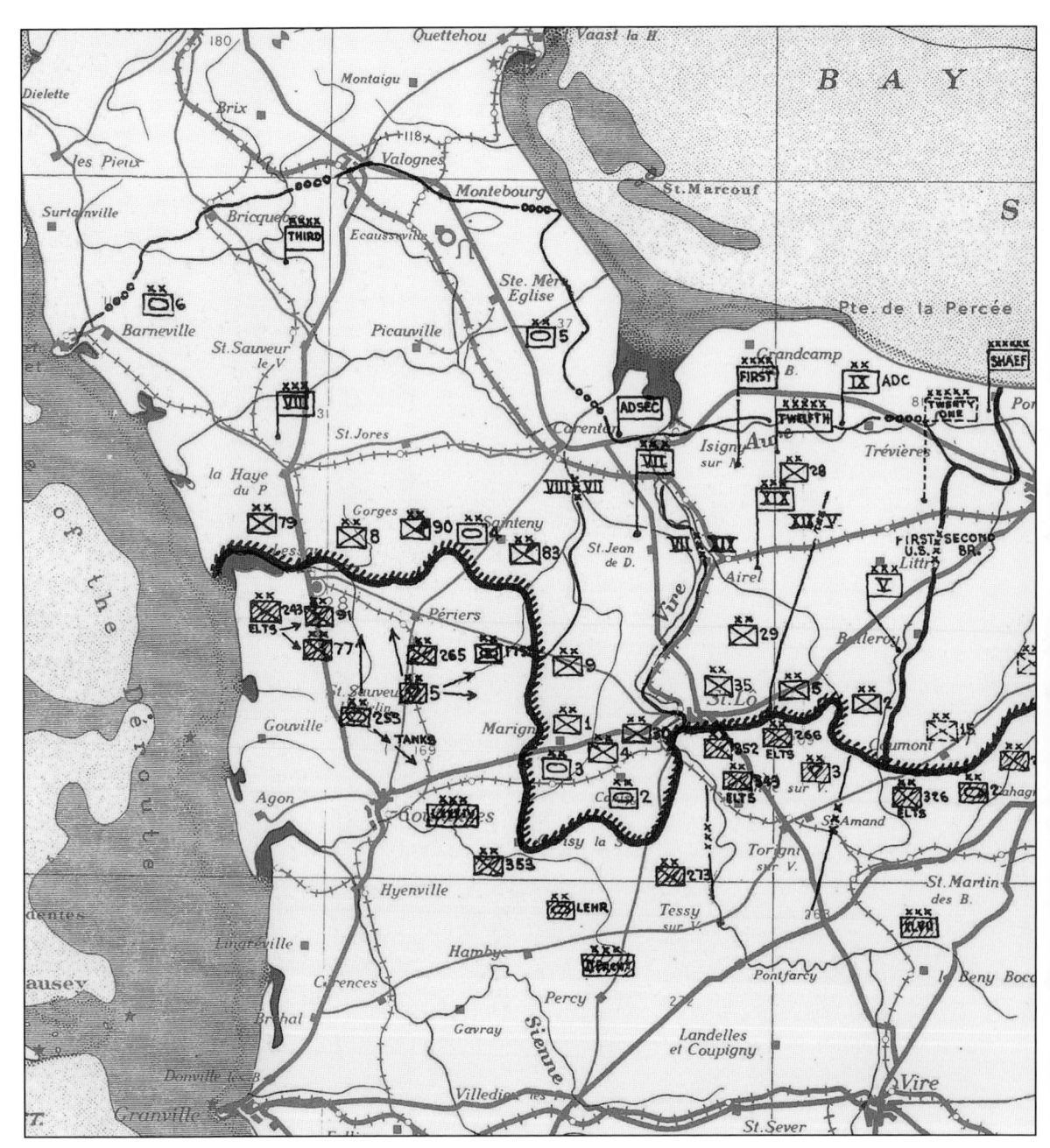

A US First Army HQ Situation Map from 2400 hours on 27 July 1944, two days after Bradley's Operation *Cobra* was unleashed. From 8 to 18 July, the 79th Infantry Division fought and captured La Haye-du-Puits, then moved on to Lessay to a site on the Périers–St Lô road, the take-off point for *Cobra*. As a result of that operation, the Panzer *Lehr* Division essentially ceased to exist after the carpet bombing, while Collins's VII Corps started their advance at 1100 hours on 25 July – after the temporary disorganization of American frontline companies from saturation aerial bombardment had worn off. On 25 July, VII Corps' 2nd and 3rd Armoured Divisions with the 1st, 4th, 9th and 30th Infantry Divisions advanced 4,000 yards creating a deep salient into the German lines. On 26 July, VIII Corps' 79th, 8th, 90th and 83rd Infantry and 4th Armoured Divisions, to the west of VII Corps, pushed the Germans back an additional 8,000 yards. On 27 July, the 2nd Armoured Division broke through into open country. (NARA)

A US M5 light tank of Middleton's VIII Corps' CCB, 4th Armoured Division, leads the entrance into Coutances, located 18 miles west of St Lô, on 29 July 1944. The previous day some German troops had slipped out of Roncey and escaped, while other German units made organized attempts to fight through the line of American 2nd and 3rd Armoured Division tanks on 29 July. However, most Nazi forces were pounded by US 9th TAF and RAF 2nd TAF with fighter-bombers after they caught the Wehrmacht traffic stationary: three vehicles abreast and bumper-to-bumper, 500 enemy vehicles were jammed around the 'Roncey Pocket'. The enemy forces were hit for six hours by an aerial array of MGs, rockets and bombs. American artillery, tanks, and TD poured shells into the area. By daybreak of 30 July, hundreds of destroyed vehicles and wagons along with innumerable dead horses lay scattered over the countryside south of Coutances. A single American armoured division, the 2nd, captured 4,000 Germans in three days and killed an estimated 1,500. By nightfall of 30 July, the HQ of SS *Oberstgruppenführer* Hausser and Wehrmacht's 84th Corps' General von Choltitz were behind enemy lines, and American tanks unknowingly passed within several yards of Hausser's Seventh Army CP, which made its way to the safety of Mortain through the regular intervals of the American tank columns. (*NARA*)

US M5 light tanks of VIII Corps' 4th Armoured Division advance into Avranches on 30 July 1944. FM Hans von Kluge had been made high commander or *Oberbefehlshaber* (OB) West in early July, following FM von Rundstedt's sacking by Hitler, and assumed FM Rommel's Army Group (*Heeresgruppe*) B command on 17 July after the Desert Fox was wounded in a strafing attack. The only contact von Kluge now had with his combat troops along the Cotentin Peninsula's western coast was through a switchboard at a telephone relay station in Avranches. Just before dark on 30 July, the Avranches signal crew reported the approach of American troops. As Collins moved his VII Corps armoured forces southward across the Sée river and cut the roads leading eastward from Avranches to Mortain, Middleton's VIII Corps, including MG John Wood's 4th Armoured Division, drove through Coutances to Avranches, where they arrived on the evening of 30 July.

The VIII Corps units moved so quickly that the Germans had abandoned Avranches. Bridges across the Sée and Sélune rivers stood intact as there was no time for the Germans to demolish them. Retreating columns of Germans, unaware of the American presence in Avranches, entered the town and set off a short-lived battle – they clearly only wanted an exit from the town. On 31 July, FM von Kluge commented that American air activities were unprecedented and that 'the Americans have ripped open the whole western front'. Von Kluge claimed the whole debacle started with Hausser's fatal decision to break out to the southeast. He railed at his situation, 'unless I can get infantry and AT weapons there [Avranches], the left wing cannot hold.' (*NARA*)

A trio of US 30th Division infantrymen run parallel to a hedgerow combating the Nazi counterattack launched from Mortain, located south of St Lô and to the southeast of Avranches. American troops streamed south of Avranches, some turning west into Brittany, others swinging east toward the eventual objective of the Seine. The Brittany ports of St Malo, Brest, Lorient, St Nazaire, and Nantes were valued by the Allied High Command to bring supplies to the expanding Allied lodgment in northwestern France, between the Seine and Loire rivers. Collins's VII Corps' 1st Infantry Division moved into the high ground in the Mortain area and easily entered the town on 3 August. Hitler wanted a counterattack launched to cut off the Allied forces headed toward the Seine. He told FM von Kluge to temporarily ignore US VIII Corps' moves into Brittany, which he would address later, and to close the gap on the German left flank by counterattacking to regain Avranches, where a new left flank was to be solidly anchored.

Kluge assembled four armoured divisions under the German 67th Corps, under the overall command of the German Seventh Army CG Hausser. During darkness on 6 August 1944, without artillery preparation in order to retain the element of surprise, the German 67th Corps was to strike westward through Mortain, to retake Avranches on the southwest coast of the Cotentin Peninsula. With the Germans again holding firmly to the Cotentin west coast at Avranches, they could build a new line and tie down the Allies once more. German intelligence was under the impression that only the US 3rd Armoured and 30th Infantry Divisions were in the way of almost 200 panzers, poised for a surprise attack. In Hitler's mind, this counteroffensive would enable Kluge to divide the US First (now under LG Courtney Hodges as of 1 August) and the newly-activated US Third Army under LG George Patton and then roll up the Allied front, which was rapidly expanding southeastward. (NARA)

A dead German soldier lies next to his disabled half-track on 13 August 1944, after the failed Mortain counteroffensive to retake Avranches forced the Germans to retreat eastward. During the night of 7 August, four panzer divisions – the 116th Panzer, 2nd Panzer, 1st and 2nd SS-Panzer divisions advanced, knocked out several American roadblocks and surged through Mortain, occupied by elements of Collins's VII Corps. Mortain, situated at the foot of Hill 317, was an excellent observation point, which Collins wanted the 1st Infantry Division to occupy on 3 August. At 2000hrs on 6 August, the 30th Infantry Division entered Mortain to free the 1st Infantry Division for a southward movement. This was four hours before the German counteroffensive began. MG Leland Hobbs, CG 30th Infantry Division, reinforced his troops on Hill 317 east of Mortain with a battalion of the 120th IR.

By dawn on 7 August, the leading German elements had advanced 7 miles and were well to the west of Mortain: Avranches was within reach. However, the Americans recovered from the initial shock of the surprise counteroffensive and used artillery fire and fighter-bomber sorties to disrupt von Kluge's attack. Collins committed CCB, 3rd Armoured Division, to support Hobbs's 30th Infantry Division at Mortain. Bradley shifted divisions from other US Corps, so that less than 24 hours after the German offensive began Collins's VII Corps had seven divisions – five infantry and two armoured. Von Kluge's tank losses mounted and the German 67th Corps commander told his troops to dig in. At that point the German attack ground to a halt and US artillery fire indicated that the element of surprise was lost. Von Kluge was severely criticized by Hitler for making his move prematurely and without waiting for three more panzer divisions to be assembled for the counterattack; however, 100 German tanks lay abandoned in the vicinity of Mortain. (NARA)

Chapter Six

The Anglo-Canadian Siege of Caen and the Falaise-Argentan 'Pocket'

The Allied capture of Caen and Carpiquet airfield slated for 6 June 1944 was allotted to the British 3rd Division landing at Sword Beach, reinforced by the tanks of the British 27th Armoured Brigade and the Canadian 3rd Division from Juno Beach. However, the task was rendered impossible when the German 21st Panzer Division counterattacked and made a push between the two Allied beach zones. German reinforcements, including the 12th SS-Panzer Division *Hitlerjugend* and the elite Panzer *Lehr* Division were put into the line around Caen on 7 June and halted the British 3rd and Canadian 3rd Divisions. The positioning of these German armoured forces soon after the landing ensured that Caen would become a simmering cauldron for the British and Canadian troops to capture, and there would be no quick Allied victory. This meant Montgomery could not make an early breakthrough advance onto the open plain south of Caen, where his armoured forces could push on towards Paris and the southeast.

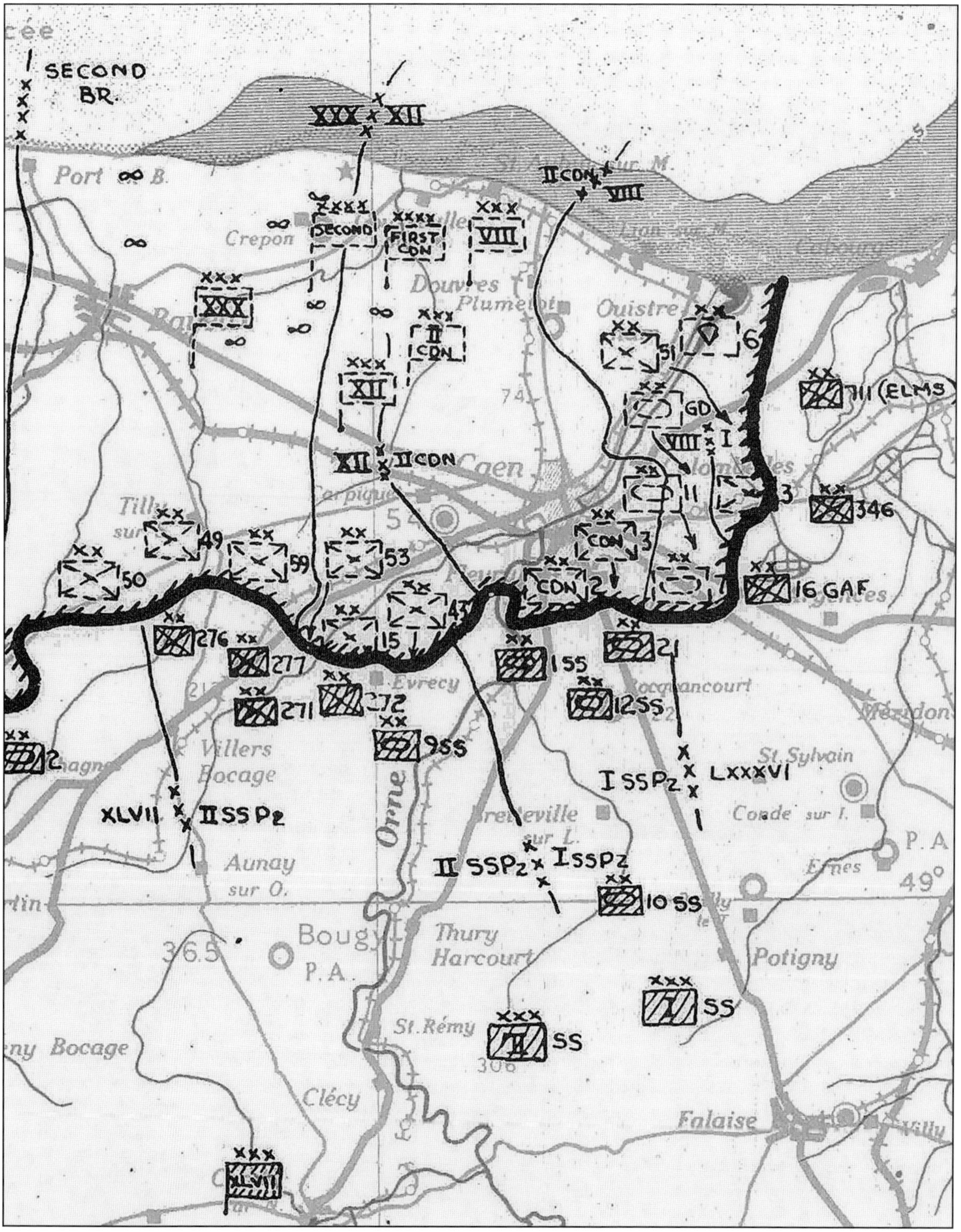
SECOND
BR.
XXX
XII
II CDN
VIII
SECOND
FIRST CDN
XXX
II CDN
XII
6
51
711 (ELMS)
GD
I
XII
II CDN
Caen
3
346
49
59
53
50
CDN 3
CDN 2
7
16 GAF
43
276
277
15
155
21
272
271
12SS
9SS
2
I SS Pz
LXXXVI
XLVII
II SS Pz
II SS Pz
I SS Pz
10 SS
SS
SS
XLVII
Port
Crepon
Douvres
Ouistre
Tilly
Evrecy
Villers Bocage
Orne
Aunay sur O.
Bougy
Thury Harcourt
St. Rémy
Clécy
Falaise
Potigny
St. Sylvain
Conde sur L.
Bocage

A US First Army HQ Situation Map from 2400 hours, 20 July 1944. Prior to the liberation of Caen on 19 July, numerous operations were aimed at the city's capture. On 12 June, the 51st Highland Division failed in an attempt to push around Caen from the east. Elements of the British 7th Armoured Division, attempting a wide encirclement to the west, suffered heavily at the hands of Panzer VI 'Tiger' I tanks in an ambush at Villers-Bocage. Operation *Epsom*, 26–30 June, took place to the west of Caen and principally involved British VIII Corps – they achieved a bridgehead over the Odon river (a tributary of the Orne, that passes through Aunay-sur-Odon south of Villers-Bocage), but failed to cross the Orne further to the east to secure the high ground along the Caen–Falaise road to the city's east. The British 11th Armoured Division did get on to Hill 112, the high ground southwest of Caen between the Odon and Orne.

Operation *Charnwood* began on 8/9 July with heavy Allied air raids on Caen's northern outskirts. Three British I Corps infantry divisions attacked Caen, leaving the city a mass of rubble but the northern part now in Allied hands. The bridges over the Orne river in the southern sector remained under German control.

Operation *Jupiter* was launched with a strengthened British 43rd (Wessex) Division on 10 July, to capture Hill 112 and get to the Orne river. After two days of fighting, the hill was captured by the British but they withdrew in the face of resistance by the German 9th and 10th SS-Panzer Divisions. From 15–17 July, British XII and XXX Corps resumed attacks along the Odon front to keep Nazi armour engaged, while a new offensive was organized for the eastern side of the Orne, from the British 6th Airborne bridgehead.

British Second Army's Operation *Goodwood* began on 18 July, involving British I and VIII Corps. The plan Dempsey had formulated and proposed to Montgomery on 12 July called for the combined resources of four corps to be employed. The three armoured divisions were to be regrouped under the VIII Corps command (O'Connor). After a saturation bombing, this massed armoured force of 750 tanks would open a salient in the German defensive line to outflank Caen from the east. Other subsidiary infantry attacks by British I (Crocker) and XII Corps (Ritchie) would coincide with II Canadian Corps' (Simonds) attack to secure Caen's southern half, while protecting the rear of VIII Corps. *Goodwood* was to start one week before the American Operation *Cobra* and, as masterminded by Dempsey, was also to be preceded by an RAF Bomber Command attack on German strongpoints blocking the approaches to the Caen-Falaise Plain.

Operation *Atlantic*, from 18 to 21 July, was a Canadian offensive launched in conjunction with Operation *Goodwood*, with two brigades, the 4th and 6th Canadian Infantry Brigades of the 2nd Canadian Division, under the command of II Canadian Corps CG, LG Guy Simonds. It was initially successful with gains made on both flanks of the Orne river, but an attack by two brigades of the 2nd Canadian Division against strongly defended German positions on Verrières Ridge to the south was a costly failure.

Caen was eventually cleared by Simonds's II Canadian Corps (comprised of the 2 Canadian and 3 Canadian Infantry Divisions and the British 7th Armoured Division) on 19 July. Attacking out of the city centre and from the area west of the city, Canadian 2nd Division pushed across the Orne and linked up with the Canadian 3rd Division, completing the encirclement of Caen. The II Canadian Corps continued driving south of the previously besieged city and the British 3rd Division reached its objective well to the east of Caen and Colombelles. However, the remainder of LG O'Connor's British VIII Corps attack faltered at Bourguébus Ridge, as the British suffered heavy tank and infantry casualties against German 21st Panzer Division's Heavy TB and SP Gun Battalion and groups of 88mm AT guns dotting every village on the plain. Torrential rains brought Operation *Goodwood* to a halt on 20 July, with a loss of 36 per cent of the Second British Army's tank strength. Allied armoured divisions still had not reached the Caen–Falaise road. (*NARA*)

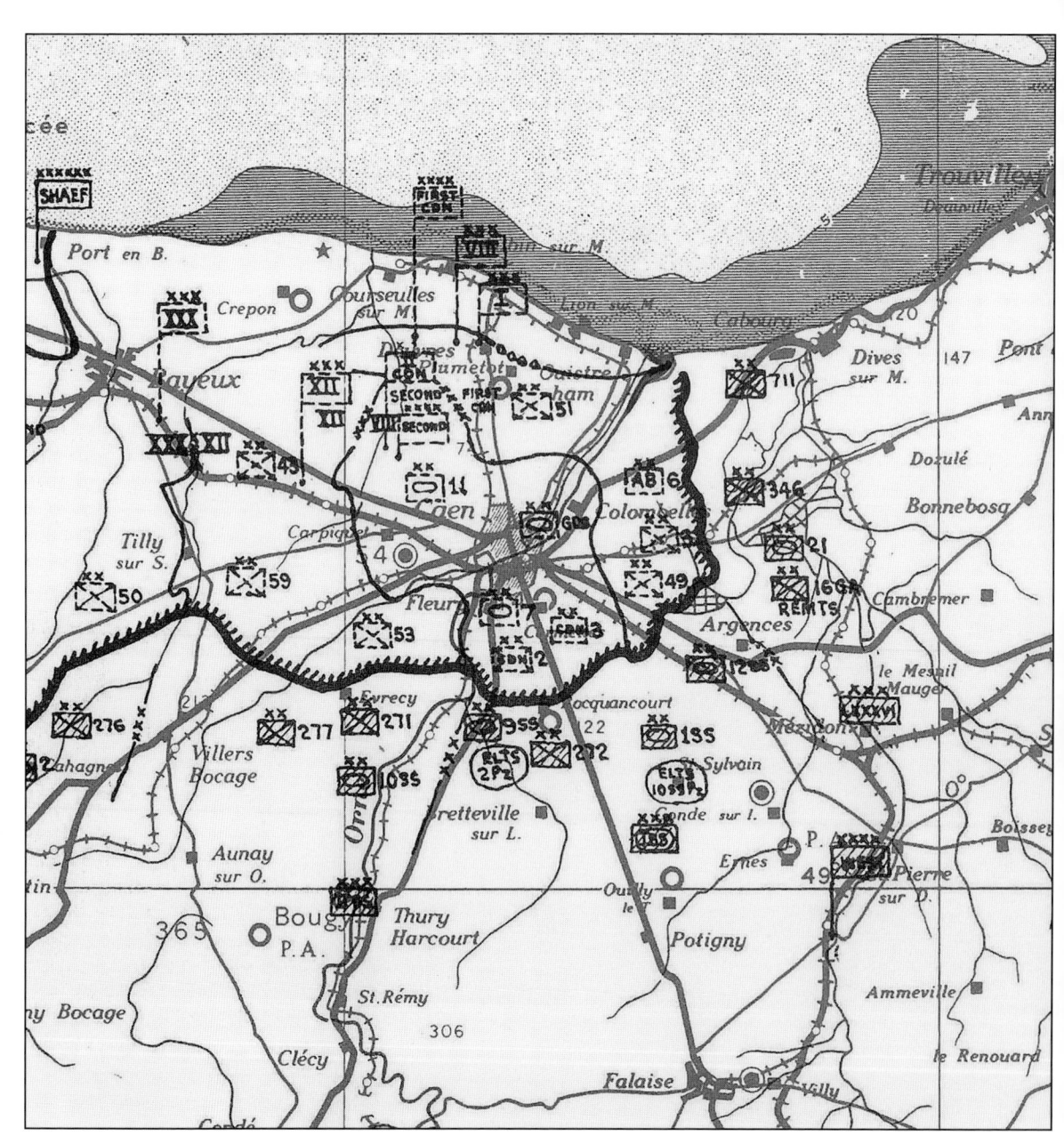

A US First Army Situation Map from 2400 hours, 27 July 1944. On 23 July, the First Canadian Army (CG LG Henry D.G. Crerar) was activated with II Canadian Corps and I British Corps. Crerar's Operation *Spring* launched II Canadian Corps down the Caen–Falaise road simultaneously with the Allied carpet bombing of the Périers–St Lô road on 25 July (Operation *Cobra*). The Canadian attack south of Caen was called off within 24 hours as the offensive stalled against the 1st SS and 9th SS-Panzer Divisions, situated respectively to the east and west of the Caen–Falaise road. On 30 July, Montgomery launched Operation *Bluecoat*, with the VIII and XXX Corps attacking southwards from the western side of the British line. Good progress was made by O'Connor's VIII Corps but the shift of three panzer divisions into the area halted the attack. As British XXX Corps performance was disappointing, Montgomery later replaced the corps commander LG Gerard Bucknall with LG Brian Horrocks and sacked the commander of the British 7th Armoured Division, MG George Erskine. (NARA)

Canadian infantry reinforcements bound for Caen in July 1944 march up a sandy track single-file, with full kit, past a watching military policeman and a dispatch rider (*right*). In mid-July, Montgomery faced a manpower crisis as he was unable to drive the Germans out of Caen. In fact, the British had started cannibalizing divisions for infantry replacements even before the invasion started. Between 6 June and the end of August 1944, 83,000 British, Canadian, and Polish troops became casualties, of whom 16,000 were killed in action. The Anglo-Canadian forces were not as well versed in infiltration tactics as the Germans. Rather, they relied on rolling artillery barrages to screen their traditional frontal attacks on enemy positions.

British Second Army was sent to Normandy with everything except adequate reserves of fighting troops. Thus, Dempsey's army and subsequently Crerar's First Canadian Army (once activated) could not afford huge manpower losses. Montgomery was determined to fight a battle that minimized infantry losses, making use instead of the Allied advantages in firepower. Failure to capture Caen soon after 6 June necessitated that he build up his own forces more quickly than the Germans could get reinforcements. His essential focus on capturing Caen drew the crack German formations to its defence, committing Second Army to a costly slogging match with the best Wehrmacht, Waffen-SS and Luftwaffe parachute troops in Normandy. (*NARA*)

(**Above**) An M4 medium British tank with dispatch rider moves quickly down a Normandy road, passing Allied infantry, between Tilly-sur-Seulles and Caen on 7 June 1944. The former locale was situated to the west of Caen on the Seulles river, which flowed northeast through the British XXX Corps' sector, comprised of the British 50th Northumbrian Division and British 7th Armoured Division. Panzer *Lehr* Division to the west of the 12th SS-Panzer Division *Hitlerjugend*, the latter opposing the Canadians on 7 June, came into the line opposite the two British XXX Corps formations. Panzer *Lehr* was one of the strongest and best-equipped Panzer divisions in France with both the Panzer V (Panther) medium and Panzer VI (Tiger) heavy tanks. Panzer *Lehr* was on the defensive as it held a section of the line in an effort to stop the British 50th Northumbrian Division advance. The subsequent fighting as British XXX Corps attempted to push beyond Tilly-sur-Seulles was extremely bitter. (*NARA*)

(**Opposite, above**) A Canadian 17-pounder AT gun fires at a water tower used as a Nazi OP. Much of the terrain facing the Anglo-Canadian forces before Caen was flat and manoeuvrable, as opposed to the *bocage* of western Normandy. The height to the top of the gunshield was over 5ft and the bulk of the 17-pounder posed problems of manoeuvre in and out of position, especially in the Normandy towns with their narrow streets. Nonetheless, the 17-pounder could knock out a Panzer VI (Tiger) tank at 1,000 yards. The gun had an overall length of 24 feet, a crew of six, and a range of 3,000 yards. (*NARA*)

(**Opposite, below**) A Canadian infantry regiment launches one of numerous attacks on Caen. Caen's value lay in its location at the centre of Normandy's road and rail communications. It was also at the northern neck of the only plain in the Allied lodgment area large enough to construction an airfield complex. The capture of Caen would serve in the development of major Allied armoured operations southwards towards Falaise, but it was a natural point of concentration for German armour. The Canadians had been observing Carpiquet Airfield since 7 June, but had not attacked its hangars or buildings as they were held in strength with pillboxes, a battery of 88mm AA/AT guns and barbed wire, defended by units of the 12th SS-Panzer Division *Hitlerjugend*, including a few companies of the 26th SS-*Panzergrenadier* and 12th SS-Panzer Regiments. On 4 July, the Canadian 3rd Division launched Operation *Windsor* with the task of capturing Carpiquet village and airfield. The next day, elements of the Canadian 8th Brigade, comprised of the North Shore Regiment, the Queen's Own Rifles of Canada, and Le Régiment de la Chaudière received 377 casualties from their attack on Carpiquet, including 132 dead. Further operations to capture the hangars and barracks at the airfield were postponed. (*NARA*)

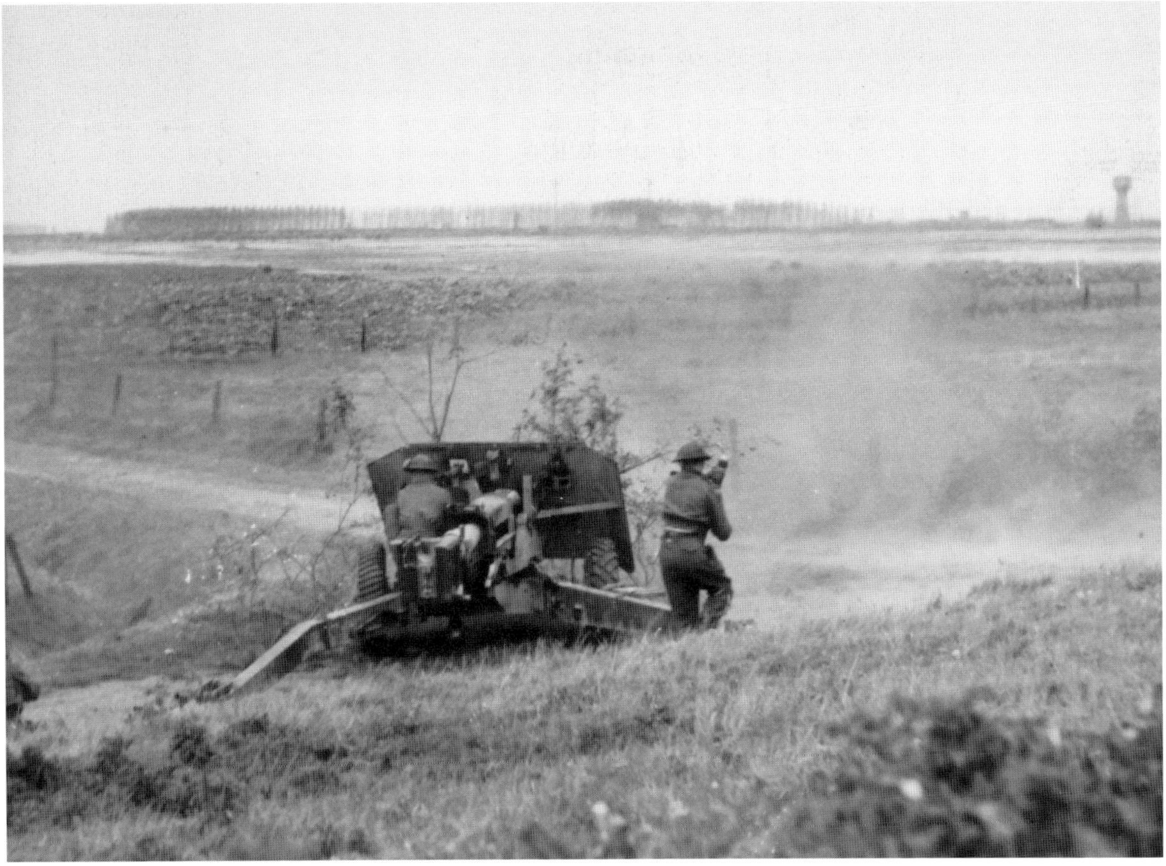

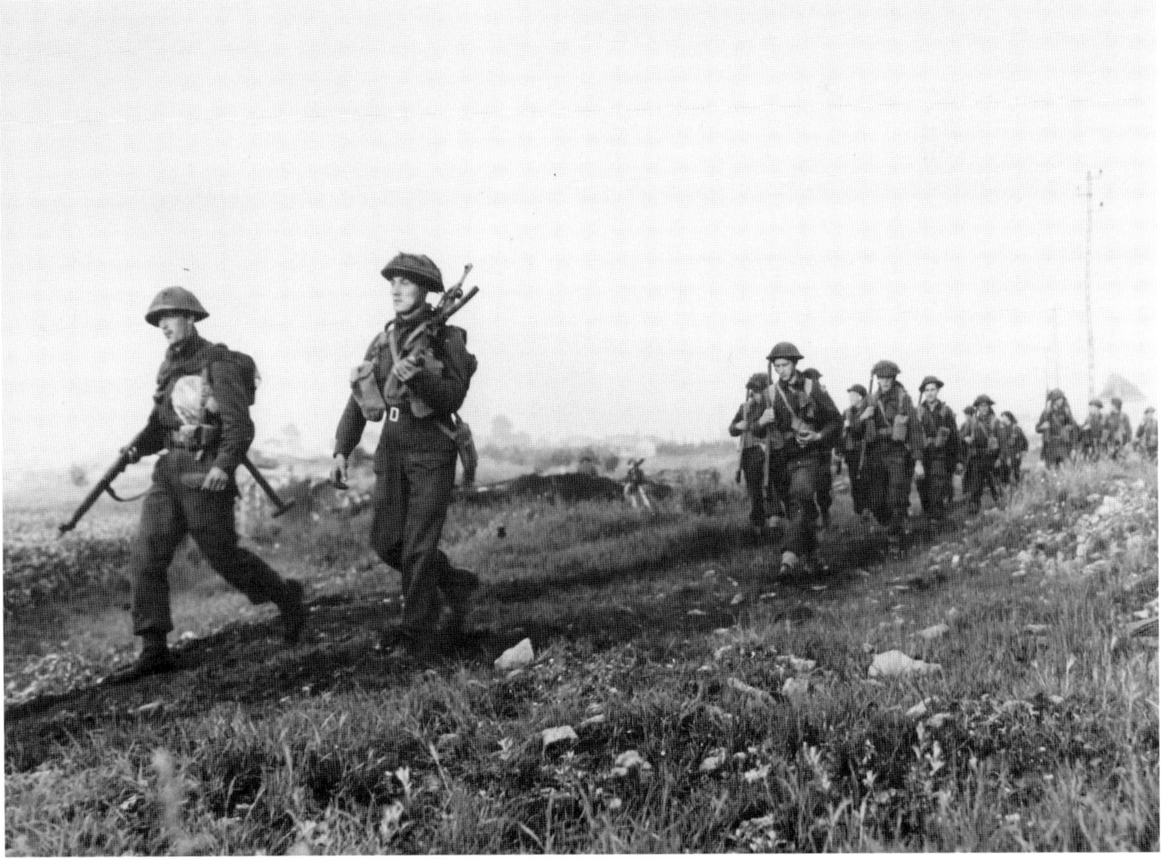

A British Second Army Cromwell 'Cruiser Tank Mk 8' raises a cloud of dust as it advances through a Normandy village in June 1944. The Cromwell was the successor to the British Crusader but did not enter service until 1944 and by then it was completely outclassed by the Panzer V (Panther). The Cromwell took a crew of five, with one 75mm turret gun and two 7.9mm Besa MGs. At Villers-Bocage on 12 June, elements of the British 7th Armoured Division swung wide across the American sector and then through a gap in the Nazi lines between Villers-Bocage and Caumont. During the morning hours of 13 June, tanks and carriers of the 4th County of London Yeomanry and 1st Rifle Brigade drove up a slope away from the town and were ambushed by Panzer VI (Tiger) tanks, led by Panzer ace Michael Wittmann. The Panzer commander knocked out the leading carrier, which blocked the road in front of the column. Wittmann then proceeded down the road towards Villers-Bocage destroying each tank and vehicle he encountered. Cromwell tanks of the British 22nd Armoured Brigade fired their 75mm shells, which bounced off the Tigers' armour. The advance of an entire British armoured division was halted within 30 minutes. *(NARA)*

A Canadian infantryman cautiously moves past a burning M4 medium tank in St Lambert, 19 August 1944. In the closing weeks of August, a critical factor for the Allies was blocking the German Army's escape. As the Americans stood at Argentan, the Canadian armour moved south towards Trun with a degree of sluggishness. The Canadian 4th Armoured Division reached Louvières, 2 miles north of Trun, on the evening of 17 August after delays caused by traffic getting jammed in the narrow streets. On that day Montgomery spoke to Crerar, reminding him how essential it was that both armoured divisions of II Canadian Corps seal the 'Pocket' between First Canadian Army and US Third Army. Montgomery gave orders that the 1st Polish Armoured Division should move past Trun to Chambois at all costs, with great speed. On 19 August, Simonds spoke to his four divisional commanders at the 4th Armoured Division's HQ emphasizing that no Germans should escape the Pocket.

There was a fierce battle on 19 August in the village of St Lambert, where two Canadian infantry companies fought all morning against elements of the Nazi 3rd Parachute Division. The Canadians gained a foothold in the village but were unable to move further. However, Canadian units managed to block German attempts to escape through Trun. On the evening of 19 August, Polish and American units met in Chambois though still the Pocket was not fully closed. *(NARA)*

(**Above**) A British M4 medium tank of the British 4th Armoured Brigade with its DD skirts up passes Universal Carrier of the King's Own Scottish Borderers (KOSB). M4 medium tanks of independent armoured divisions and armoured brigades were primarily intended to function as close support for the infantry. As the campaign progressed, Anglo-Canadian infantry increasingly took to riding into the battlefield and 'de-bussed' when within range of the enemy. Universal Carriers, produced by Vickers-Armstrong and sometimes referred to as 'Bren' Carriers because of their LMG armament, were issued to support companies in infantry rifle battalions for carrying support weapons and increased threefold in number from 1940 to1943. (NARA)

(**Opposite**) An AVRE of the British 79th Armoured Division, RE, carries wooden fascines to quickly span an enemy AT ditch for more rapid crossing. Thanks to the military foresight and creativity of MG Percy Hobart, CG British 79th Armoured Division, RE, a variety of speciality armoured vehicles arrived during the Normandy invasion. These included DD tanks that, under the right surf and tide conditions, could swim ashore; 'Crocodiles' and 'Wasps' – Churchill I tanks and Universal Carriers turned into tracked flamethrowers, respectively; 'Crabs and Scorpions' – flail tanks fitted with heavy chains on a rotating cylinder that cleared minefields; 'Bobbins' – tanks that rolled out a reinforced canvas road to drive on as they moved forward; and 'Armoured Ramp Carriers' (ARKs) – tanks that carried deployable ramps instead of turrets, as well as other variants. (NARA)

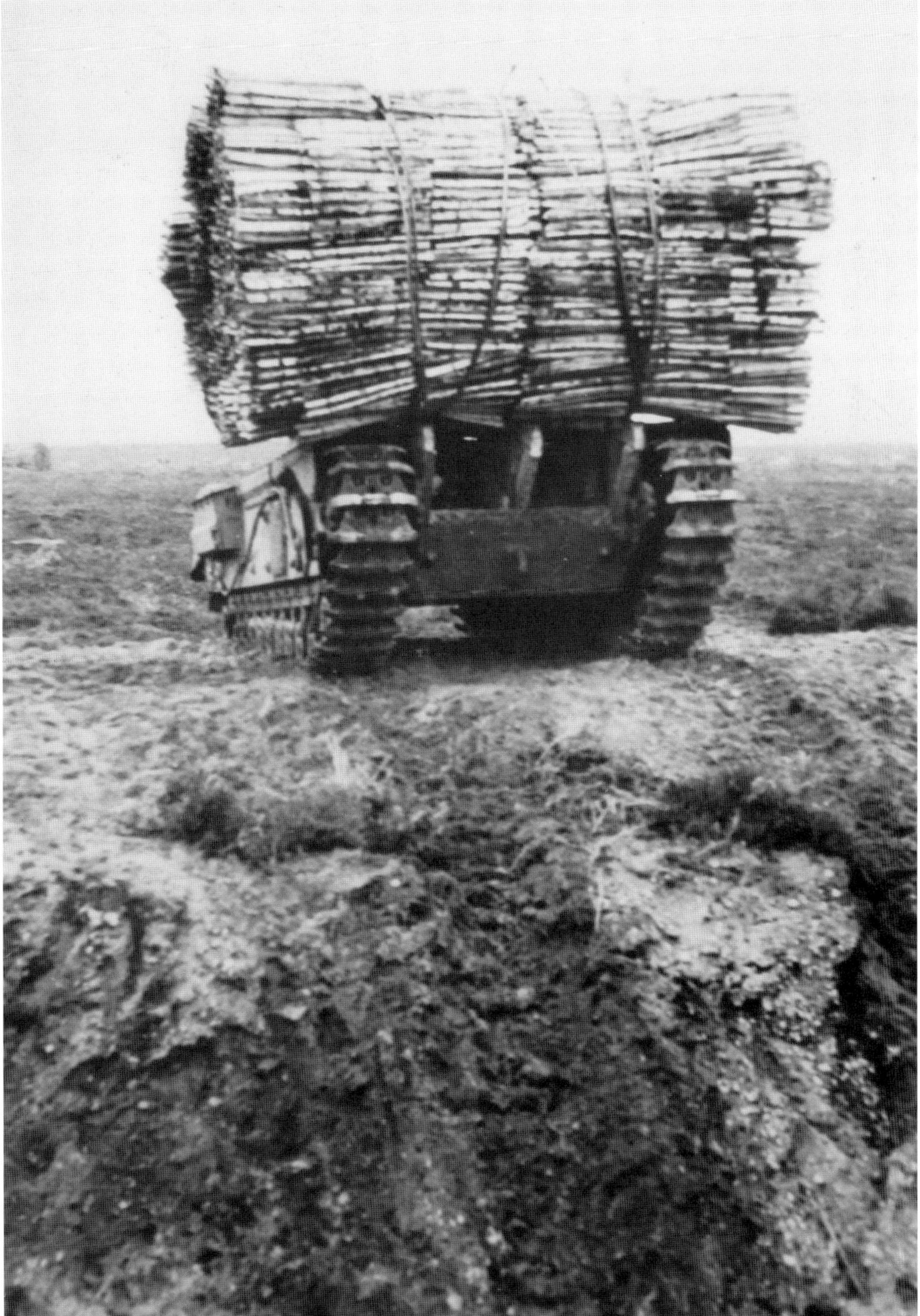

A British flamethrower mounted to a Universal Carrier, known as a Wasp Mk I. The flame nozzle was in the front of the vehicle and the two fuel tanks inside. Wasps were eventually used in infantry Carrier Platoons, and the first vehicles were ready for action in June 1944. Lightweight armour, open-topped design, and relatively low range of the flame equipment made it vulnerable to mines and AT weapons. Here the Wasp spews its flammable stream onto a German fortified position in Normandy. *(NARA)*

A 17-pounder self-propelled Achilles TD of an RA AT Regiment fires on a German pillbox. The British variant of the US M10 3in GMC TD, the Achilles was armed with the British Ordnance QF 17-pounder high-velocity 3in AT gun in place of the M10 TD's less powerful 3in M7 gun. Over a thousand M10s were converted to the Achilles, making it the most numerous AFV to carry the 17-pounder gun following the M4 Sherman 'Firefly' tank. In addition to its open turret gun, it had a 0.5in calibre and a 0.303in calibre MG. It had a crew of five and an operational range of almost 200 miles with a maximum speed of 32 miles per hour. These tanks went ashore on 6 June 1944, equipping units of the RA and Royal Canadian Artillery. *(NARA)*

Canadian infantrymen examine German 4ft-thick outer and 3ft inner reinforced concrete strongpoints at Carpiquet Airfield after its capture. On 8/9 July 1944, the opening of Operation *Charnwood* bombed and shelled the northern outskirts of Caen. The city of Caen was turned into a mass of rubble. On 8 July, the Canadians attacked the villages of Buron and Gruchy, where they had been defeated a month earlier. Throughout the day, the Canadian 3rd Division pressed the 12th SS-Panzer Division *Hitlerjugend*, then moving south against Authie and Franqueville before joining with the troops in Carpiquet. Moving eastwards, the Canadians attacked Ardenne Abbey, the site of a *Waffen* SS massacre of Canadian POWs by elements of the 25th SS-*Panzergrenadier* Regiment. The Regina Rifles advanced during darkness and as the abbey was pounded by artillery the SS troops withdrew into Caen, abandoning the hangars on the eastern side of Carpiquet Airfield. (*NARA*)

(**Above**) Two Churchill Mk IV Infantry Tanks were modified as AVREs with their turret weapon a 29mm spigot mortar or 'Petard' that fired a 40-pound warhead with a practical range of 150 yards. 'Petard' is a sixteenth-century word of French origin describing a 'bomb to breach'. This AVRE tank version dealt with many fortifications of the Atlantic Wall which had been missed by Allied aerial or naval bombardment. The spigot mortar is clearly visible in the turret as the tank passes a British soldier leaning against a truck at a village roadside. The spigot mortar was specially designed to fit the existing mantlet of either 6-pounder (57mm) or 75mm gun-armed Churchill I tanks. During inland combat, its purpose was to clear concrete bunkers and all kinds of enemy fortifications and obstacles. (*NARA*)

(**Opposite, above**) Canadian gunners ready their 5.5in medium gun for firing, south of Caen in late July 1944, in temporal concert with Montgomery's new offensive, Operation *Bluecoat*. This gun is firing in support of II Canadian Corps, combating the remnants of elite German panzer forces on the Caen–Falaise road. It fired a 45kg 5.5in shell to a maximum range of about 15,000 metres, and was more effective against dug-in German fortifications. Each medium artillery regiment, a corps level asset, had sixteen of these guns and used them to supplement the infantry divisions' own field regiments of 25-pounders. (*NARA*)

(**Opposite, below**) British 2nd Army's Guards Armoured Division's No. 4 Company, 1st Welsh Guards of the 32nd Guards Brigade are shown spotting German 21st and 12th SS-Panzer *Hitlerjugend* Divisions' positions near Cagny, on 19 July 1944, during Operation *Goodwood* to capture ground southeast of Caen. The Company Commander, Major J.D.A. Syrett is seen indicating a mortar target to Sergeant Veysey. Guardsman Fenwick holds the Bren gun (*to the major's left*), while Guardsman Kitchen is the first soldier in the foreground. Major Syrett was killed a few days later on 22 July. A dispatch rider stands near his motorcycle on the right. (*Author's collection*)

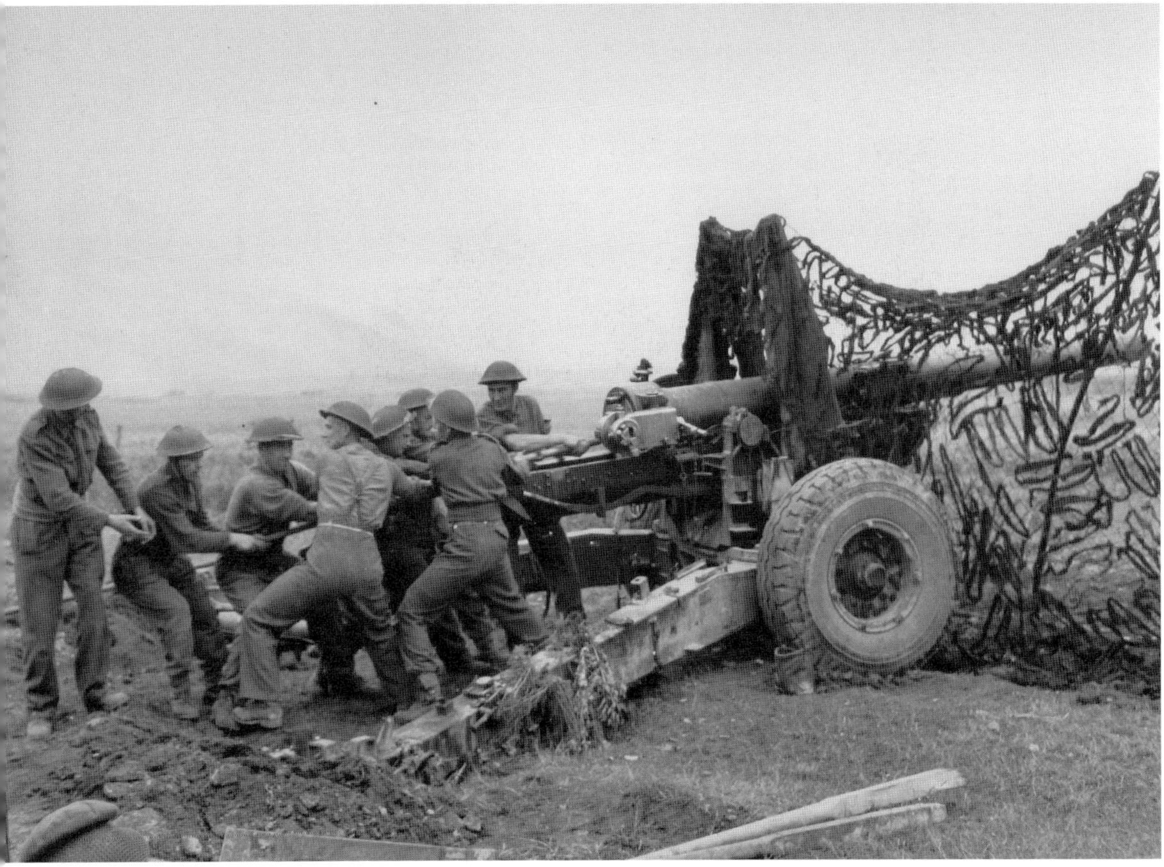

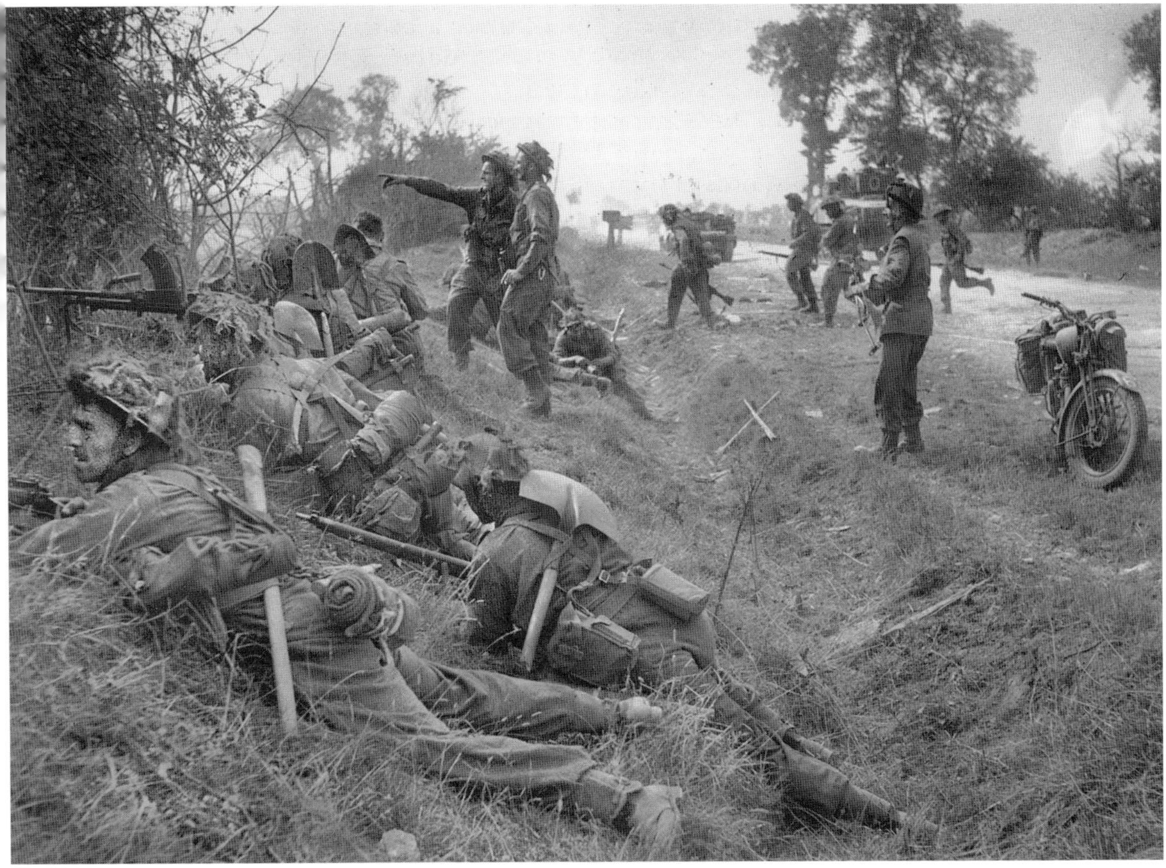

A British sapper searches for mines by a destroyed Universal Carrier in Tilly-sur-Seulles during Operation *Perch*, which took place from 7 to 14 June 1944, one of Montgomery's earliest attempts to capture Caen with his Anglo-Canadian forces. The plan was to encircle and seize Caen with a British XXX Corps advance to the southeast of the city. After a lack of Allied success, the operation was expanded to include British I Corps in a pincer attack on the town. On 11 June, XXX Corps in the west advanced south to Tilly-sur-Seulles, which was defended by the Panzer *Lehr* Division. The Normandy village was repeatedly captured and re-captured, changing hands no fewer than 23 times. I Corps' movement was delayed due to attacks by the 21st Panzer Division. With no major breakthrough, a persistent German defence, and mounting British casualties, Operation *Perch*'s offensive east of Caen was terminated on 13 June. (NARA)

A Canadian mortar section direction crew in a Normandy village spot where rounds are falling and relay the information to the firing crews in the rear via a field telephone. The 3in mortar was the standard used by Canadian infantry battalions. The weapons were grouped into a Mortar Platoon, first as part of HQ Company and from 1942 as part of Support Company. Six 3in mortars comprised an infantry battalion commander's artillery. Transportation was usually done by a Universal Carrier, on which sixty-six bombs could also be carried. The mortar fired HE and smoke rounds and generally had a minimum crew of three. (NARA)

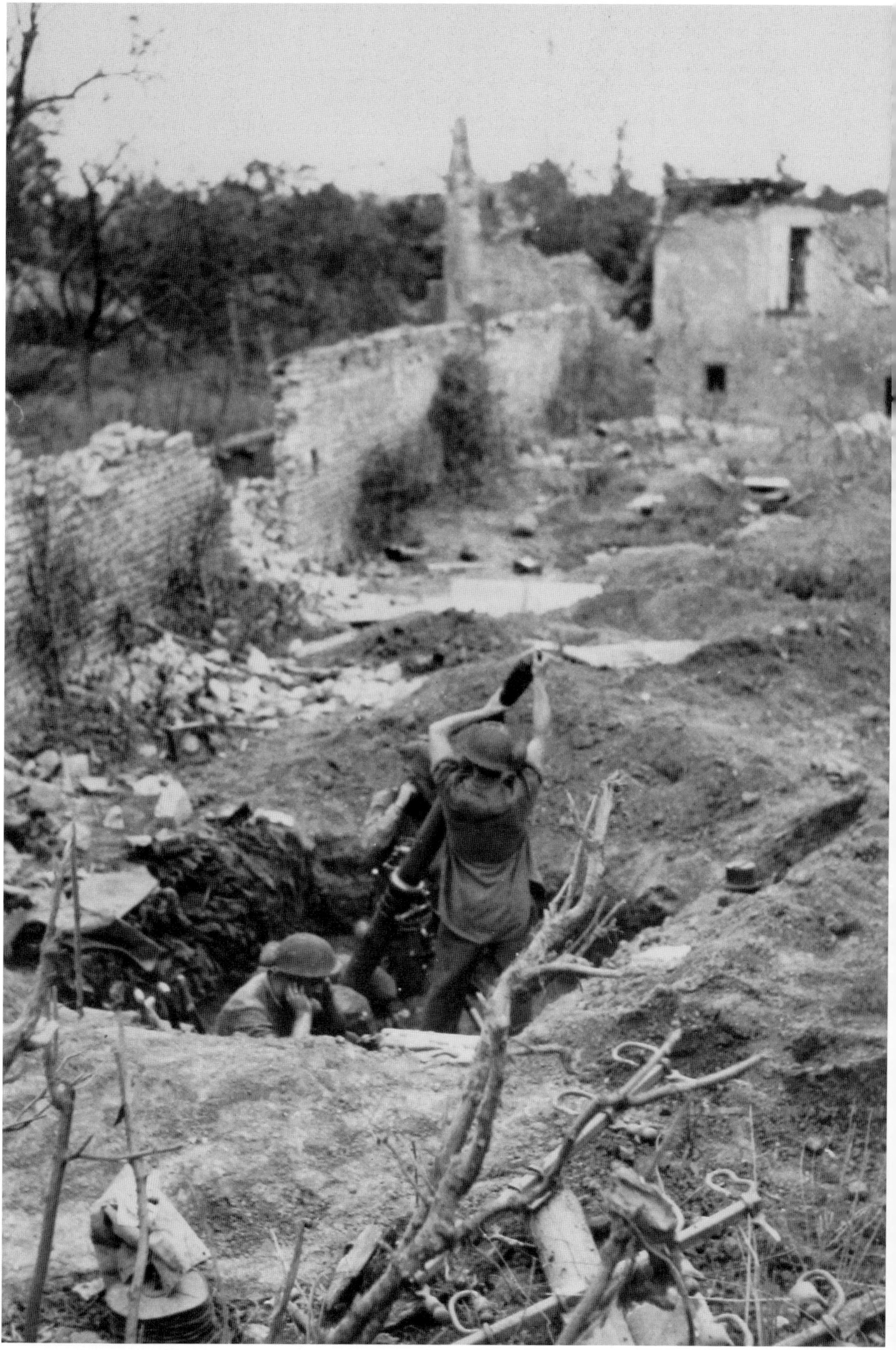

(**Opposite**) A Canadian 4.2in mortar fires at Nazis a short distance away defending Verriéres Ridge from a pit amid ruins of a French farmyard. On 25 July 1944, Canadian First Army CG Crerar launched Operation *Spring*, coinciding with Bradley's Operation *Cobra* to the west. A week earlier, Operation *Goodwood* had started and ended abruptly just two days later, when Dempsey's British VIII Corps' armoured forces, under O'Connor, slammed into the German-controlled Verriéres-Bourguebus Ridge, 5 miles south of Caen. However, a small rent did appear in the German line at the westernmost end of the feature, Verrières Ridge. The II Canadian Corps CG, LG Guy Simonds, called for the capture of the Ridge in order to outflank the 1st SS-Panzer Division. However, on the morning of 25 July, the two lead infantry divisions in Simonds's Corps suffered 1,500 casualties, including 500 dead. One-fifth of the casualties came from just one battalion of the Black Watch (Royal Highland Regiment) of Canada. (*NARA*)

(**Above**) Canadian soldiers aim their Projector, Infantry, Anti-Tank (PIAT) weapon at the enemy in Normandy. This spring-loaded weapon based on the spigot mortar system projected a 2.5-pound shaped charge using a cartridge in the tail of the projector. It came into service during the Tunisian campaign of 1943 and had an effective range of 115 yards in a direct fire AT role, and 350 yards in an indirect role. The PIAT was able to penetrate 4 inches of armour with the force of a 75mm gun. It weighed 33lb and could be brought into action within seconds. For most German tanks in Normandy though, the PIAT gunner had to manoeuvre to get a side or rear shot from close range. An after-action analysis of the Normandy Campaign found that 7 per cent of all German tanks were knocked out by PIATs, compared to 6 per cent by rockets fired from aircraft. (*NARA*)

(**Above**) A German Panzer V Ausf.A Panther tank, stopped by Canadian troops armed with PIAT rocket launcher and hand grenades. As early as 8 June 1944, elements of the German 26th SS-Panzer Regiment of the 12th SS-Panzer Division *Hitlerjugend* drove from Rots in the east along the Caen–Bayeux road, in a left flanking attack against the Regina Rifles at Norrey and Cardonville, and the Royal Winnipeg Rifles and Canadian Scottish at Putot. About midnight, German tanks came to within 300 yards of the HQ. Two Panzer V Panthers came into view and this German tank was hit by a PIAT round fired from behind a stone wall at a range of 15 yards. Another PIAT projectile crashed into it after the panzer continued to advance another 30 yards. The German tank stopped and backed up, but was hit again by another PIAT round and spun out of control only to be hit by a torrent of Canadian hand grenades, causing the crew to abandon the tank. (*NARA*)

(**Opposite**) A Canadian infantryman of the Royal Regina Rifles, 7th Infantry Brigade comprising Canadian 3rd Infantry Division, is shown holding a captured German *Maschinenpistole* (MP) 40 ('Schmeisser') 9mm Parabellum SMG with its stock folded, during house-to-house combat in Caen on 10 July 1944. The MP 40 had a rate of fire of 500–550 rounds per minute with an effective firing range of 100–200 metres. It usually had a 32-round detachable box magazine. It was often called the 'Schmeisser' by the Allies, after Hugo Schmeisser, who had designed the MP 18 but not the MP 40.

The Regina Rifles landed on Juno Beach on 6 June 1944 at Courseulles-sur-Mer, the most heavily fortified enemy position that Canadian troops would face on D-Day – they suffered over 100 casualties, including two company commanders killed. The Regina Rifles became the first and only unit of the Allied invasion force to reach and hold its final 6 June objective, the high ground on the Caen–Bayeux road at Bretteville l'Orgueilleuse. (*NARA*)

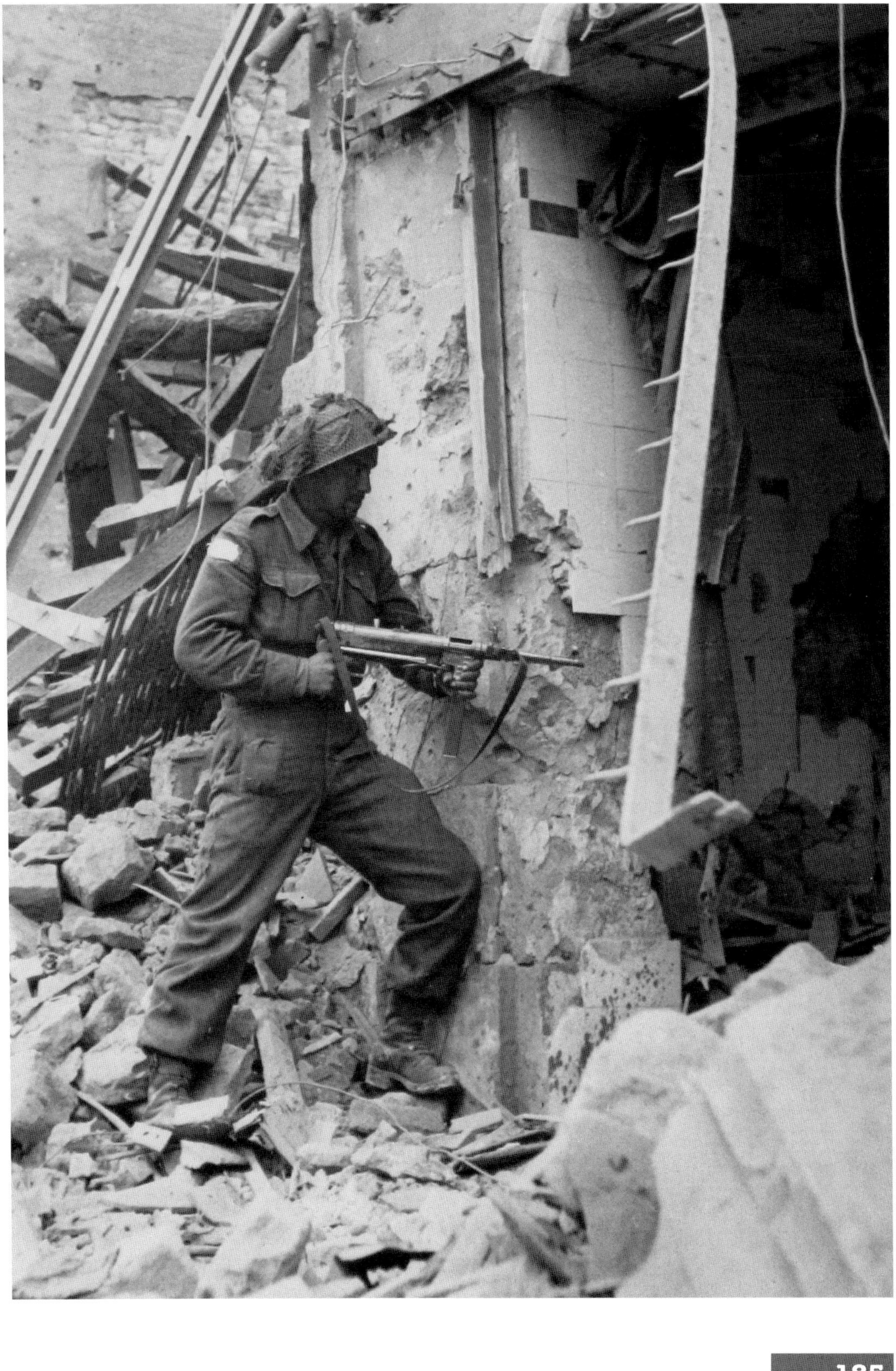

Canadian infantrymen of the Royal Regina Rifles are involved in heavy street fighting in Caen, 9 July 1944. Operation *Charnwood*, on 8/9 July 1944, unleashed heavy Allied bomber raids on the northern outskirts of Caen. This was followed by the three Canadian infantry divisions attacking the city en masse; it was reduced to rubble, with large areas completely obliterated, which tanks and infantry had to negotiate. Canadian 3rd Division fought fiercely on the western side of Caen to enter the city. This was an area that had previously been given up to 12th SS-Panzer Division *Hitlerjugend* in June. Now the Regina Rifles were ordered to take Ardenne Abbey, the HQ of SS MG Kurt Meyer's 25th SS-*Panzergrenadier* Regiment. After intense night combat with accompanying Canadian armour the abbey fell, with extremely high Canadian casualties, and the Nazis withdrew into Caen in a southeastwards direction. One Canadian battalion suffered 11 officers and other ranks casualties, 36 of them fatal. The capture of the abbey by the Regina Rifles helped pierce the defences of Caen. On 9 July, advance units of the Regina Rifles followed the Germans into the city and engaged in house-to-house fighting amid the widespread debris of destroyed buildings and obstructed streets, which initially precluded the use of armour. On 10 July, bulldozers and engineers cleared some paths through, allowing M4s from the Canadian 2nd Armoured Brigade access to the street combat. (*NARA*)

A Canadian 6-pounder AT gun of the II Canadian Corps is towed by a Loyd Carrier tracked vehicle with its crew south down the Caen–Falaise road on 21 August 1944. The Loyd Carrier was named after its designer, Captain Vivian Loyd, in the late 1930s. Its upper hull was enclosed at the sides and front but was open at the rear without a roof. There was an option to attach a canvas roof to protect the occupants from the elements, which was supported by a three-piece framework. A single Bren LMG was sometimes carried for defensive purposes. The Ford V8 engine was located centrally in a box-like structure at the rear of the Carrier, with the radiator behind it (as seen between the two soldiers at the back). Passage into the crew compartment could be accessed on each side of the engine. The Tracked Towing (TT) type was the most produced variant of the vehicle and it was predominantly used to tow heavy armament such as the Ordnance ML 4.2in Mortar and the Ordnance QF 2- and 6-pounder AT guns, as well as carrying their respective crews. It was equipped with four seats for the gun crew. From 6 June 1944 onwards, the Loyd Carriers were in action throughout Normandy, towing 6-pounders from battlefield to battlefield.

The Canadians used Loyd Carriers far more commonly than the Universal Carrier for towing purposes, although the Universal Carrier with its more sophisticated steering mechanism holds the record for the most produced armoured vehicle, with 113,000 built by Vickers-Armstrong. Universal Carriers were usually used for transporting personnel and equipment, mostly support weapons, or as MG platforms. The 2nd and 3rd Canadian Infantry and 4th Canadian Armoured Division led the drive. To the east of the Canadians was the 1st Polish Armoured Division, while the British 53rd Infantry Division was to the Canadians' west, at the northern shoulder of the Falaise-Argentan Pocket. (*NARA*)

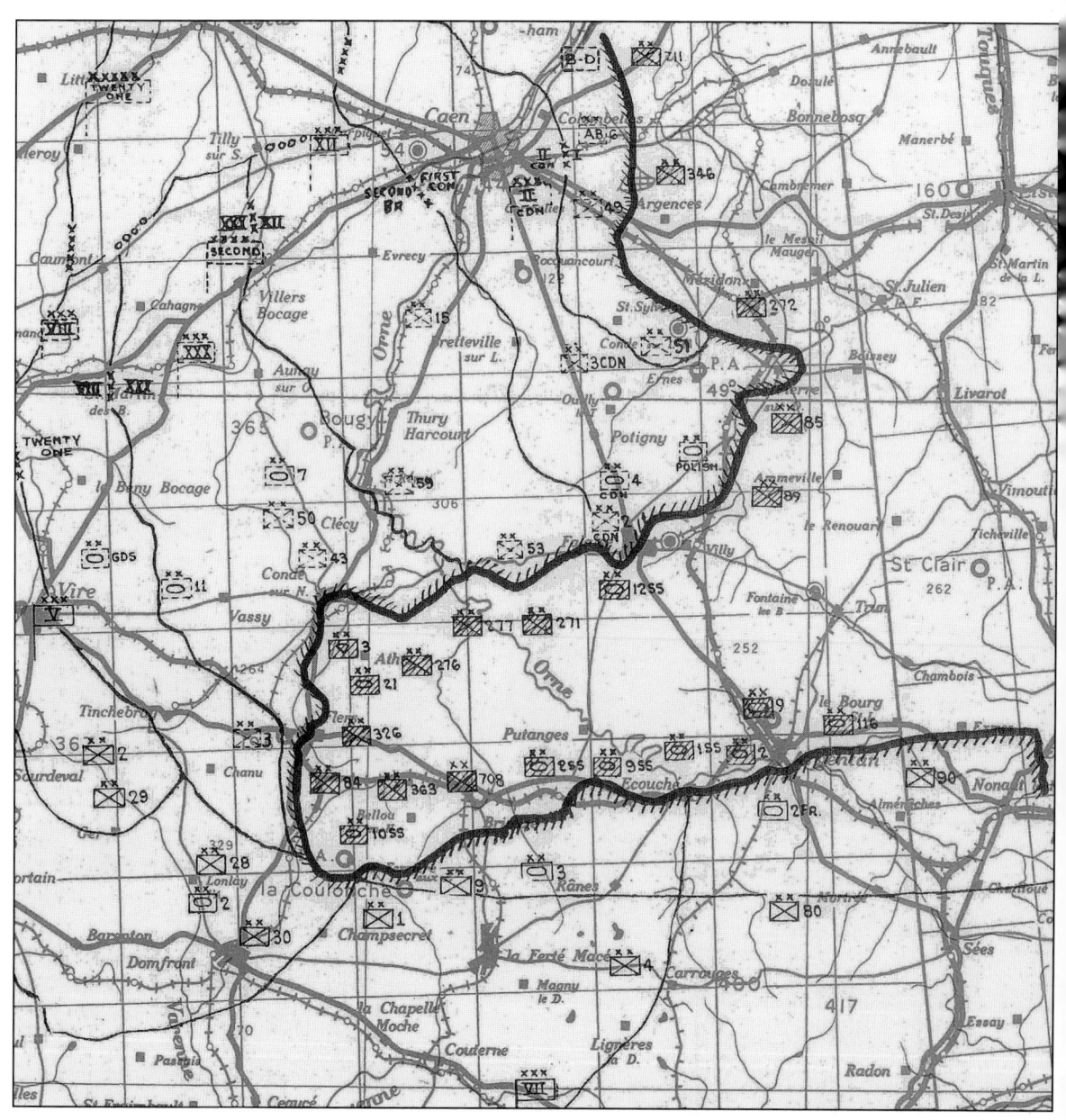

A US First Army HQ Situation Map at 2400 hours on 17 August 1944 demonstrating the Falaise-Argentan Pocket. Prior to that, on 4 August, the British established a new line running from the Orne river at Thury Harcourt (just east of Bougy) southwest through Vire, where US V Corps was situated. The new realignment enabled British XII Corps (HQ situated to the west of Caen near Carpiquet) to advance rapidly across the Orne south of Caen. On 7 August, Operation *Totalize* was launched by II Canadian Corps after heavy aerial bombardment of German defences south of Caen. The Canadians attacked along the line of the Caen–Falaise road but were stopped after three days of fighting with an ad hoc force from II SS-Panzer Corps. Also on 7 August, Operation *Lüttich*, the German counterattack Hitler ordered to capture Mortain and then Avranches, started but was almost immediately halted by the US VII Corps' 30th Infantry Division with few gains; it continued until 13 August without a breakthrough.

On 8 August, Patton's US Third Army liberated Le Mans and he moved his XV Corps (under MG Wade Haislip) northwards towards Argentan, arriving on 12 August at the southern end of the

Pocket east of Écouché and southeast of Falaise at the northern end of the Pocket. II Canadian Corps, comprised of the 2nd and 3rd Canadian Infantry and 4th Canadian Armoured Divisions, attacked towards Falaise down the Caen–Falaise road on 14 August, in Operation *Tractable*. After slow progress, Falaise was reached on 16 August. That day, Patton's forces liberated Orléans and they reached Chartres two days later. The US 79th Infantry Division, part of Patton's VIII Corps now, reached the Seine and seized a bridgehead across the river on 19 August at Mantes-Gassicourt.

The shrinking German escape route from the Falaise-Argentan Pocket was now confined to the area between Trun and Chambois along the Dives river, which ran parallel to the Orne to the west, just southwest of St Clair. Trun was captured by the Canadians moving southeast along the Falaise–Trun road on 18 August while the 1st Polish Armoured Division, to the east of the Canadians, seized Mont Ormel, overlooking the German escape route through the Dives river valley on a southeastward line from Trun to Chambois. The Polish tankers met the Americans in Chambois on 19 August in an attempt to seal the Pocket; however, insufficient troop strength prevented a complete closure. Fighting continued among escaping Germans fleeing eastward and the Polish 1st Armoured Division on Mont Ormel on 19/20 August. The Poles, resupplied by Allied aerial drops, fought off retreating II SS-Panzer Corps counterattacks that were trying to keep the eastern end of the Pocket open. By 21 August, the gap between Trun and Chambois was finally closed by additional Allied troops. No other German troops were able to escape. (NARA)

(**Below**) Two Canadian soldiers with their helmets camouflaged are shown reading a road sign indicating the direction of Caen, where they had been in brutal combat with the Nazis from 6 June to 19 July 1944. Their next destination was a drive south down the Caen–Falaise road, the Canadian 2nd and 3rd Infantry Divisions and the Canadian 4th Armoured Division against the northern end of what would become the Falaise-Argentan Pocket. (NARA)

An M4 medium tank of the Canadian 4th Armoured Division moves south along the Caen–Falaise road, part of II Canadian Corps' advance after the fall of Caen on 19 June 1944. By 8 August, the Canadians had penetrated the German defences for 3 miles, but then the attack bogged down. Crerar's 1st Canadian Army committed two more divisions that were not battle-tested and the Canadians gained 5 more miles before the advance came to a complete stop 8 miles from Falaise. Bradley's new strategic plan of 8 August entailed the US First and Third Armies wheeling and driving north towards the army group boundary, specifically the towns of Flers, which would comprise the western end of a 'pocket', and Argentan, at the eastern end. Since both towns were within Montgomery's 21st Army Group zone, the Americans would stop just short of the east–west line of Flers–Argentan, where they would form the southern shoulder of the pocket and, with the Anglo-Canadian forces creating the northern shoulder, a trap would catch the Germans in-between. Bradley ordered Patton to direct Haislip's XV Corps, which was securing Le Mans, to the north towards Argentan. *(NARA)*

Massed Anglo-Canadian armoured forces are seen here, moving into action south of Caen towards Falaise on 8 August 1944. The terrain was much more suitable for mechanized warfare than the *bocage* of western Normandy and the villages surrounding the city of Caen. The tank in the foreground is a Cromwell, a Cruiser Tank Mk 8. On 11 August, US Third Army's XV Corps under Haislip moved as ordered from Le Mans toward Alençon, both south of Argentan. FM von Kluge, C-in-C West, knew he was threatened with a double envelopment.

Also on 11 August, Montgomery realized that the bulk of the German forces in Normandy were west of the north–south line that ran from Caen through Falaise and Argentan, and then southwards to Alençon and Le Mans. As the Canadians attacked south towards Falaise and US XV Corps attacked north towards Alençon and then Argentan, the gap through which all German supplies and reinforcements arrived would become precariously narrow. Allied occupation of Falaise and Argentan would limit the opening of this gap, giving the Germans only one major highway for their movements, the road through Flers–Écouché–Argentan, from west to east along the southern part of the Falaise-Argentan Pocket. The Germans were well aware that if the Canadians reached Falaise and the Americans took Argentan these two Allied forces would be only 15 miles apart, a short gap keeping the German Army in Normandy from complete encirclement. On 13 August, Haislip received orders from Bradley and Patton to stop his offensive on Argentan and take up blocking positions while awaiting further orders. At this time, with the Canadians several miles north of Falaise and the Americans several miles south of Argentan, less than 25 miles separated them. (*NARA*)

(**Above**) Canadian armoured cars pass a disabled German SPA on the road from Caen to Falaise in early August 1944. The vehicle in the lead is either a British Humber Mk III or a Canadian 'Fox', one of the most important Anglo-Canadian armoured cars of the Second World War, a total of 5,400 being produced. It had one 37mm M5/M6 gun or one Ordnance QF 2-pounder 40mm gun and one 7.92 Besa MG, and a crew of three or four depending on which mark it was. Mk III had a three-seater turret and could accommodate a crew of commander, driver, gunner, and radio operator. Like most British-produced armoured cars, the Humber was rugged, reliable and operationally sound. The Canadians produced a vehicle identical to the Humber Mk III called the Fox.

Behind the Humber armoured car is a Humber Mk IIIA light reconnaissance car (LRC) that was used to gather intelligence by Royal Canadian Engineers' field squadrons and companies, as well as Royal Canadian Army Service Corps bridging companies for short special reconnaissance missions and for motor transport. The LRC was also used in the Armoured Car Squadrons of the RAF Regiment in northwest Europe It typically had a crew of three and its four-wheel drive gave it off-road capability. As for armament, it had one 7.92mm semi-enclosed Bren II MG, situated within a rear top swivel turret that had 8mm of armour on three of its sides, a 4in smoke discharger for concealment, situated at the left front side where the windscreen in a normal vehicle would be, and sometimes an antiquated Boys AT rifle coming out of the same port as the smoke discharger. (*NARA*)

(**Opposite, above**) A French MP directs an M4 medium tank of a French 2nd Armoured Division mechanized convoy in Écouché towards the Falaise-Argentan Pocket. On 12 August 1944, the 2nd Armoured Division, commanded by General Philippe Leclerc, began its advance northwards in the direction of Écouché to participate in the closure of the Pocket in which 110,000 Germans were trapped west of Falaise. On 13 August, the 501st Battle Tank Regiment began the infiltration of Écouché without preparatory artillery bombardment, both for surprise and to limit French civilian casualties. In the centre of Écouché, the French reconnaissance unit discovered a column of the German 116th Panzer Regiment of the 2nd SS-Panzer Division *Das Reich*, which was engaged with heavy enemy losses. However, several Nazis managed to escape, covered by the action of a Panzer V Panther tank that maintained the high ground and delayed a French advance for a whole week. On 20 August, the Pocket was closed at Hill 262, located northeast of Chambois, and most of the German soldiers within it surrendered to the Allies. (*NARA*)

(**Below**) An M4 medium tank of the French 2nd Armoured Division, under the command of General Philippe Leclerc, leads a Loyd Carrier towing a 6-pounder on the outskirts of Écouché, which was located at the southern shoulder of the Falaise-Argentan Pocket on the Orne river, to the west of Argentan. American divisions in the vicinity supporting the French armoured drive into Écouché were the 80th and 90th Infantry Divisions to the south and east, respectively. (*NARA*)

(**Above**) An M4 'Firefly' of B Squadron, 10th Armoured Cavalry Brigade of the 1st Polish Armoured Division at the start of Operation *Totalize*. The line of tanks are waiting to be called forward to support the attack of the British 51st Highland Division, south of Caen on 8 August 1944. The censored marking on the left of the tank's hull next to the unit marker 51 was 'PL' an abbreviation of Polish Lancers or the historical designation 'Winged Hussar'. The Firefly was fitted with a powerful 17-pounder gun which gave this M4 variant a capable edge in knocking out heavily-armoured Panzer VI Tiger and Panzer V Panther tanks. In Montgomery's armoured units, there was one Firefly per troop of four tanks. However, it had the unenviable reputation of tending to burst into flames when hit. (*NARA*)

(**Opposite, above**) Canadian M4 medium tanks rendezvous at the northern end of the Falaise-Argentan Pocket during late July's Operation *Spring*. An M4 Sherman flail tank or 'Crab' (*left foreground*) is about to clear a path on the dirt track beneath one of the undulating hills that alternated with flat plain in this region south of Caen. MG Percy Hobart requested that this specialized tank go into full production. A mine flail is a vehicle-mounted device that makes a safe path through a minefield by deliberately detonating land mines in front of the vehicle that carries it. The flail consists of a number of heavy chains ending in fist-sized steel balls attached to a horizontal, rapidly rotating rotor which is mounted on two arms at the front of the armoured vehicle. The rotor causes the flails to spin wildly and pound the ground violently. The force of a flail strike above a buried mine mimics the weight of a person or vehicle and causes the mine to detonate, but in a manner that did little damage to the flails or the tank. 'Scorpion' tanks were 'Matilda' II tanks fitted with a flail that operated in the Second Battle of El Alamein in October 1942. Churchill Infantry tank flails were used in northwest Europe, notably at Arnhem in 1945 when the Dutch city was occupied by Allied forces. (*NARA*)

(**Below**) A British infantry column and three Universal Carriers move though Vassy, between Villers-Bocage to the north and Domfront to the south, just outside the closed western end of the Falaise-Argentan Pocket, on 15 August 1944. British formations in the vicinity included the 11th Armoured Division and the 43rd (Wessex) Infantry Division's 4th Battalion King's Shropshire Light Infantry (KSLI). Vassy was taken by the 11th Armoured Division's 159th Brigade. (*NARA*)

Canadian infantrymen in Falaise have been stopped by snipers and wait behind cover of walls for an M4 medium tank to ferret the Germans out. A wounded Canadian soldier is being tended to the right of the tank's rear. It was difficult for Allied armour to negotiate some of the narrow Normandy town streets and lanes. Within the Falaise-Argentan Pocket, the II Canadian Corps was pitted against SS-*Obergruppenführer* (Colonel General) Josef 'Sepp' Dietrich's Fifth Panzer Army, comprised of SS-Panzer Divisions.

The Canadians pushed south from Falaise on the night of 16/17 August 1944, after a heavy bombing raid by the RAF and while the Canadian forces moved into the northern outskirts of St Lambert the next day, heavy Canadian field artillery units were drawn up. When the Alberta Regiment of the 2nd Canadian Infantry Division started to advance into St Lambert, the Germans heavily counterattacked – with the capture of Trun, the German Army was now confined to only three escape routes with access to crossing points of the last natural obstacle to their escape, the river Dives, and the most northerly and best of these crossings ran through St Lambert. Although the town of Chambois, to the southeast of Trun, was occupied by the US 90th Infantry Division on 13 August, the Germans were anxious to keep possession of as much of it as the Americans, and the town was the focus of fierce combat until the Canadians finally fought their way down into the town, meeting the American forces there on 19 August. (*NARA*)

British troops of the 3rd Infantry Division, VIII Corps; comprised of the 1st Battalion Suffolk Regiment, 3rd Battalion Royal Northumberland Fusiliers Reconnaissance Regiment, and an M4 medium tank of the British 11th Armoured Division liberate Flers on 16 August 1944. Approximately 80 per cent of the town had been destroyed by Allied bombing on 6–7 June to reduce the advance of German reinforcements to the beachhead. Flers is situated on a tributary of the Orne and was located at the western end of the Falaise-Argentan Pocket. The Germans had only one major road to escape through the Pocket, on a line of Flers–Écouché–Argentan. *(NARA)*

US XV Corps troops of the 318th IR, 80th Infantry Division in Patton's Third Army enter Argentan on 20 August 1944. A huge American flag was hoisted on that day in the presence of Colonel Harry Mac, commander of the 318th IR. On 8 August, Bradley had ordered Patton to turn Haislip's XV Corps, which was securing Le Mans, to the north toward Alençon and, eventually, Argentan since the Allied commanders were confident that Collins's VII Corps would hold at Mortain. On 11 August, XV Corps swerved toward Alençon between Le Mans to the south and Argentan to the north. When Haislip reached the vicinity of Argentan on 13 August, he ran into firm German positions there. He was preparing a stronger, coordinated attack to take Argentan, but received orders from Bradley and Patton to stop offensive operations and assume blocking positions while awaiting further orders from Bradley – who in turn was waiting for Montgomery to authorize the entrance of American units into the 21st Army Group area to avoid 'friendly fire' incidents. Montgomery wanted the Canadians to close the Falaise-Argentan Pocket from the north as the Canadians were ready to make a second attack on Falaise, and then beyond to Argentan.

The Canadians launched their attack on 14 August and with the 1st Polish Armoured Division they broke through German Fifth Panzer Army defences and advanced to within 3 miles of Falaise. With Haislip's troops idle south of Argentan, 15 miles still separated the converging Allied drives. Bradley, on 14 August, having waited 24 additional hours for Montgomery to let American forces cross the Anglo-Canadian 21st–US 12th Army Groups' boundary and drive north through Argentan to rendezvous with the Canadians and Poles, told Patton to have Haislip leave half of his XV Corps at Argentan and take the rest through Dreux, well to the east. The Canadians entered Falaise, which was reduced to rubble, on 16 August. Montgomery proposed now that the Canadians and Americans close the Pocket by meeting at Trun and Chambois, villages northeast of Argentan. On the night of 16 August, seven German corps were trapped in the Pocket. The shortest road distance from the westernmost point of the Pocket to the eastern point of escape, Flers to Trun, was 40 miles. (NARA)

A Cromwell tank of the Canadian 4th Armoured Division that moved south from Falaise converges with US XV Corps' 80th Division's infantry and motorized troops in Argentan, 20 August 1944. On 18 August, Canadian troops took Trun and threatened St Lambert. At the same time, the 1st Polish Armoured Division coming from the north and the Americans moving up from the south threatened to take Chambois – in doing so they would close the escape gap. The Allies took 50,000 prisoners and counted 10,000 German troops killed in action. Within the Pocket the roads and fields were littered with thousands of enemy dead and wounded, wrecked and burning vehicles and smashed artillery pieces, as well as dead animals decomposing in August's sweltering heat.

The other half of Haislip's XV Corps had reached Dreux on 16 August, and then ultimately Mantes-Gassicourt on the Seine, where they established a secure bridgehead on 19–20 August, when Haislip's 79th Infantry Divisions crossed the river. One regiment walked across a dam, another paddled across in small assault boats and rafts and a third regiment crossed over a treadway bridge that was constructed overnight. While Haislip quickly moved east and across the Seine with his troops, MG Leonard Gerow's V Corps HQ temporarily led the remainder of XV Corps at Argentan. *(NARA)*

Epilogue

British troops carry their river assault boat through a street in Vernon for the Seine river crossing by the 5th Battalion, Wiltshire Regiment and 4th Battalion, Somerset Light Infantry of XXX Corps' 43rd (Wessex) Division, on 25 August 1944. Once across, the 5th Wiltshires faced a counterattack by the Germans including three Panzer VI Tiger tanks of the 205th Heavy TB. From Rouen in the north to Paris further south, the Seine is 250 yards wide and all the bridges had been damaged previously by Allied air attacks to hinder enemy movements. British losses were 600 men over the four days of the Seine crossing at Vernon, with 1,600 Germans killed on the east bank. (NARA)

(**Above**) Another group for the Seine crossing included the 1st Battalion, Worcestershire Regiment, 214th Infantry Brigade, 43rd (Wessex) Division. They had travelled to Vernon in DUKWs and began assembling on the night of 24 August. In the photo, British troops from this unit cross a road bridge partially demolished by previous Allied air strikes at dawn on 26 August 1944. After climbing up a ladder to one end of the damaged bridge, the Worcesters crossed towards Vernonnet on the Seine's far bank, treading carefully on wooden planks laid down by engineers the previous night. Sappers then built a Class 40 Bailey Bridge and alongside it a Class 9 Pontoon Bridge. (NARA)

(**Opposite, above**) American soldiers of the Third Army's 5th Infantry Division in Walker's XX Corps follow an M10 3in GMC TD of the 818th TD Battalion, moving forward to Fontainebleau on 20 August 1944, in preparation for its Seine river crossing to the south of Paris. Fontainebleau was liberated on 23 August. XX Corps seized bridgeheads over the Seine at Melun, to the north of Fontainebleau, and at Montereau. (NARA)

(**Opposite, below**) American soldiers cross the Seine river on a pontoon ferry, 20 August 1944. On the night of 19 August, the first Third Army units reached the Seine, with elements of the US 79th Infantry Division, XV Corps (Haislip) crossing at Mantes-Gassicourt to establish a bridgehead. XX Corps (Walker) also reached Fontainebleau on 20 August for a later crossing. By 25 August, four Allied armies had reached the Seine. (NARA)

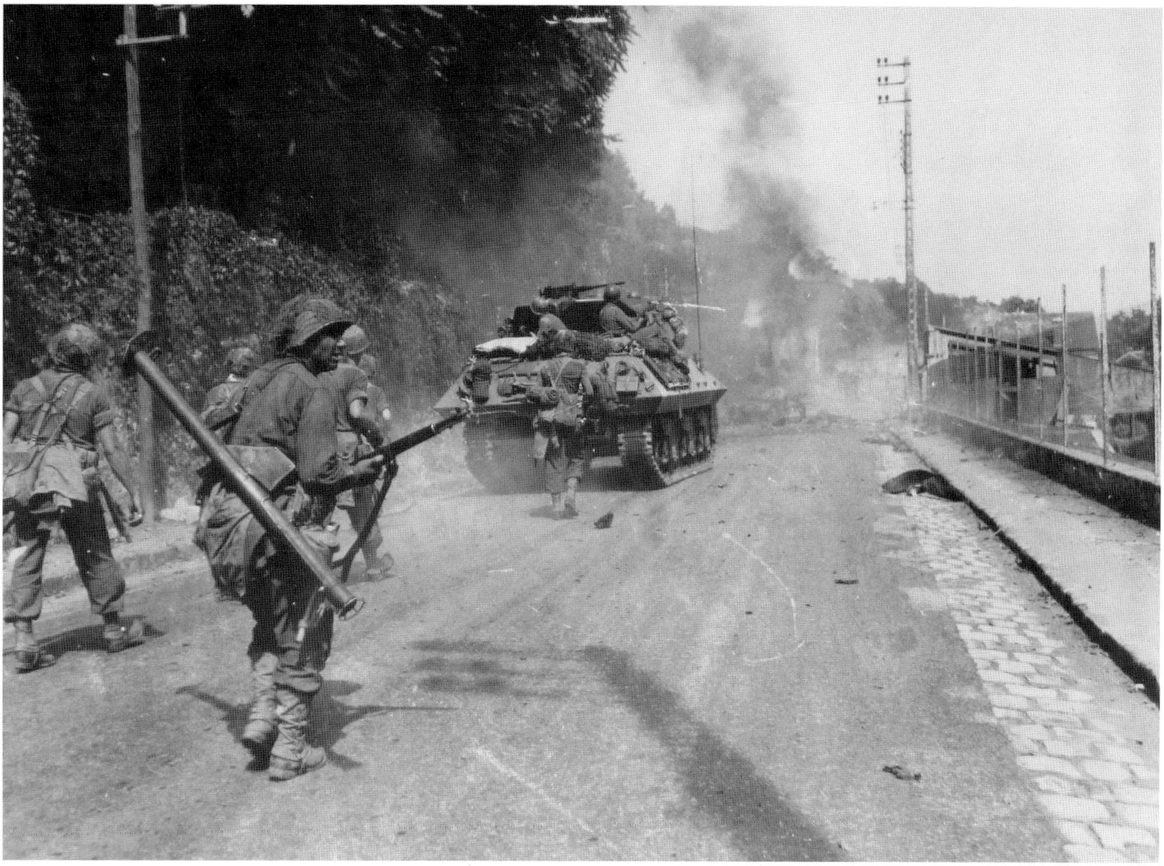

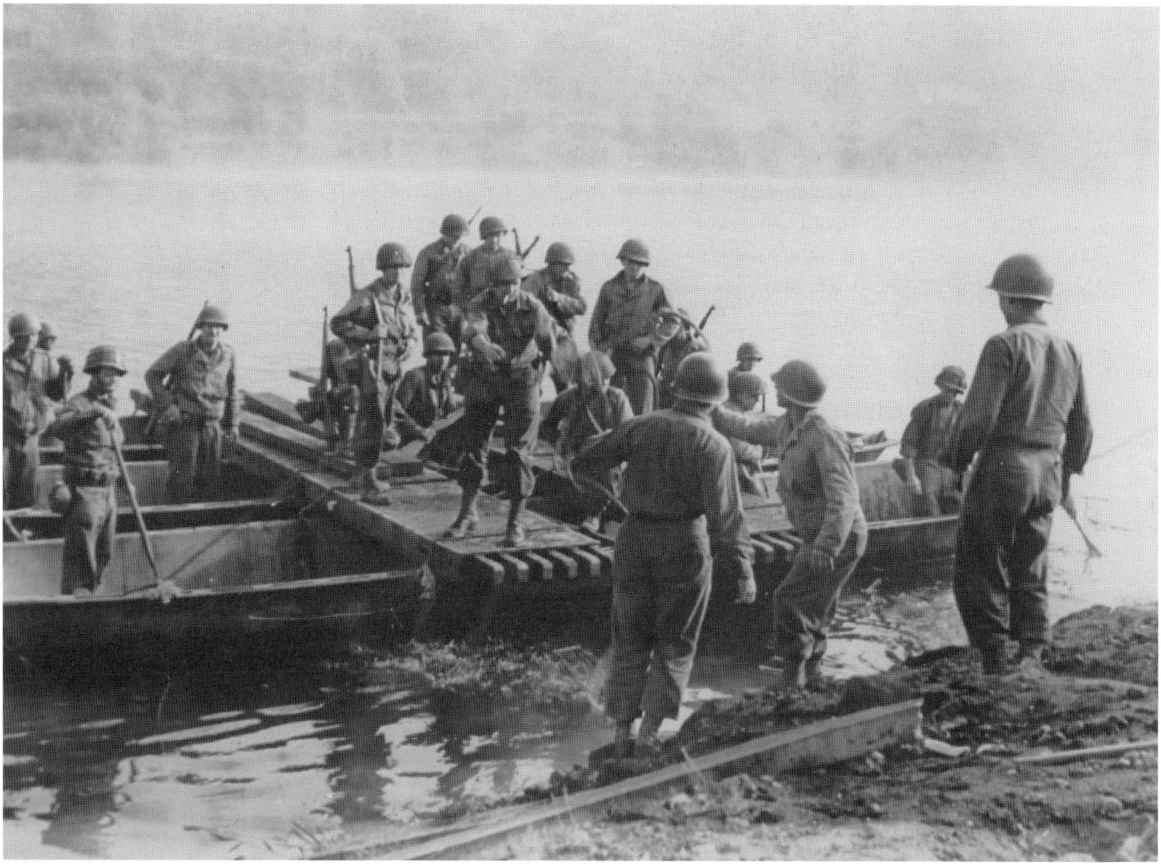

(**Above**) Canadian artillerymen are shown easing an Ordnance QF 6-pounder AT gun into the middle boat of three light river assault boats to cross the Seine. The vessel to the right has already had a jeep loaded on board and is about to be pushed into the river. The boat on the left has treadway planks ready to load a wheeled structure on to it. All three assault boats have outboard motors. The First Canadian Army's II Canadian Corps reached the Seine river at Elbeuf, northwest of Vernon and south of Rouen on 26 August. The next day, Canadians of the Royal Hamilton Light Infantry met up with elements of the US 2nd Armoured Division in Elbeuf. The British I Corps, also a part of LG Crerar's First Canadian Army, was to secure the Le Havre Peninsula. (NARA)

(**Opposite, above**) General Philippe Leclerc, CG French 2nd Armoured Division, walks down a road in Rambouillet with staff officers, for the approach to Paris on 23 August 1944. Leclerc accepted the surrender of the German garrison in Paris under German General Dietrich von Choltitz on 25 August. Leclerc joined Charles de Gaulle's Free French Forces early in the war and was promoted to colonel by de Gaulle having achieved victories in French Equatorial Africa. Following his promotion to BG, he staged a 1,000-mile march from Chad to Tripoli, Libya, to join forces with Montgomery's British Eighth Army, capturing Italian garrisons along the way. He was promoted to MG in 1943. (NARA)

(**Opposite, below**) Parisians scatter under Nazi sniper fire, part of a last ditch German resistance effort to disrupt ongoing celebrations in the French capital, at the Place de la Concorde on 26 August 1944. The Germans had officially surrendered to Allied forces the day before, but pockets of French collaborators and German soldiers remained at large. (NARA)

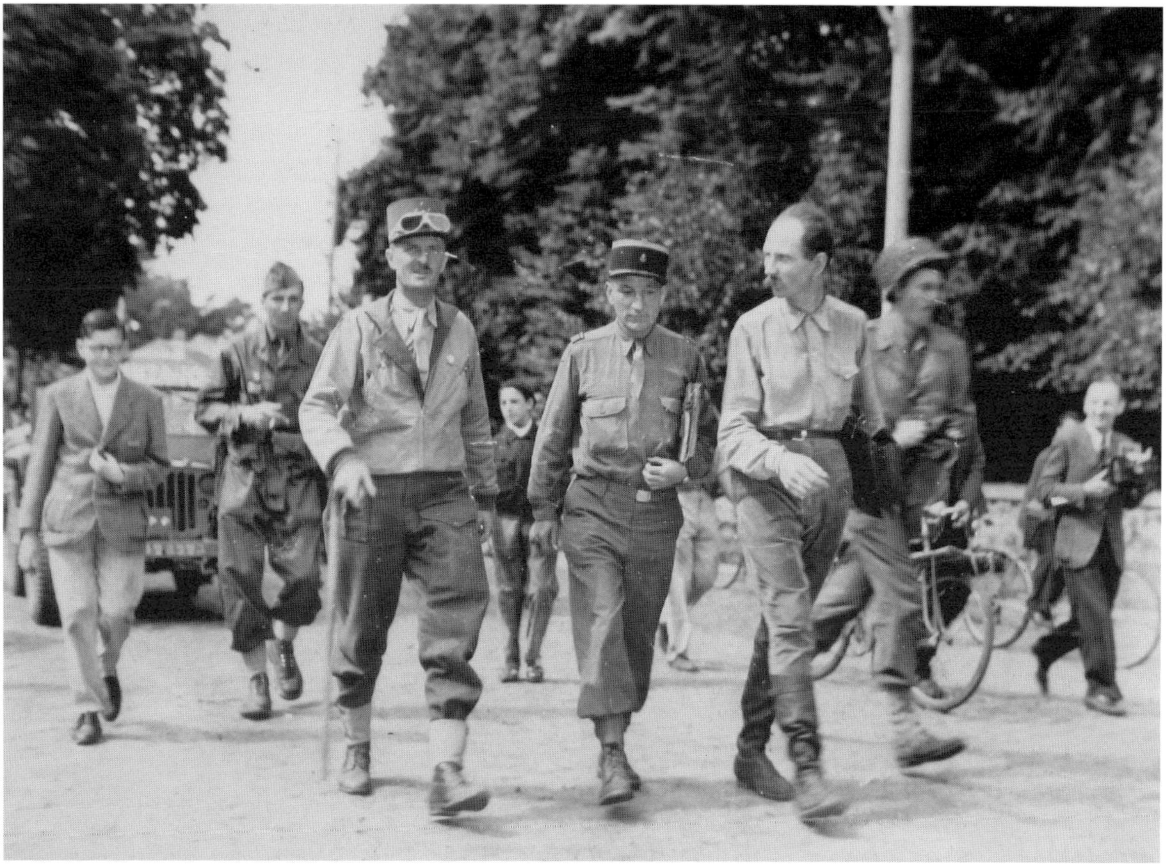

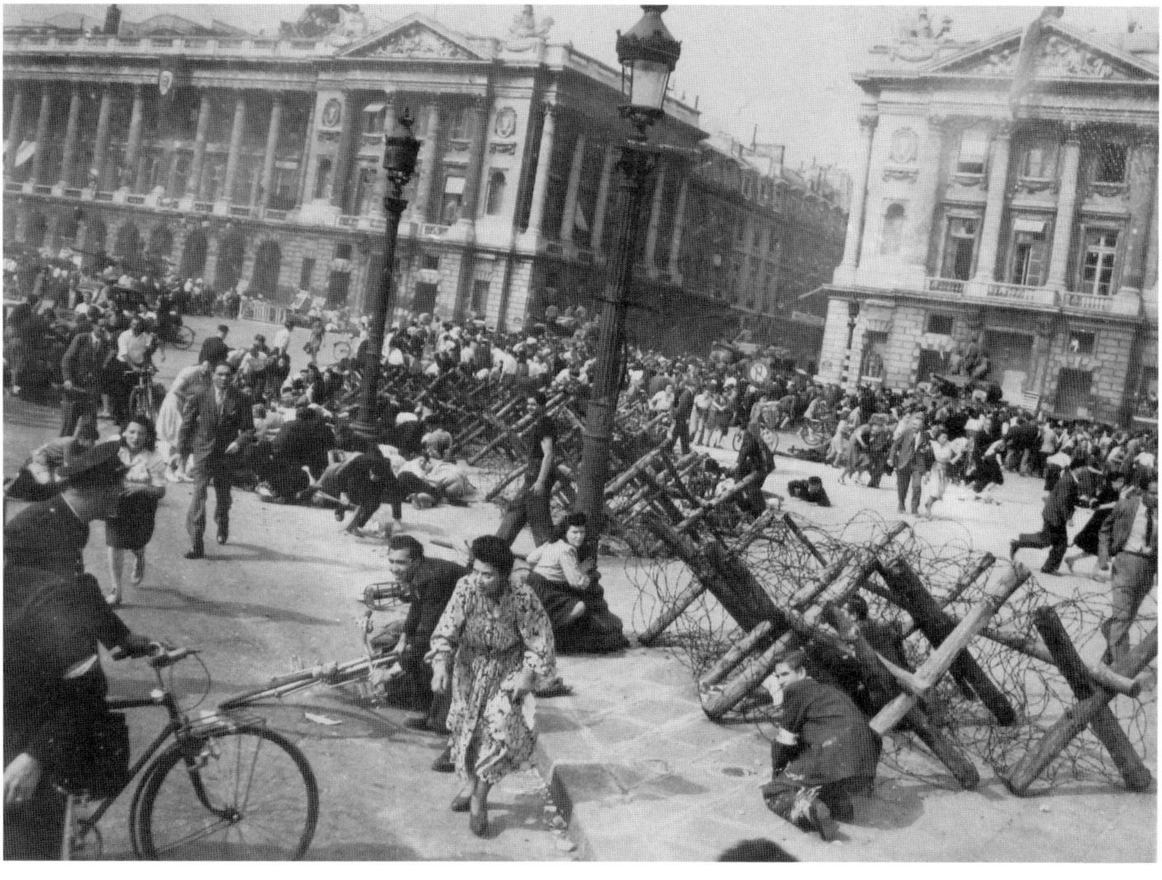

The US 28th Infantry Division's participation in the victory parade down the Avenue des Champs-Élysées, with the Arc de Triomphe behind them, began on 29 August 1944, four days after the liberation of Paris. The parade was escorted by American jeeps of the division in the vanguard. (NARA)

Bibliography

Badsey, Stephen, *Normandy 1944: Allied Landings and Breakout*, Campaign Series 1 (Osprey Publishing, Oxford, 1990).

Balkoski, Joseph, *Beyond the Beachhead: The 29th Infantry Division in Normandy* (Stackpole Books, Mechanicsburg, 1989).

Beevor, Antony, *D-Day: The Battle for Normandy* (Viking Penguin, New York, 2009).

Blumenson, Martin, *The Duel for France 1944: The Men and Battles that Changed the Fate of Europe* (Da Capo Press, Boston, 1963).

Blumenson, Martin, *US Army in World War II. The European Theater of Operations: Breakout and Pursuit* (Center of Military History, Washington, D.C., 1993).

Crosby, Francis, *D-Day*, Images of War Series (Pen & Sword, Barnsley, 2004).

D'Este, Carlo, *Decision in Normandy* (Harper Perennial, New York, 1994).

Diamond, Jon, *Montgomery's Rhine River Crossing: Operation Plunder*, Images of War Series (Pen & Sword, Barnsley, 2019).

Ford, Ken, *D-Day 1944 (3): Sword Beach & the British Airborne Landings*, Campaign Series 105 (Osprey Publishing, Oxford, 2002).

Ford, Ken, *Caen 1944: Montgomery's Breakout Attempt*, Campaign Series 143 (Osprey Publishing, Oxford, 2004).

Ford, Ken, *Falaise 1944: Death of an Army*, Campaign Series 149 (Osprey Publishing, Oxford, 2005).

Gilbert, Martin, *D-Day* (John Wiley & Sons, Hoboken, NJ, 2004).

Harrison, Gordon A., *US Army in World War II. The European Theater of Operations: Cross-Channel Attack* (Center of Military History, Washington, D.C., 1993).

Hastings, Max, *Overlord: D-Day and the Battle for Normandy 1944* (Simon & Schuster, New York, 1984).

Holland, James, *Normandy '44: D-Day and the Epic 77-day Battle for France* (Atlantic Monthly Press, New York, 2019).

Lewis, Adrian R., *Omaha Beach: A Flawed Victory* (University of North Carolina Press, Chapel Hill, 2001).

Mason, David, *Breakout: Drive to the Seine*, Ballentine's Illustrated History of World War II, Campaign Book, No. 4. (New York, 1968).

Tucker-Jones, Anthony, *Armoured Warfare in the Battle for Normandy*, Images of War Series (Pen & Sword, Barnsley, 2012).

Zaloga, Steven J., *Operation Cobra 1944: Breakout from Normandy*, Campaign Series 88 (Osprey Publishing, Oxford, 2001).

Zaloga, Steven J., *St Lô 1944: The Battle of the Hedgerows*, Campaign Series 308 (Osprey Publishing, Oxford, 2017).

Notes